MEDITATIONS FOR BUSY PEOPLE

MEDITATIONS FOR BUSY PEOPLE
HOW TO STOP WORRYING AND STAY CALM

Stephen Bowkett

Thorsons
An Imprint of HarperCollins*Publishers*

Thorsons
An Imprint of HarperCollins*Publishers*
77–85 Fulham Palace Road
Hammersmith, London W6 8JB
1160 Battery Street
San Francisco, California 94111–1213

Published by Thorsons 1996

10 9 8 7 6 5 4 3 2 1

Stephen Bowkett asserts the moral right to
be identified as the author of this work

A catalogue record for this book
is available from the British Library

ISBN 0 7225 3358 6

Printed in Great Britain by The Bath Press, Bath

To Wendy, who lives as though she means it.
Love always.

Acknowledgements

To David Brawn who set the ball rolling.

To Elizabeth Hutchins for sensible suggestions, chatty asides and a professional job of editing.

To David and Helen Lesser and all at the AQCH for guidance and good grounding.

And to all friends and colleagues at 'Healthways' for a sense of direction and an expanded perspective.

Long may we flourish!

The best cure for worry is to observe a worried man.

Traditional Chinese saying

❂

Worry is an insidious poison. It contaminates the flowing stream of our conscious thoughts and, because of its habitual, mechanical nature, it passes negative messages back continually to the deeper levels of our mind. There is an intimate and reciprocal connection between thought, belief, attitude and behaviour – including the 'behaviour' of our physical appearance. Beauty may be skin deep, but worry can sink to the very core of our being.

In observing a worried man or woman, we are really looking at a worried life, at a worried *way* of life. And the irony is that the sufferer, while investing a huge amount of time and energy in the act of worrying, remains always the passive victim of the pains and difficulties it brings. All of that effort for such a mean and unwanted outcome!

If you can see worry by looking in the mirror, think about what it is doing to you… Or, more usefully, what you are doing to yourself.

Today I will begin to cure my worry.

Sitting quietly, doing nothing,
Spring comes and the grass grows by itself.

Taoist poem

❻

When I was a young boy, I would not dare to fall asleep in the car, fearing that somehow my father would not be able to drive it and it would crash. It was, I suppose, a kind of superstition – that I needed to be there, watching, to make sure the world worked as it should.

It was a childish fear. But many adults are still full of them. This particular one stemmed from a sense that I was at the centre of my world – I was responsible for it; I needed to control it, to make things turn out right.

Many people find it hard to let go, simply to let the world unfold as it should. We each of us carry a vision in our head of how things ought to be – how we would like them to be. So there is always a pressure to turn the world in the direction we want it to go. That pressure is the source of much of our worry and dissatisfaction and rage.

Things are as they are. What is going to happen will happen.

To say this is not to abrogate any responsibility or to adopt an uncaring attitude. It is just to relax for a while and let the driver do the driving.

Today I will sit quietly, doing nothing. Spring still comes. The grass grows by itself.

Stretching his hand out to catch the stars, he forgets the flowers at his feet.

Jeremy Bentham

⑥

We live in a world where ambition is equated with courage, strength and determination. Grand dreams have always fired the imagination and driven men and women on to great endeavours. And yet, if a fine line is crossed, we are accused of being naïvely idealistic, of having our heads in the clouds, of shooting for the moon, and people cease to take us seriously.

Such conflicting signals may cause confusion and can certainly make us wary of taking that next step, of reaching out just a little farther to catch the stars.

Most of us, perhaps, dream large, but live small. That should not and need not lead to any sense of disappointment or diminish what we do achieve in our ordinary day-to-day existence. In reflecting habitually on the stars that may forever be too far away, we miss out on the tiny successes of each day and on the triumphs available to us at ground level.

Today I'll take time to notice the beauty of the flowers at my feet.

Life is the art of drawing sufficient conclusions from insufficient premises.

Samuel Butler

⑥

What do we ever know for sure? A great deal of our brain capacity is given over to accumulating, editing and storing a picture of what the world is like 'out there'. We do this, of course, in order to survive.

But this picture of the world is more than simply a route map which allows us to recognize that fire is hot and an orange is edible. The data builds to form 'truths', 'beliefs', 'convictions' and 'certainties' about what is and what is not so.

And yet, how easy it is to live a lie, to kid ourselves that we will do such-and-such someday or that so-and-so will become possible when the conditions are right.

This happens consciously, but it also occurs more profoundly, and perhaps more dangerously, on a subconscious level. Fears, uncertainties, misapprehensions, long forgotten or outgrown, can still run like dark threads through the emotional tapestry of our lives and the fragile fabric of our being.

So how can we ever draw 'sufficient conclusions' from premises which are never perfect, which in some regard must always be inadequate?

The answer is an ancient wisdom which has existed for as long as humanity has recognized its imperfections. What is the bedrock on which we can stand, despite the essentially inconclusive nature of life? Love, hope, awareness of the moment, the exquisite joy of simply being alive.

Today I will notice these things!

> Carpe diem! *Seize the day.*

Horace

❻

The motto of mottoes – short, simple and to the point. *Carpe diem* epitomizes the nature and purpose of affirmations. And, like all good affirmations, it can be repeated often, so that the idea percolates down to the deeper layers of the mind and eventually, with increasing power, takes effect.

But let's be clear about what it means to 'seize the day'. It does not involve, I think, struggling in our everyday existence to fulfil our most heartfelt ambitions. Neither do we need to strive to find importance in our every small action, our every casual word. (Besides which, 'striving' and 'strife' are too closely related to pursue one while naïvely assuming we'll avoid the other!) It's plainly true that days are not laden with grand significance: they are composed of prosaic sights, ordinary people, mundane tasks, timetables, sameness…

Yet, what variety is to be found in skyscapes, minute by minute, or the slower shift of the weather through the week. How greatly our thoughts and moods affect one another, and are affected by the people we meet, the things we say on a routine basis…

That, of course, is the nub of the problem and the secret of the affirmation's power. What is routine is what we *see as routine*. Seizing the day means no more than shifting our perception to realize that the sum total of our life, the ultimate structure of existence, is composed of unique and irretrievable instants. We are made by each moment, by how we live it.

Today – starting now – I appreciate the seething world of which I am a living part!

Why not grasp the pleasure at once! How often is happiness destroyed by preparation.

St Augustine

⑥

Buddha once told this parable:

> A man was riding across the countryside when he encountered a hungry tiger. He bolted for his life with the tiger closely pursuing him. Soon he came to a precipice and, seeing no other option, flung himself over. Desperately he grabbed at a vine growing from the lip of the precipice and there he hung with the tiger snarling down at him – and the tiger's ravenous mate gazing up! The man had been lured into a clever and inescapable trap.
>
> It so happened that a wild strawberry plant was growing nearby. That summer it had produced a single delicious fruit. Without warning, the vine to which the man was clinging began to tear free. In the last fleeting moments of his existence, he reached for the strawberry, picked it and ate it.
>
> How sweet it tasted!

In this case, the rich rewards of the spontaneity of life arose through extreme circumstances. Strawberries have always tasted as sweet, it was simply the man himself who had changed.

The capability for such change is always within us and can be brought about merely by being. Action undertaken on the moment, *for* the moment, will see happiness enhanced rather than destroyed.

Today I will grasp the pleasure at once!

As the generation of leaves, so is that of men.

Homer

⑥

We live in a world that is changing at an astonishing rate, indeed, one wherein the pace of change is itself increasing. The writer and academic Alvin Toffler brought the concept powerfully into the public imagination in the 1970s when he coined the term 'future shock' – the phenomenon of feeling helpless and overwhelmed by the sheer rush of humankind into an unpredictable and largely unknown future. It is a real phenomenon, of that there can be no doubt.

To feel swept away passively by the vast chaotic stormtide of time can bring with it the impression that we are minute and vulnerable beings, with barely a breathing space between the cradle and the grave. We may view our lives as being unremarkable and insignificant, as well as brief, and all set against the background of an impossibly large and uncaring universe.

But this is no more than a perception more likely generated by words and images than by experiences. It is an attitude of pessimism – something which it is all too easy to develop. To be sure, attitudes are powerful things – but they, unlike the broad sweep of the future, are under our control and are amenable to change.

The first step to such change might be to reflect upon those generations of leaves, which, in time, are swept away to oblivion. Because who could deny that without their existence the limitless forest itself would never have come into being?

Today I celebrate my uniqueness and my place in the grand scheme of the Cosmos.

It is because everyone recognizes Beauty as Beauty that the idea of ugliness exists.

Tao Te Ching

☙

We might well yearn for a world where ugliness does not exist and where pain and hatred cease to have purpose or power.

It is not likely to happen. The very fact of life and death is testament to the cyclical nature of all-there-is. Without one, there could be no other. Thousands of years ago human beings recognized the essential duality of Creation, which has as its balance and counterpart the equally important state of Non-existence, the Void of the unmanifest. Each of us is, as it were, woven up from the soil and drawn back down through the mould once our day is over. That is reality's fabric, of which we form the smallest threads. This state exists at all levels, on all scales, from microbes to stars.

In coming to see the twofold nature of everything, we can quite easily take the next imaginative step and realize that beneath the duality lies a unity. Beauty-and-ugliness is actually a single state; one thing not two. Each gives the equivalent opposite its essential meaning.

This is not to say that we have to love ugliness any more than we need condone evil in any form. It is simply that these are necessary components of life that allow us to appreciate what is vital and positive, beneficial and good. What matters is perceiving the beauty against the backdrop of ugliness and deriving from it a necessary joy.

**Today is embedded in yesterday and tomorrow.
Now, in the midst of my life, what beauty do I see?**

We suffer from the delusion that the entire universe is held in order by the categories of human thought.

Alan Watts

❦

The history of human learning very largely comprises the growing realization that we are not at the hub, or the sole purpose, of creation. The progress of astronomy has been that of relegating the Earth from a position of central importance to that of a tiny planet orbiting an unremarkable star, one of billions in an ordinary galaxy. It has been said that there are more stars in the universe than there are grains of sand upon the beaches of our own planet. So the likelihood is that we are nothing special.

Likewise, biology has taught us that life, whether created by God or arising as the random product of physical laws, will appear wherever the conditions are suitable and will then struggle remorselessly to survive. It is life itself that is important, rather than the small and fleeting concerns of any individual being.

That jewel of wisdom, 'Desiderata', quite rightly says that each one of us is 'a child of the universe, no less than the trees and the stars' – but equally, no *more* than the trees or the stars.

So perhaps when our ego, with its shallow sense of self, places our problems at the centre of things, we should step back for a moment and try to imagine, quietly and with no undue effort, where we really stand on the immense glowing canvas of infinity.

Today the world does not revolve around my worries. Sitting quietly, doing nothing, I marvel at this wider view.

Rejoice at your life, for the time is more advanced than you think.

Lao Tzu

☾

There is without doubt something ominous about that thought, as we realize that all of our hopes and dreams, our ultimate ambitions as well as our short-term goals, need to be packed into a finite amount of time.

As children we simply accepted time and played our way down the years. We didn't think much about it. Time possessed a different quality then. Perhaps you found, as I did, that it was more elastic – boredom stretched seconds to the limit as we waited for the dull school lesson to end; an afternoon spent with friends sped by in moment. We rarely spent any time worrying that it was slipping through our fingers... The world, as they say, was our oyster, and we the pearl of wonder and optimism within.

Things can change. Time is no different now, but for some people, as adults, the fact of their mortality is not only conceivable, but also fills them with dread, panic, helplessness. Yet the sheer inexorability of time's passage makes any agonizing futile. There is, of course, never enough time in a busy life, but if we have done something worthwhile then it is never lost.

And whether or not we believe that something of ourselves continues after our lives here have ended, what a waste of that life it is to regret what might have been or anticipate with misgiving what may never even happen.

Today I rejoice at my life.
Each minute is precious to me.

What we have to learn to do, we learn by doing.

Aristotle

⑥

So much of our education consists of being *told* – often about what we are getting wrong! This can easily lead to an attitude which persists throughout life: that we can only learn through the authority of others; that learning is the slow and painful process of decreasing the number of errors we make; and that in order to succeed we must attain the standards previously set by those who would purport to educate us.

This process embodies certain benefits, especially if the teacher is fired with enthusiasm and a love of both the subject and the students. But it remains one limited way of learning *some* things – driving a car or mastering a formal subject at school, for example. Many areas of life – the internal life of the mind, as well as our necessary interactions with the outside world – are not amenable to that kind of instruction.

How do we learn to boost our self-esteem or increase our confidence?

How do we succeed in becoming happier?

Where do we look to to become more sensitive and positive towards the people around us?

How can we best make use of much of the advice offered in these pages?

Realizing the nature of true authority is a vital first step. That 'true authority' comes from whatever empowers us rather than narrows our thinking and in such empowerment we become authorities over ourselves.

Today I tell myself that my actions give meaning to my words.

What the superior person seeks is in himself;
What the small person seeks is in others.

Confucius

✿

The tale is told of the noviciate who one day went to his master. He said, 'Master, I have been here for seven years and I feel that I have learned nothing. I was hoping to find my god, but where do I search from here? How can I point to the Buddha I seek?'

The master nodded and shrugged. 'I cannot tell you where to point,' he replied, 'because the Buddha is in the finger with which you are pointing.'

We are accustomed to looking for answers in certain ways, searching in certain directions – usually beyond ourselves, relying on the given wisdom of others. There is a saying that can act as a reminder that this is not the only way of solving problems: 'We change the problem or we change ourselves.'

Think now about what you would need to do to change a typical problem you may have. Would winning a fortune solve it? Would moving to another part of the country? Would being younger work? Or being someone else entirely? How likely are these possibilities?

Now consider what you would need to do to change yourself, given the limitations placed upon you, and all of us, in changing the problem itself.

Whom would you ask?

Where would you look?

Today I am the superior person. I do not point towards the answer.

Hope is a good breakfast but a bad supper.

Francis Bacon

⑥

Each day is a *new* day, something quite unique and fleeting. It's another page in the book of our lives, turned irresistibly by time, but blank and fresh for us to make our mark upon it.

To start a day with hope is no bad thing, depending upon the kind of hope it is. For hope is a sharp-edged emotion – like a knife it can be an extremely useful tool or can cut badly.

Focus on hope and consider whether, today, your hopes are modest or spectacular. Are they realistic or false? And do you really hope to achieve your goals or, deep down, do you know that they are fantasies, born of envy or previous disappointments perhaps and driven on by wishful thinking? Will you still have hope at the end of the day – when it is more commonly known as regret?

All of this assumes that you wake up hopeful in the first place. If not, then at least you will not find yourself stumbling on the futile hopes which some people scatter like stones along the path. Make the most of wherever you start from.

Learning to hope well is a matter of seeing a clear way to achieve what's possible, being alert for positive opportunity, reflecting on past successes and using their momentum to put a spring in your step as you move through the day.

Learning to hope well is a small, quiet, subtle thing – but something that accumulates day by day into a towering, unstoppable force.

Today I will enjoy a good breakfast of hope.

Become what you are.

⑥

- Sit or lie down and pay attention to your breathing. Make it slightly deeper and slower than usual.

- When you feel more relaxed, imagine that you are sitting beside a stream.

- Imagine that the stream represents your flow of conscious thought – that ceaseless rush of mental activity so frequently called the 'monkey mind'. Let it run and scamper; do nothing either to slow it or analyse its activity.

- When you are familiar with this state and at ease, imagine you are watching yourself observing the flowing stream. Now ponder just who it is that is watching the water – and what part of you does that flowing water represent?

- Now create another viewpoint – a part of you watching the part that watches the part that watches the water. Is this just a mental trick? Or can it be that what we really are, our innermost mind, is something other than what we observe in this tranquil state?

- Whether you find an answer for yourself or not at this stage, let that busy stream carry all your worries away. Then bring yourself back with a slow count of 3, 2, 1 and open your eyes…

Today I will begin to become what I am!

An enemy with troubles at home is ripe for conquest.

Sun Tzu

☯

Sun Tzu's *The Art of War* is a well known classic, written by the Chinese warrior-philosopher over 2,000 years ago. It is a manual for conflict, following the principles and practices of the great spiritual tradition of Taoism, and thus is as much about harmony as it is about conquest.

We meet many conflicts and situations that provoke us to anger or frustration. Often our immediate reaction is to lash out. Do we indeed strike out? Do we back down in humiliation? Or do we attempt to 'bottle up' our temper and internalize what our emotions tell us needs to be released? Whichever way we choose, it seems that we have lost the battle. Our adversary – that stupid careless driver, that insolent child, that uncaring employer – has, directly or by default, won the day. We have ended up simply hurting ourselves!

It is undoubtedly true that we are frequently our own worst enemy and many of our troubles are 'at home' inside our own head. Therefore, conquest is easy for those who would seek to thwart us, insult us, belittle our efforts or deny what we have achieved.

Sun Tzu also said: 'The one with many strategic factors in his favour wins.'

What are the strategic factors you have in conquering your own anger and worry?

Perhaps a useful weapon in the armoury is this final piece of wisdom from Sun Tzu: 'To win without fighting is best.'

Today I will observe my most insidious enemy – the enemy within – and learn how to win.

What I do is me: for that I came.

Gerard Manley Hopkins

❦

Hopkins was a man of profound religious faith, although that faith was not unshakeable. He doubted, as we all doubt sometimes, the habitual certainties of our lives. But one thing remained constant in Hopkins' mind and that was the conviction that all things are unique.

It is not difficult to test this assertion. Look at any two trees, faces, stones, sunsets… They may sometimes seem almost identical, but closer observation will always reveal their small and subtle differences.

Hopkins coined the term 'inscape' (inner landscape) to describe the individuality of every created thing – both of itself and in the sense of the moment-by-moment changes that characterize the existence of things through time. For him, the inscape of an object was nothing accidental, nor was it passive or meaningless. Everything, he said, is as it is for a reason.

Today I will allow myself to see that 'What I do is me.' I will see this right now!

Yet they, believe me, who await
No gifts from chance, have conquered fate.

Matthew Arnold

⑥

I love the idea of 'synchronicity' – the congruence in space, time and circumstance of two or more events that, on the surface of things, seem to be entirely disconnected.

Take, for instance, the farmer's wife who lost her wedding ring in the fields while out potato picking, only to find it 25 years later in the centre of a potato she was chopping up for supper… Or the professor of statistics demonstrating the random and chaotic laws of chance, took a coin from his pocket and flipped it, asking, 'Heads or tails?' The coin landed on the polished floor, spun a few times, and – to great applause – came to rest vertically on its edge! The odds against this happening are apparently of the order of one thousand million to one.

The human urge to believe there is some kind of unifying pattern beneath the supposedly orderless tumble of events in the world is the basis of all religion. It provides at least a feeling of comfort that we tiny elements in this vast entirety are nurtured beneath the wing of the Omnipresent. At best, it drives us through life with a profound sense of purpose and a consuming joy at the opportunity we have been given of life.

Yet whether we believe in a universe that is designed or accidental and whether or not we feel that the unifying force of synchronicity exists, it is surely the height of foolishness to invest emotional energy in the hope of chance bringing us easy rewards. Rewards might come our way … or they might not.

Today I will take my chances and enjoy myself!

November 15th, Sunday. I walked in the morning. The
valley in its winter yellow, but the bed of the brook still in
some places almost shaded with leaves – the oaks brown in
general, but one that might be called almost green.

Journals of Dorothy Wordsworth

☖

Our life is composed of a million moments. Most of them are unspectacular. Most cannot be recalled as moments of high emotion. And yet, as a jigsaw is made of individual pieces that seem to have little meaning or significance by themselves, when put together they form a picture that is complex and elaborate.

Our ordinary day-to-day moments, mundane thoughts and incidents, by and large, can be likened to the scattered pieces of a puzzle. We work so hard to complete the picture, to glimpse the final meaning fitted in the frame, but all too often pay no heed to the seconds and minutes and hours that collectively make up our lives.

When are we ever complete? What meaning does any frame possess, except in relation to what it contains?

The details of life are as perfect and finished as life in its entirety – no puzzle at all, if I don't keep searching for the solution.

Today I pause in my puzzling and look at life's single moments, ordinary yet unique.

To believe only possibilities is not faith, but mere philosophy.
Thomas Browne

❻

'Mere philosophy' in this sense means the thinking of our conscious, rational mind. Its job has always been to receive information, weigh it up, compare it with previous experiences (those it can recall) and decide on a course of action. But it can also generate scepticism and its dark sibling, cynicism. It can easily set up feedback loops of negative or unhelpful thinking which may over time percolate down to even deeper levels.

The process works in both directions, of course. Our intuition is constantly sending signals up to the conscious mind, which may or may not listen to this factless, unspoken wisdom. For our conscious egos like to feel that they are in control and know where they are going.

Faith, on the other hand, exists often without recourse to reasoning and is, in that regard, irrational. It is subtle and powerful, greater than belief, but incorporating belief. It demands no proof and, like the water of a mountain spring, may be tasted and relished or allowed to trickle by unnoticed. It does not deal in possibilities, but sinks its roots deep into certainty. It is a tree and the troubled thoughts of worry nothing more than lichen on its surface.

Today, in a quiet time, I will look gently for the source of faith.

We sat together, the forest and I,
merging into silence.
Until only the forest remained.

Li Po

⑥

Many of us occasionally like to be alone with our thoughts. But sometimes thoughts cut us off from the tide of life of their own accord. They can create a barrier between ourselves and all that is outside. More insidiously, they may separate who we think we are from what we really are. Such thoughts – concerns, anxieties, frustrations, disappointments – throw up a dim window, through which we are then forced to look.

For centuries people have come to this realization and devised a number of ways for doing something about it:

⑥ Smash the window by hurling yourself into an activity which leaves you no time or opportunity for troubled thinking.

⑥ Reason out the causes of your difficulty. If you can correct or change those causes, set about planning the steps of your journey to success. If they cannot be corrected, set about planning how best you can accommodate them in your life.

⑥ Ignore the window for a while. Sit quietly in a pleasant place and, without effort or expectation, absorb the qualities of tranquillity and existence-for-its-own-sake…

What does it feel like, 'Annihilating all that's made/To a green thought in a green shade…' (Andrew Marvell)?

Today we sit together, the forest and I.

Real slavery is that you have learned to endure it.
Adapted from Rabbi Hanokh of Alexander

☾

We like to feel that we have a high degree of freedom in our lives. Most people hold democracy to be among the noblest political ideals of the civilized free world. And on a philosophical level, the notion of predestination – that our pathway and purpose in life have already been set out in the minutest detail – can fill even the most easy-going of individuals with a sense of suffocating claustrophobia.

But when it comes to the things that irritate, concern, worry or distress us, many people suffer the chronic stress of a host of problems without even bothering to consider how the situation could be improved, let alone acting to achieve that improvement.

Is this slavery? Certainly, according to the *Concise Oxford Dictionary*, which equates slavery with 'drudgery', the toleration of a distasteful state over a long period of time.

Perhaps in some cases the situation has been going on for so long that the sensibilities have been dulled to the point of numbness and the imagination is unable to look beyond the horizon of unhappiness. But most often people know what's worrying them and but for the want of a way out would do something about it. They know well enough that if the same energy were spent in solving problems as putting up with them, sufferance would soon be a thing of the past.

This book offers what will hopefully be some useful doorways.

Today I reaffirm my intention to break the shackles of worry!

The fall of a leaf is a whisper to the living.

Russian proverb

6

Achieving happiness is easy if you trade in your old car for a brand new model with all the added extras. Likewise you can purchase security by spending more on an insurance plan. And if you had the perspicacity to invest a sizeable proportion of your life savings in a timeshare villa, then Paradise on Earth could be yours just about whenever you wanted it...

Or so the advertisers would have us believe. And millions of people do believe it, too, defining the canvas of their emotional landscape by the latest possession, the newest special offer, the next seductive promise in an endless sequence of such promises.

Our culture has encouraged us to accept that more + bigger = better. We are embedded in a philosophy of acquisition to the extent that even the greatest and most elegant gifts of life – peace, happiness, fulfilment – can be ours for the investment of just a few more hard-earned dollars.

Of course ownership brings pleasure. I delight in the clever machine I use to compose these words. But it's refreshing to step back, to stand away from it all and reaffirm a healthier sense of perspective. Behind the brash buzz and glitter of the modern post-industrial world lies a deeper, quieter significance. Travel to your nearest park, or right out into the country, and allow the solitude to whisper its vital message.

Today I listen to the leaf fall. I know I am alive.

Daring ideas are like chessmen moved forward.
They may be beaten, but they might start a winning game.

Goethe

⑥

Being a writer, I find it handy to live by a few treasured mottoes which help me to get a handle on my work. One of the most useful is: 'To have good ideas, you must have lots of ideas.' This means that every page I'm happy with is the result of many false starts, rewritings and discarded words.

The maxim might be altered to read: 'To have successful ideas, you must have lots of failed ideas.' I find this a healthy perspective, since it takes the sting and venom out of 'failure' and reinstates it as a necessary element in the process of succeeding.

It is important for me in my writing to realize that a failed plan does not make *me* a failure. Failure is an attitude, a state of mind. It can, admittedly, be brought about by a succession of failed ideas – in which case a self-reinforcing negative feedback loop has been created and the situation becomes serious.

But by cultivating a positive attitude, one of taking pleasure from every small achievement and affirming my intention to succeed, I dare to look failure in the face and move beyond it.

Today I do not fear a failed plan, for beyond it lies success.

For everything you have missed, you have gained something else.

Emerson

⑥

When I was a young boy, every Friday I would be given my pocket money and sent off to school. I wouldn't spend a penny of it in the tuck shop, but would wait until the final bell and then run up the hill to the local newsagent's in a state of great excitement. Because Friday was the day when the latest batch of comics from America would arrive. Batman, Superman, Spiderman, Hulk – I loved them all and wanted every issue.

I had enough money to buy two and a half comics. The newsagent would put my third choice aside until next Friday came along. But how I hated it if there were four comics in the pile I wanted that week! What a strange, tearing hurt it was to feel that I was going to miss one!

We miss opportunities all our lives, chances to *say* and *be* and *do*. That's just the nature of things and there's nothing we can do about it. What is possible, though, is to determine to make the most of what we have gained. It's the old but ever-pertinent question again: do we see the cup as half full or half empty? The cup is the cup is the cup – but the choice of viewpoint is ours.

Remember that regret dims the sun and those pernicious words 'if only' drain all the colour from the day.

Today – and every day – my cup is half full.

A man shows his character by what he laughs at.

German proverb

⑥

The notion that 'laughter is the best medicine' is a cliché, of course. And like all good clichés it contains some powerful wisdom. In the same way that we behave as we think, so we think as we behave. Thus, if we allow ourselves to take the opportunity of laughter, this can only result in a beneficial uplifting of our thoughts.

But *what* we laugh at is a more complex issue. Negative-minded people laugh at others' misfortune and failure in a vain and twisted attempt perhaps to bolster the illusion of their own success.

What we learn from this is that laughter is a powerful force – either to hurt or to heal. In the latter case, take the experience of Norman Cousins, who cured himself of ankylosing spondylitis by laughter. Through hiring videos of Marx Brothers' movies and *Candid Camera* clips, he achieved a remission of the illness at odds of over 500:1. Even more astonishing is the fact that Cousins subsequently did the same thing in recovering from a massive heart attack.

There is no doubt that Norman Cousins possessed remarkable inner resources, but he is still only a human being with a capacity for laughter. That laughter, according to Dr Paul C. Roud, is 'a symbol for the therapeutic value of all positive emotions'.

While we laugh, unashamedly, unselfconsciously, we turn automatically towards the light of health.

There is laughter in my life today. I will recognize it and use it.

Wind, flag, mind moves…
When the mouth opens, all are wrong.

Mumon

❻

The Zen story goes that there were two monks arguing over a flag flapping in the breeze. A patriarch happened by and witnessed this.

One monk said, 'The flag is moving.'

The other monk said, 'No, the wind is moving.'

The patriarch took a stick and thrashed them both. 'You fools!' he told them. 'It is your minds that are moving.'

We all see the world from the viewpoint of ourselves, negotiating our way through life with the route map we have been creating in our mind since Day One. What we think, say, feel and do – our entire being – is a subjective thing. There is no way that we fail to put the stamp of who we are on every perception. We speak and spell ourselves: 'What I do is me: for that I came.'

It is in part our individual vision that makes us unique. So it is no bad thing to accept that our minds are moving – and that if I say it is the flag and my friend says it is the breeze, in a very important way we are both absolutely right.

Today I will reflect upon the way my mind moves.

If you are going to kill a snake, kill it once and for all.

Japanese proverb

⊚

Worry lies coiled in quiet places. If you have a tendency to let it nag away at your life, then when you sit down to relax, or during a train journey, or if you need to do some ironing or washing up, suddenly it's there, running through all the worst-case scenarios of what might happen.

But have you noticed how those thoughts and feelings seem to vanish if ever you're actively thrown into a situation? If, for example, you're called upon to concentrate intensely upon some task at work or if you're amongst friends, enjoying their company and conversation?

Worry is mechanical thought. It operates on a conscious and subconscious level. Consciously, it circles in the head like an irritating tune that won't go away. Subconsciously, it can set up 'programs' in your map of reality which ultimately lead to a detrimental shift in your perception of things.

To a large extent it can be combated by deliberate thinking – by consciously working out short-term goals towards solving the larger problem: and by subconsciously clearing a time and space for yourself where you can use a variety of techniques for reprogramming your outlook at deeper levels. Such mental techniques are enhanced if you set them running and then forget them by launching yourself into a busy routine of work and leisure. Worry thrives on inactivity and lack of choice.

So if you're going to kill the snake, do it once and for all with deliberate intention and determined action.

Today I will seek out the serpent.

Habits are first cobwebs, then cables.

Anonymous

❻

A habit often begins as a deliberate act. It ends as mechanical behaviour – 'mechanical' in the sense it keeps running in the background, often without us being aware of it at all. Sometimes it is merely neutral, like whistling a tune as we walk along the street. Sometimes it's indicative of deeper tensions, such as grinding our teeth or drumming our fingers on a tabletop. More seriously, mechanical behaviour can sink its roots deep into our world-view, so that we automatically react in a negative or detrimental way when faced with certain circumstances or situations. In this case, what would not be a difficulty for some people, or indeed might be a positive challenge, is seen by the worrier as an insoluble problem.

Such a 'problem' is fuel to the fire. Its presence feeds the worry, which flourishes as the sufferer fails to see any viable way out – indeed, can see only the worst that might happen. What began as a cobweb has turned into an apparently unbreakable cable of response.

In considering this, I am put in mind of my mother. She has never been overly houseproud, but will dust regularly and flick away strands of cobweb before they proliferate and become noticeable.

Now *that* is a habit worth cultivating!

My first job today, and at the start of every day, is to flick away the cobwebs of worry.

There are essentially four kinds of risk:
the risk one must accept
the risk one can afford to take
the risk one cannot afford to take
the risk one cannot afford not to take

Peter F. Drucker

⑥

From the distorted perspective of worry, almost anything can be seen as a risk. I have an acquaintance who's worried about going on holiday in case the house gets burgled. Someone else I know worries about going to parties because if only he could build up the courage to ask a girl to dance, she might say no. And another friend of mine is worried about giving up smoking in case she puts on too much weight, which could result in a fatal strain on her heart…

These are not 'risks' in the normal sense. They are not hazardous. The fear is entirely inside the worriers, tangled up in the way they see the world. And even if some slight chance of the unfortunate consequences *did* exist, there are plenty of tools in the mental toolbox both for learning positively from the experience and for minimizing the chances of such circumstances happening again.

Having said all of that, there's no denying that most aspects of life carry some sort of risk. Accepting the *concept* of risk is a necessary first step in perceiving the *kinds* of risks that exist – and in sharpening up the both the reason and the imagination to distinguish usefully between them.

Today I begin to see which risks I cannot afford not to take!

This universe appears as a juggling, a picture show;
To be happy – look upon it so.

Ancient Sanskrit manuscript
(transcribed by Paul Reps)

Ⓖ

Many different metaphors exist to describe the nature of the universe and of the lives of individuals upon this Earth. For several hundred years, science was dominated by the precise clockwork nature of the Cosmos – until a totally new level of reality unfolded through discoveries and developments in the field of quantum physics. To Fritjof Capra (author of *The Tao of Physics*) and Gary Zukav (*The Dancing Wu Li Masters*), the universe is indeed looking 'less and less like a great machine, and more and more like a great thought'. Their perspective unveils a universe that is holistic, organic, purposeful. And the bedrock of such a viewpoint allows for a towering optimism to be erected upon it.

Our view of 'life, the universe and everything' is of course of supreme importance in providing a background colour for day-to-day existence. For if we can feel happy about creation on the largest of scales, then our capacity for joy – and enjoyment – moment by moment is informed and fed by that overall framework.

And can we verify that such a framework is true? Look within rather than without – and remember the words of Marcel Proust: 'Do I believe that a God exists? I don't know – but I live as though He does.'

Today, if only for a short while, I try to see the picture-show nature of this world.

I await the moon's rising – the moon does not hasten:
I watch the river – the river flows on.

Li Po

⑥

The conscious and subconscious aspects of the mind are often likened to a rider on a horse. The rider likes to feel he's always in control, yet the horse is by far the more powerful. The horse that is our subconscious mind has a very easy-going and yet a fiercely protective nature. It always attempts to act in a way that serves the best interests of the individual. So it is in a very real sense our best friend and guardian angel. We could all improve our well-being enormously by striking up a more meaningful dialogue with it.

Problems, although they can stem from the subconscious, arise far more frequently in the conscious mind – the rider who likes to feel he knows just where he's going and just how to get there. It is the conscious aspect of the mind that suffers from the delusion 'that the entire universe is held in order by the categories of human thought' and grows frustrated if things do not behave as it would wish.

One simple and positive step which can be taken to bring horse and rider more closely into harmony is to accept that some things are quite beyond our control. As the saying goes, 'Change what you can change and accept what you can't…' The writer/philosopher Arthur C. Clarke summed it up more succinctly when he maintained that we should all 'co-operate with the inevitable'.

Today I feel easy with the thought that the moon will not hasten and the river flows on.

Sometimes the best teacher teaches only once...

Anonymous

⑥

Having trained and worked as a teacher for many years, I was often reminded of the fact that teaching does not always imply learning. Indeed, poor teachers rarely succeed in imparting anything useful or significant to their students and children learn vast amounts *despite* what is ostensibly being taught in schools, absorbing 'the hidden curriculum', soaking up ways of negotiating the winding pathway of their lives.

Worry is not a good teacher. It wears the gown of hopelessness and wields the stick of dismay. Its daily, mechanical lessons all too frequently only inculcate a vague sense of claustrophobia. But it is a teacher nevertheless. Its lesson might remain unvarying and deadly dull, but if we do not learn from it, the fault is usually ours.

So what can be done? Good students ask plenty of questions – *precise* questions so that the answers are clear and unambiguous. Good students learn despite a poor teacher; they are aware, alert, self-motivated and tenacious in their quest for knowledge.

How can we fail to become good students, knowing the success of the rest of our life depends on it?

Today I take heed of the lesson worry teaches me.

I have asked to be
Where no storms come,
Where the green swell is in the havens dumb,
And out of the swing of the sea.

Gerard Manley Hopkins

⑥

Escape is not to be sneered at if it's used as a temporary shelter from the bustling routines of life. But, as the boat leaves the harbour just as soon as it can, so it's good practice not to linger in a place that is calm but limiting – because the eventual return to the open ocean will then be all the more difficult to make.

But there's a simple technique which can be practised, more or less anywhere, and as required, which makes for a rest that's as good as a change:

⑥ Sit or lie down. Take a few deep, calming breaths. Let your eyes close.

⑥ Imagine a place that is to your liking – a favourite room, a much-loved spot by the sea or on a wooded hill; anywhere in fact where you feel safe and comfortable, relaxed and serene. It can be a mixture of a real location and the product of your fantasy… Look up and set a rainbow galaxy spinning in your sky; make a silver-white unicorn gallop silently through your woodland fastness; change the colour of the rocks and the sea; make music visible as glassy shapes in the air.

⑥ Enjoy your personal, private ashram. Visit it often.

Today I will go where no storms come…

Within us all there is another person – the inner person, the friend, the noble person.

Meister Eckhart

(6)

Science has progressed by cultivating an attitude of open-minded scepticism, wherein the enquirer allows the possibility of a phenomenon, but will not accept it as true until sufficient evidence has accumulated to demonstrate its existence.

Learning about the inner world of the mind, and beyond the mind, the spirit, is not so easy. Taking an objective stance is like attempting to make a chalkmark on water. The subjective nature of ourselves as individuals makes detailed exploration difficult in the scientific sense, because all that comes to me from the outside is filtered through the lens of my unique perception, which has been evolving since birth – or even way before that, some would maintain.

Yet detailed exploration of ourselves *by* ourselves is eminently feasible. In search of the 'inner being', perhaps we could use the method of science: be open-minded, gently doubtful, until the weight of evidence tips the scales of acceptance. On this journey we must remember that 'proof' will always be entirely personal – but at its most potent will possess the qualities of revelation and unfold the essential meanings of faith.

What is assuredly true is that the attempt must be made. For consider where the world would be if people of science had not set out on a similar, but external journey – enduring an endless, purposeless age of darkness.

Today I admit the possibility of my inner being and begin my search.

The peculiar symptom of worry is that even when you observe its stupidity and futility and resolve to stop – you cannot. It is the mind – your master – that worries, not you.

Barry Long

⑥

Here Barry Long distinguishes between who we think we are, and our true and essential natures. In the same way that a photograph of myself is a plain two-dimensional representation of me, so my mind – and in particular my limited, mechanical, conscious mind – simply reflects the surface features of who and what I really am. Consciousness is like ripples on a pond, hinting at depth without revealing it.

To look beneath requires commitment, but no effort. And who better to make a commitment to than ourselves? The easy, gentle discipline of daily tranquillity and quietude is not hard to establish, once the bluff and persistent protestations of the ego-centred conscious mind are ignored and overridden: 'I simply don't have enough time for it… It's going to be so *boring*, just sitting there… All this wishy-washy meditation stuff is nonsense anyway… OK, so what happens after a month of sitting quietly, doing nothing brings no results? Go on, answer me that if you can!'

Ripples. Ripples on the surface of a pond…

It doesn't even matter what you call the object of your search: your conscience, your inner being, the Superego, subconscious programming, the Overmind, the soul…

Achievement exists for its own sake.

And happiness goes beyond words.

Today I let the pond lie still and look within.

After the action of imagination ... follows the action of understanding.

François de Sales

⑥

In the course of my work as a writer one of the most frequently asked questions is: 'Where do you get your ideas from?'

I am not so much surprised or puzzled by the question itself, as the way in which it is asked, as though 'writers', or artists of any kind, are somehow special people who 'get' these mysterious things called 'ideas' (from goodness knows where) and have the astonishing capacity to turn them into 'real' things like stories or pictures or pieces of music.

My usual first reply is something like: 'Well, that question is an *idea*. Where do *you* think it came from?'

The fact is that ideas come from *everywhere*. Our whole life experience supplies the raw material and creativity is as natural to all of us as breathing. Every act is conceived before it is carried out. What we think, we do. And what we do, we are. There is no mystery.

Writers, artists and musicians are simply ordinary people who have tilted their imaginations a certain way and opened up the dialogue between this deeper level and the conscious mind, so increasing the flow of usable ideas.

And make no mistake, ideas *are* real things – as real as the Mona Lisa, New York, the Sphinx, the Apollo moonshot, the ascent of Mount Everest, the automobile…

Today I consider the proposition that I am less and less like a great machine, and more and more like a great thought…

Nothing great was ever achieved without enthusiasm.

Emerson

⑥

Watching children at play is a perfect example of this aphorism. They throw themselves actively into a world of imagination, have fun, strengthen friendships and as a bonus by-product learn a lot about how the world works and their potential place within it. Play and enthusiasm go hand in hand… Did you ever meet a kid who played with great energy and was *not* enthusiastic about it?

Of course, the minds of children are still elastic. They do not yet suffer from the 'hardening of the categories' that can be so limiting to most of us adults. While kids can achieve perfect, unselfconscious Zen simply by dropping into a world of fun-filled fantasy, we struggle to suspend the great weight of our disbelief long enough to enjoy a movie or a couple of chapters out of a paperback novel …

The mistake we make is, having drawn the lines, we never again dare to step across them. We become fixed in the way we think. This occurs more tragically in the wasteful vicious circles of worry, which is not even evolving thought, but rather downward spirals leading nowhere in particular.

And yes, we'd like to change if we could…

So let's grab that idea of *wanting* to change – grab it with enthusiasm, which is the fuel we'll use to drive the vehicle of our choice.

I can achieve something great today, because I'm ready to play!

Do not say with regard to anything, 'I am going to do that tomorrow.'

The Koran

❻

Worry thrives on delay and procrastination. It grows and flourishes over time, in the rich soil of inaction and low expectation, increasing its grip on our ability to reason clearly and on our capacity for joy. Like an unchecked vine, it gradually develops a stranglehold on our life. What seemed once to have been a background distraction is suddenly a stifling, dominant force, quite out of control, bending us under its weight.

Putting things off until tomorrow is, like worry itself, an attitude, a state of mind which builds up its own momentum. We delay because we think we'll fail, and that thought, projected into the future, allows worry to replay in our mind's eye the worst case scenario of what might happen. Thus we spiral further into worry's self-fulfilling prophecy... Then, *because* we do nothing, we don't just worry about the problem itself, but also about its inevitability – and later we may regret our lack of action and say, 'It'll be different next time...'

Until next time arrives.

It is of course so easy to convince ourselves that problems will go away by themselves. Indeed, sometimes they do. But think back over what has worried you in the past year, and consider how effective swift and direct action would have been in helping problems to go away by themselves...

Start small, but start now.

Not tomorrow, but *today*, I take action against anything that's worrying me.

We can believe what we choose – but we are answerable *for what we choose to believe.*

John Henry Newman

⑥

To me this is not entirely true. Some beliefs begin modestly, as incidents or something as small as a scrap of conversation, accidentally overheard and having no significance at the time. The information enters the subconscious mind, without necessarily passing through the analytical filters of consciousness. Or it may be that if the incident happens during childhood, the unsophisticated conscious mind might easily misinterpret what has been said or done. Information in the subconscious is always active, so that something accepted by the deeper levels, even if misinterpreted, is treated as true and the seeds of belief are sown.

In this sense, although we suffer the consequences of our beliefs – which may result in subconscious responses on a mental, emotional or physical level – we do not always choose those beliefs. Nor, sometimes, do we realize that the source of a problem is a belief at all.

Coming to this realization, however, is the first step in knowing which direction to take in rooting out limiting beliefs. And once those beliefs, and the incidents which gave rise to them, come to light and are perceived afresh by the adult mind, then the reason why they exist is no longer valid and their effects can disappear.

Today I look deeply into what I believe, in order soon to find out why. When I choose my beliefs, then I am happy to be answerable for the consequences.

He that will not apply new remedies must expect new evils.

Francis Bacon

⑥

Worry is a double evil. It damages *of* itself, leading to much of the dis-ease which these days we know as 'stress-related illness'. But it also feeds the illusion that there is no way out of the situation. The nature of worry, its incestuous self-fuelling fire, militates against us realizing that problems can have many solutions and that worry as a problem *per se* can be defeated in any number of ways.

The victim of worry is surrounded by closed doors and exists in a tiny featureless room. Sometimes the doors are not even recognized: more often, the sufferer dare not ease one open a little to see if it leads to a way out. Worry is entrapment and solitary confinement, its own gaoler and judge.

Even though problems sometimes disappear of their own accord (usually because they were not problems in the first place!), because worry, like Nature, abhors a vacuum, others come along to fill their place... And the worrier does not so much expect their arrival as dread it. Surely anything must be better than the endless churning hurt of worry...?

So try anything, as long as it's positive. The world is full of remedies that have worked. And while the first of them may not work for you, or the tenth or the fiftieth, the fact that you are taking positive direct action to fight the enemy of worry might just be enough by itself.

Today I turn my attention to finding new remedies.

At 50, everyone has the face he deserves.

George Orwell

❦

Infuriatingly true – and the truth can hurt. But it's never too late to change.

Using Orwell's assertion as a starting-point, it is plain to see that *at this moment* we are the outcome of the days, months and years through which we've lived. We are moulded by our experiences – and, more fundamentally, by our perceptions of those experiences. We are what we think we are, as a result of what we think happened!

As I have maintained elsewhere in this book, thoughts, beliefs, attitudes and behaviour are inextricably connected. And so, not just our habitual expression, but our posture, the spring (or not) in our step, our whole demeanour, whatever our age, is affected by our outlook on life.

If you are happy in your outlook, then that happiness shines through in your expression and enhances your features, however old you are.

Do you have the face you deserve? Do you need to do something about it?

Today I will look in the mirror and reflect on what I see.

Pause sweetly and gently ... not to employ, but merely to calm and fix the mind.

Madame Guyon

⑥

Think of the conscious mind as a TV set. Except in sleep, it is always turned on. Its programmes are continuous and of all kinds. They may be absorbing, frightening, entertaining, boring, fresh and original, or tedious repeats, screened one after the other, again and again. Thankfully perhaps, there are no commercial breaks...

Ironically, while many of us are selective in what we sit down to watch on the television, we may show no discrimination at all in the TV of the conscious mind, taking it for granted that what we see is all there is. Sometimes we may not even be watching at all.

Thinking of the television set analogy puts me in mind of a friend who went out and bought a fancy new VCR with all manner of sophisticated functions. Unfortunately, he never bothered to learn what his clever machine could do and used it simply to record and playback, usually when two programmes he wanted to watch were running simultaneously.

Consider a little further. Nobody would keep a TV running for no reason and we question the intelligence of buying a VCR with all those facilities which are never utilized. And yet we treat our conscious mind in just that way – rarely bothering to find out what it can do, and employing its full range of functions for our benefit.

Today I will press pause – merely to calm and fix the mind.

Let us leave the beating and turning over of empty straw.
Let us ponder by night in view of the stars.

Richard Jefferies

⑥

Worry closes doors and narrows horizons. It is a fruitless activity, the turning over of empty straw, pointless but tenacious in the grip it has on our minds.

Horizons, of course, can be mental or physical. It is possible, indeed desirable, to widen our mental horizons and use determination, ambition or a fondly nurtured dream to drive us towards them. But we need to have a sense of direction and purpose, and before that we need to realize that the journey is possible.

Physical horizons can help us here. Worry loves routine. It draws strength from the boredom or frustration we may feel at being trapped in the workaday world. It takes advantage of the similarity of our days to strike the spark of dissatisfaction and then fan the flames of our perceived confinement.

Break the cycle by breaking the routine. Everyone has *some* free time. Use it to do something different – anything different, even something quite out of character. A holiday in another part of the country would help enormously, but if this isn't possible, choose a more modest diversion – a walk, a movie, contacting a friend you haven't seen recently … or simply stepping outside on a clear night, in view of the stars.

Today I relish a break in my routine and the thought of the unexpected.

The most important pursuit is making that person, the one standing at your side, happy – for that alone is the pursuit of life.

Leo Tolstoy

⑥

We occupy a world that is shrinking by the day. Our community is the rest of the human race, not just the neighbours living on the same street. And that community, at this moment, is being washed by the tides of war and tyranny, poverty and disease.

Happiness is not a quality or gift that is dependent solely upon a person being rich or clever or beautiful. These might help – but equally they might not. Neither is happiness an emotion often experienced in isolation. The deliberate recluse might find contentment 'out of the swing of the sea', but most of us would discover only loneliness, however wonderfully peaceful the first few days might be.

I have in many of these meditations personified worry in order to define it. It was my enemy for years, along with its brother, whose name is selfishness. They are often seen together and when they visit, they don't like to find other company already there.

Worry wants you for itself. Its brother whispers in your ear, 'Why should I care about those refugees halfway across the planet? I've got problems of my own!'

If you listen, if you turn away from the harrowing images on the TV screen, you turn inward. But by looking outwards and, however modestly, by helping others, you end up helping yourself – and showing worry and selfishness the door.

Today I find happiness in myself by offering it to others.

They who lived in the concentration camps offer sufficient proof that everything can be taken from you but one thing, the last of the human freedoms – to choose one's attitude in any given circumstances: to choose one's own way.

Viktor Frankl

⑥

The prisoners in the camps represent the extreme end of human suffering. The hardships they must have faced are almost inconceivable – and yet their tragedy is compounded by the common knowledge that people in many parts of the world are being victimized as horrifically, right at this moment.

It may or may not help any given individual to be told that there are others worse off. And indeed, my intention today is not to do that. Worry preys on the ego, that sense of self we embody in the simplistic concept of 'I'… 'My problems are happening to me… I am suffering… Why do these hassles come my way?' It would be patronizing to suggest that the problems which worry us are minor in comparison to those caught up in the maelstrom of war. A problem is a problem is a problem…

But every self-improvement guide you ever read will assert that human beings possess depths they may never have glimpsed, strengths they may not be aware of, until they come to the brink. That realization can in itself be a source of energy, as beneficial as the knowledge that, in the face of surpassing evil, the fortitude of the human spirit can still prevail.

Today, in a quiet, private moment, I celebrate the courage of my kind.

The world without wonder – the world without mystery!
That indeed is the rainbow without colours, the sunrise
without living gold, the noon void of light.

Fiona Macleod

(6)

Two centuries ago, as the White Man was forging west across the plains of America, he came across many native tribes and settlements, and was eager to prove his superiority and dominance over the Red Man.

On one such occasion, the White Man came riding into camp with his guns and liquor and coloured trade beads. Sliding down off his horse, he demanded to see the tribal chief, an old man who seemed far too bent and frail to lead his warriors.

To make the message plain and simple, the White Man took a stick and drew a circle in the dust outside the chief's tepee. Through an interpreter, he said, 'This is what the Red Man knows.'

Then he draw a larger circle around the first.

'And this is what the White Man knows, so you should be respectful.'

The old chief considered this carefully. Then he took the stick and drew a huge circle around the other two, that filled the encampment's central clearing.

'And this,' he replied, 'is what none of us knows. So we should all be respectful...'

Today I reflect on the idea that the mystery of life is not a problem to be solved, but a reality to be experienced... (Alan Watts)

Beyond my visible nature is my invisible spirit. This is the foundation of life whereby the universe has its being.

Iolo Morganwg

⑥

Beyond happenstance there is coincidence; beyond coincidence there is serendipity; beyond serendipity there is synchronicity… And beyond all of these is what modern scientists are calling 'the Anthropic Principle of the universe'.

In talking of the universe, we must invariably use large numbers. Astronomers and quantum physicists have, in the past few decades, come upon several so-called 'large number coincidences' which stretch the notion of randomness beyond the limit of credibility.

These, and other, relationships begin to seem as though they are fundamental characteristics of a Cosmos 'fine-tuned' to allow for – perhaps, indeed, make inevitable – the appearance of sentient life. If this is true, then these basic mechanisms and qualities must have been designed, built in to the Big Bang which created our universe 15 billion years ago.

Perhaps the most remarkable aspect of the Anthropic Principle is that creation can produce entities capable of understanding it and the matrix from which they arose.

And perhaps that understanding is only a scratch on the surface: that what we presently perceive is no more than a faintly illuminated corner in a vastness of staggering complexity and light.

Today I ask, 'How can I begin to see my invisible spirit?'

What is the sound of one hand clapping?

Zen koan

⑥

It was the rationalist philosopher René Descartes who came up with the powerful maxim *Cogito ergo sum* – 'I think, therefore I am' – and went on to describe a universe based upon strictly mechanical models and mathematical principles. Furthermore, he asserted that the universe could be known to the ultimate degree by the use of the reasoning capacity inherent in humankind.

There is no doubt that man's ability to think logically has led to great advances in our understanding of the physical world. But Ambrose Bierce's definition of logic is apropos here: 'The art of thinking and reasoning is in strict accordance with the limitations and incapacities of human misunderstanding.'

Any conscious thought represents the use of just one among many faculties in our mental repertoire, a single viewpoint from a house of many windows. Conscious thought is often spoken of us though it were a pure and isolated phenomenon, occurring apart from the great seethe of gut-feelings, intuitions, guesses, hunches, gambles, bets and superstitions which compose the inner landscape of us all. It is regarded as a clear light shining confidently forward into a future where the universe behaves much the same as it does now, and has always done. But the brightest light always casts the darkest shadow.

Reasoning has given us access to the moon and planets; it may not of itself be enough for us to attain the stars.

Today I do not *think* about the sound of one hand clapping!

I move along the columns of age,
Along the streams of inspiration…
Along the fair land of knowledge…
Along the hidden land, which by day the moon inhabits…
Eleanor Hull

⑥

Dreams have been a source of fascination, mystery, fear and hope for thousands of years. People have used them to prophesy and to look back into lives and ages past. They intrigue us with what they tell, tantalize us with what they don't tell. We keep journals and diaries of those fragments we remember and try to achieve intrusive lucidity so that we can direct their course. Above all, we attempt to understand them by dragging them out into the open.

Dreams are neither a function nor a product of the conscious mind and are not easily – or perhaps even ultimately – amenable to surface logics. If we use the computer analogy of the mind, then dreams become the machine code on which the final message upon the screen is dependent. They operate at a deep level, according to their own rules, for their own purposes.

And yet 'their' purpose is our purpose too. Belonging to the subconscious realms, dreams serve our best interests. They constitute an inner dialogue between aspects of our mind to which we are not privy. The performance continues consciously on stage, while this vast activity goes on behind the scenes – and *only* while it goes on. Because when we cease to dream, we die.

Am I a butterfly dreaming he's a man? It's something I never worry about.

Today I move along the hidden land, but don't trouble to seek the moon.

If some great Power would agree to make me always think what is true and do what is right, on condition of being turned into a sort of clock and wound up each morning … I should instantly close with the offer.

T. H. Huxley

❦

Human beings have been wryly, but accurately, described as 'bundles of contradictions wrapped up in paradox'. We are fickle, fleeting, unpredictable, chaotic. We utilize the great power of language to say things we don't mean, generate enormous tensions within by acting in opposition to the way we feel. We lie to each other and deceive ourselves. We often desperately seek to maintain control of our lives and yet, with a passion, wish for the unexpected so that we can break the mundane routines of our existence. We cry with joy, laugh with bitterness, have the capacity to be delighted and disgusted within the same moment. We celebrate the triumphal achievements of technology, but avoid walking on the cracks in the pavement.

Being what we are is to be *all* that we are. Moving towards our limits does not reveal any astonishing new qualities, nor, in finding our true selves, do we lose any element or aspect of what we have been. The undiscovered country still exists, even before the explorer begins the journey to the interior. Likewise, anger, resentment, envy and the rest of the demons will always be a part of us. Trying to leave them behind is like attempting to outrun your shadow. We can never be perfect, nor would ever want to be, I suspect, knowing that the price would be the loss of our essential humanity.

Today I accept what I am. That is the basis on which progress is built.

Go and sit over there and get on with something!

Mollie

❻

No, not Molière, but Mollie, one of my schoolteachers of many years ago.

I was born and brought up in the mining valleys of South Wales, and upon my entry to secondary education the attempt was made to teach us the Welsh language – a daunting prospect indeed! Actually, I made reasonable progress, but for financial reasons my parents decided, in my thirteenth year, to move to the Midlands where I was put into a French group at my new school.

Mollie, as she was affectionately known to her students, realized that I spoke not a word of French and that there was no way I could possibly catch up with the studies. She sent me over to sit by myself in the 'naughty' corner, where I was expected to occupy myself during every French lesson from then on. All I could do to while away the time was write in the notebook my form tutor had given me.

So I wrote anything and everything I could think of: poems, jokes, diary extracts and longer journal entries, stories which were, for me, a potent mix of observation, fantasy and wishful thinking, scraps, fragments, new words I'd learned, then more stories, poems and plays...

I looked forward to every French lesson, when I could 'sit over there and get on with something'. Years later, I realized that that fortuitous tumble of circumstances formed the basis of a career and a lifelong love of writing.

Today I consider the notion that serendipity is no accident for those who are sensitive to opportunities.

Forgiveness is the answer to the child's dream of a miracle,
by which what is broken is made whole again.

Dag Hammarskjöld

🌀

Two brothers had grown apart.

One afternoon, the older brother was playing in the bedroom they shared. He had spent over an hour painstakingly positioning dozens of tiny plastic soldiers in readiness for a play battle. The room was quiet; he was deep in his world of make-believe.

There came a clattering on the stairs, then footsteps hurrying along the landing. The younger brother swept in, kicking the carefully arranged ranks of toy soldiers across the carpet.

'Where's my boat? I've come for my boat,' the younger boy said.

His brother, in a fury, scrambled up and snatched the brittle battery-powered speedboat off the toy shelf. He held it high above his head.

'You stupid idiot! Look what you've done... I'm going to smash your boat for that!'

There was a moment's stillness, absolute stillness when more than just the fate of a toy hung in the balance.

'No – please – ' said the younger boy.

His brother, quite deliberately, threw down the boat and smashed it on the floor.

Forgiveness was a long time coming, but because we were children, when it arrived, it was effortless and instantaneous. And I have carried the guilt with me for years – but use it daily to reaffirm my closeness to the brother whose boat I destroyed.

Today I will make, however modest, a small act of forgiveness.

Your destiny shall not be allotted to you, but you shall choose it for yourselves.

Plato

⑥

You have probably seen that simple executive desk toy of a spherical metal ball on a string which hangs above two magnetic disks. Take the ball and lift it upwards and outwards, then release it. It will swing between the two magnets, first being attracted to one, then the other, performing an intricate chaotic dance on the end of the string before coming to rest above one or other of the disks.

Astonishingly, it is not possible to predict the ball's destination. The starting conditions are far too precise to be reproduced.

This understanding is one of the consequences of chaos theory, the study of disorder expressed through complex systems. It touches the public imagination via a number of powerful icons, most notably the heart-shaped image of the Mandelbrot Set where, at every edge, rainbow spirals swirl down towards infinity.

A lesser-known pattern is that of the line which splits, each split dividing, each division splitting once more – so that within remarkably few steps, the branching structure becomes infinitely complex. This is the true nature of reality which underlies the apparent clockwork precision of the universe.

And so, while none of us can predict any outcome in the impossibly manifold field of the future, at each instant we have the capacity to choose which path we will take. There lies destiny, created anew each second, and self-determination amidst the chaos of the world.

The rest of my life starts now. Today I choose my path.

Nothing will be attempted if all possible objections must first be overcome.

Tom O'Brien

❻

Think of a problem. Write down possible ways or methods of solving that problem. Let's take as an example quitting smoking:

> Simply stop and get by on will-power.
> Wean off by cutting down.
> Wean off with patches, nicotine gum, etc.
> Try complementary therapies, e.g., hypnotherapy.
> Use 'diversionary tactics', such as taking up a hobby.
> Avoid smoking contexts until the habit is broken
> (stay away from the pub, for instance).
> Investigate the underlying *reason* for smoking,
> if there is one...

And so on. Now what do you do?

STOP, sit quietly ... and listen to the conscious mind reeling out all the reasons why your plan is not feasible. It will cost time, money and effort; it will disrupt your routine; smoking hasn't hurt you yet, so why give up anyway; besides, you enjoy it and all of your friends smoke; and you're bound to put on weight or start biting your nails and...

When you have listened to the monkey mind jabbering for a while, you can, if you're interested, jot down its objections. One or two of them may be worth listening to.

After that, act quickly and decisively to achieve your aim.

Today I will not attempt to overcome the objections of my monkey mind.

A pipe gives a wise man time to think and a fool something to stick in his mouth.

Source unknown

🌕

A friend of mine decided to give herself what she called 'a physical, mental and emotional MOT'. She began by cutting out meat from her diet, buying a couple of vegetarian cookbooks and rustling up some tasty 'body friendly' meals. She also thought that jogging would be a good idea, so equipped herself with a stylish pink-and-purple jogging suit and some special air-cushioned Reeboks, and set out each evening on a preplanned route around the local park.

Round about the same time, she began visiting a lay psychotherapist, in conjunction with reading a few books about putting meaning into your life. She felt that she really needed to get back in touch with her inner self and wanted to regress to childhood in order to maintain significant contact with all of her life-path.

To supplement the synergistic nature of her body/mind enhancement programme, my friend took up meditation and Tai Chi classes, where a fellow explorer told her that she was deeply psychic and possessed a wonderfully vibrant aura. Perhaps a couple of weeks in retreat would allow her to develop this gift in a holistic way, so that she could tap into the universal energies of the Overmind and channel them through the purified lens of her being…

She might have taken up the suggestion, too, if she hadn't met this guy at a car boot sale and become involved in his all-consuming passion for breeding Koi carp.

Do I smoke the pipe today or just stick it in my mouth?

No gate stands on the public road.
Those who pass this barrier
Walk freely throughout the universe.

Alan Watts

❻

We create gates for ourselves all the time, barriers, obstacles along the path of the life we walk. Self-lies, excuses, denials, all helping to nourish that sense of inertia which prevents us moving freely forward. It is eminently feasible to think of all manner of reasons why we *shouldn't* do something to lift ourselves out of the rut of the daily routine. Perhaps it wouldn't work… We use that very word 'perhaps' as a justification for never even attempting to change direction by changing ourselves or our circumstances. It is always easier to do nothing, to let things roll on just as they are.

Alan Watts is talking about something rather more profound here than the barriers which keep us penned in a lifestyle that we may bemoan, but rarely seek to transform. Even so, the metaphor is a useful one.

We have all seen gates barring the way to a winding country lane or a particularly beautiful stretch of coastline. Often they are wreathed in barbed wire and bear signs such as: 'Private Property – KEEP OUT! (This means you!)'

But our existence here with all the other travellers of Earth is a public road and the only trespass we can commit is against the unhelpful momentum of our own mechanical thinking.

Today I walk freely and no gates bar my way.

Old age is always fifteen years older than I am.

Bernard M. Baruch

Ⓑ

One of the most sinister quotations I ever came across was George Bernard Shaw's: 'Old men are very dangerous, because they don't care what happens to the world.'

The cliché that we are as old as we feel makes sound sense. It is so incredibly easy for dotage to become a self-fulfilling prophecy. With advancing years, we expect our faculties to fail, as we sit quietly with a rug across our lap, nodding in the gentle sunshine of our declining years… The very language we use to frame the concept embodies these unhelpful expectations. Why should our years be 'declining', for instance?

I take my inspiration from individuals who subscribe to Bernard Baruch's philosophy, people like a distant aunt and uncle who ride motorbikes to go to dances together at age 60 (you should see them jive!) Or my wife's grandmother, who read at least two books a week, one fiction, one non-fiction, and enjoyed the sense of fun of a 10-year-old. She died in her late eighties with a love of life still shining in every smile.

But some people begin to die in their minds before even middle-age is upon them. We all know them – the ones to whom everything is serious, the ones who drape the accoutrements of age around themselves like drab clothes, the grey people.

And it occurs to me, you know, that *because* they don't care about the world, or themselves, old men – and women – *are* dangerous…

And for 'old', read 'as old as you feel'.

Today I take a look at how old I really am.

When it is not necessary to make a decision, it is necessary not to make a decision.

Lord Falkland

⑥

One of the most useful and readable books about dealing with worry is Dale Carnegie's *How to Stop Worrying and Start Living*, which I bought years ago when I was full of hormonal turmoil and adolescent angst. A technique which Carnegie describes is to make a list of present problems and seal it in an envelope. Six months later, read through the list. You can guess what you'll find:

Some of the problems will have been dealt with long ago.
Some of the problems will never have materialized in the first place.
Some of the problems will be quite unrecognizable.
Some of the problems will have got worse (in which case you look for other solutions).

This is a valuable exercise which teaches a lot about the nature of problems. But, apart from the act of sealing the envelope, it is a passive one, and on no account should be used as a method of dealing with problems. Know your enemy, but don't ignore him.

And so, when you don't need to make a decision to solve a problem, decide quite definitely *not* to make one.

Today I reaffirm my decision to live deliberately.

When bird passes on –
like moon,
a friend to water.

Masahide

⑥

Choose a quiet time when you will not be disturbed. Be prepared to drift effortlessly into a daydreamy state of deep tranquillity. In such a state, with the conscious mind idling, the door to the subconscious swings a little farther open. Pleasant memories might arise spontaneously from the depths or delightfully fresh and vivid associations could appear. For you are glimpsing now the seething currents of your creative sea – what I call 'the Imagine-Ocean'.

Take four slow, deep breaths.

Count yourself in: one-sleep-two-sleep-three-sleep-four-sleep-five-sleep… Time each count with subsequent breaths.

Focus your mind on a swinging object – a crystal on a thread, a child's playground swing, the pendulum of a slowly ticking grandfather clock.

At this point, just before those wonderful recollections emerge, speak to your subconscious mind directly. There's no need to articulate mentally – visualize instead.

Now you are a willow leaf carried on the stream of life, never dreaming of fighting against the current. Tomorrow … the endless Imagine-Ocean is yours to explore.

Today I allow my life to unfold naturally, just as I breathe in and breathe out. (*Tao Te Ching*)

It felt like morning, and the freshness of the world-to-be intoxicated us.

T. E. Lawrence

❻

The psychologist Abraham Maslow wrote a paper in 1950 called *Self-Actualizing People: A study of psychological health*, in which he proposed the idea that all of us behave in accordance with a hierarchy of needs. Our 'deficiency needs' – food, warmth, shelter, sex – must be satisfied before we can attend to needs further up the hierarchy – intellectual stimulation, the cultivation of friendships, artistic expression and others.

If we imagine the needs hierarchy as a pyramid with deficiency needs at its base, then the pinnacle exists in the form of what Maslow termed 'the peak experience', a sudden and spontaneous upsurge of pure joy which floods the being and creates, if only fleetingly, a profound sense of *rightness*, the unshakeable conviction that the universe is unfolding as it should.

Maslow proposed that peak experiences are the norm in psychologically healthy people whose basic needs are catered for. Moreover, such people (whom Maslow designated 'alphas' or 'self-actualizers') were prone to peak experiences regularly. He concluded that once self-actualizers become aware of their peak experiences, they begin having more of them.

The writer/philosopher Colin Wilson has called the state of mind during a peak experience 'spring morning consciousness'. It is not a subtle or mystical state, but, like the butterfly in the hedgerow, it can go largely unnoticed by the driver speeding by in his car, hell-bent on reaching his destination.

Today, this morning, I recognize that the world-to-be is the rest of my life.

Needs are a function of what other people have.

Source unknown

❦

I remember, as a young boy, my mother explaining to me the difference between 'want' and 'need' – usually in a toy shop. 'You *want* that toy, Stephen, but you don't *need* it…' I had to agree. My mother, bless her, usually bought me the toy.

Now, many years on, I am prompted to look again at the distinction and to wonder whether, in this obsessively materialistic society, we have confused what we need and what we merely want.

There is a powerful tendency for many of us to compare ourselves unfavourably with others – someone who is better looking, has a bigger car, seems more popular, enjoys a richer lifestyle. And we may think that if only we had what they had, life would be fine and our problems would disappear forever.

Such thinking is most likely fallacious, but it is also *wishful* thinking, which the conscious mind immediately counters with thoughts of how little we have, or how unsuccessful we are. In such a mental deadlock, not only do we fail to see the glass as half full, but the danger is that we perceive it as being all but empty.

It is easy to be cynical, as in the oft-repeated adage, 'I'd rather be rich and happy than poor and sad.' But in the world as it stands, we have what we have, most of our basic needs are satisfied, and what we want we can work towards much more effectively if our mental compass needle points toward optimism.

Today I look practically at what I really need, at what I truly want.

If you can't measure it, I'm not interested.

Source unknown

❦

No one knows who first said this, but you might reasonably ascribe the saying to a scientist or a banker, rather than to a philosopher, mystic or priest. Such a viewpoint is extraordinarily limiting and denies the multifaceted nature of the world we live in.

Take sunshine. You can use a thermometer to measure the temperature of the air that's been heated by it or a Campbell–Stokes recorder to measure the duration and variation of sunshine through the day, you can measure the amount of energy in the sunlight reaching the surface of the Earth (the sun at the zenith delivers the equivalent of 1,600 kilowatts per hectare) and you can measure it in connection with other factors such as humidity or air pressure. But you can't measure how sunshine makes you feel good when you draw the curtains open in the morning. You can't measure how it might boost the self-esteem of someone who's complimented on their tan. You can't measure that wonderful feeling of anticipation upon hearing sunshine forecast for the weekend. You can't measure the exquisite beauty of a sunset – or the uniqueness of that sunset.

We live in a world of immeasurables. To deny them is self-delusion. And whenever I encounter a view of the 'if you can't measure it, I'm not interested' kind, then I always respond with a far wiser epithet: 'If it happens, it exists.'

Today I'm interested in what can't be measured.

⑥

The old man lived alone on the hillside. All he needed was his peace and solitude, plus a few pots and pans to cook his meals, and the hens and fruit trees beside his hut to provide him with food. He also owned a pair of sandals and would wear these when walking down to market in the town; there he would barter some eggs or plums for fish or bread.

One evening the old man returned home. He hurried, because the full moon was due to rise over the distant mountains very soon and he did not want to miss that.

Upon arriving at his hut, he was surprised to see a thief sneaking out with his best cooking pot. Caught in the act, the thief raised the pot above his head, as if to strike the old man.

'Don't hurt me,' the old man pleaded. 'And if you need the pot more than I do, then by all means take it.'

The thief frowned, then glanced at the old man's sandals.

'And since you have no sandals of your own,' the old man said, 'then take mine.' And he removed his leather sandals and handed them over.

The thief ran off, puzzled yet delighted at his good fortune. The old man put his fish and bread indoors, then hurried out to face the east, as the moon rose and flooded his soul with silver.

'What a pity,' he thought, 'that I could not have given that thief the beauty of this moonlight...'

Today I look around to see what I can give to myself ... and I will know if I am happy.

Better than a thousand words –
One word which brings peace.

The Dhammapada

❻

If you stand before the mirror each morning and say, 'Every day in every way I am getting better and better,' chances are it won't work, because you're getting the conscious mind to talk to itself.

The conscious mind is good at some things. It can pay attention and concentrate intensely; sift information, weigh it up, analyse it and reach a decision; then act upon that decision. But it is that critical capacity that is the undoing of 'affirmations' rendered solely on the conscious level.

Day One – you make your affirmation and put some effort into making it work. Day Two – you don't detect much difference, but these things take time. Day Three – still no change and you're constantly checking yourself to see if the affirmation is taking effect. Day Four – you are in a rush and forget to do the affirmation. Day Five – doubt is beginning to creep in. Day Six – it's OK for the author of the book you read it in, he's doing well for himself!

Words are power if they can be accepted by the most powerful part of your mind, the subconscious. In a quiet time, when your conscious is lazily idling, make your affirmation without effort or expectation.

Over time, with your doubting consciousness 'off duty', you will find the weight of repeated affirmations accumulating and producing results.

Today I begin to build the word which brings peace.

For the moon, there is the cloud,
For the flower, there is the wind.

Zen saying

⑤

This is the Oriental equivalent of Donne's famous 'No man is an island.' Nothing exists in isolation: everything has a context. Both sayings embody a holistic perspective, wherein small beginnings can produce large-scale consequences, and where the interconnectedness of things makes those consequences largely, delightfully, unpredictable.

Unpredictability is not the same as randomness or even implicitly an argument against design. Accepting the view of such a 'networked' universe leads inevitably towards an optimistic outlook. We are not accidental beings cut adrift and struggling alone in a haphazard world: what we perceive is *flexibility within a structure.* Moreover, the inconceivably diverse linkages between each of us and everything else makes the context of our lives a support structure of surpassing complexity and elegance. It all has a purpose. Even the isolating force of worry, if properly channelled, can lead towards understanding and self-progress.

My mother often says, 'Everything turns out for the best,' which is her way of summing it up. Is this putting your head in the sand or allowing for the possibility of a purposeful macrocosm? It depends upon your cosmology.

Today I open my mind to the belief that for the moon, there is the cloud...

We are guests in the world, here only for a short while.
Those who know this truth do not waste their time with
quibbling or gossip.

The Dhammapada

☙

If all of this is here for a purpose, then the notion of being 'guests' in the world is not just romantic rhetoric. If, in some sense, the universe 'knew we were coming', then we are not just here to have lived and died without some personal evolution having taken place. In which case, how we treat our world and our fellow guests is as important as how we treat ourselves. Large consequences arise from tiny beginnings…

So learn large from small actions, past or present. Try not to let mechanical thoughts and behaviour – or actions encouraged by others with vested interests that are not your interests – ossify into unwanted and unhelpful attitudes.

Worry draws us unthinkingly into such attitudes – and into maltreatment of ourselves. We bemoan our lot and envy the lot of others – those more successful and beautiful. Such wasted time quibbling and gossiping!

Our mortality is a two-edged sword, our sense of transience sharpened on the strop of fear, or a honed blade that cuts swiftly through the ties of worry that bind – because there is so much to do in the time that is left.

Which it will be for any of us, our hosts have allowed us to choose.

Today I look back at the litter of wasted moments
and forward at the clear road ahead.

But I, being poor, have only my dreams.
I have spread my dreams under your feet.
Tread softly, for you tread on my dreams.

W. B. Yeats

⑥

When I was 10, I wanted to be an astronaut – an aspiration that intensified in my teens as I watched wonderstruck while men walked about on the moon. Around the same time I dreamed of being a world-famous author.

At 21 I became a schoolteacher, already cynical because I knew that superheroes didn't really exist and that the Apollo moonshot programme was driven by politics and cancelled when the TV ratings dropped.

But then, amongst children, I rediscovered the point and pleasure of dreaming.

On the larger scale, I realized that the dream always comes before the hardware. Everything we see and which exists to sustain our lives was once *imagined*.

Similarly, we sustain ourselves with dreams. Wishful dreams – yes – of winning a fortune and quitting the day job – but also more 'reasonable' dreams, driven by hope which fuels our actions and informs our decisions, moving us with a purpose through the mundane succession of our days.

I became an author, so dreaming has an added piquancy and importance to me now. And while I cannot claim to make a living from it, I do make something much more valuable.

A life.

Today I tread softly, not letting cynicism trample through my mind, because dreams are vital, precious things.

Three sparks that kindle love: a face, demeanour, speech.

The Triads of Ireland

🌀

Discovering and practising techniques for dealing with problems like worry and negative emotions is one broad front on which to attack. The other, no less effective way is to ignite within ourselves all the *positive* emotions of which we are capable and which are ours to experience as a right.

Love, properly considered, is the most powerful human feeling imaginable – not the love of things or the mealy self-love perpetuated by the ego, but a deeper and more fundamental force: the sheer unashamed love of one person for another and the experience of life which allowed them to come together.

It is often said that relationships need hard work. But perhaps more importantly, relationships require sensitivity and awareness on the part of the participants. It is not necessary to 'work hard' in cultivating a beautiful garden, although commitment is a prerequisite of success.

Similarly, a commitment of time and devotion leads to the cultivation of an improved relationship: each partner looking anew at the other and experiencing the delightful surprises of rediscovered love.

Like worry itself, time spent together can become mechanical and bland. See with new eyes, hear with new ears; recall that very first encounter when excitement and curiosity and deeper, subtler blends of feeling stirred inside. These are not lost, but perhaps dormant through routine and the surface perceptions we allow ourselves to suffer.

**Today I see and listen and appreciate once more –
igniting the sparks that kindle love.**

If the beginning is not right, a thousand practices will be useless.

Eihei Dogen

☯

The metaphors of chaos theory have been touched upon earlier. Perhaps the most elegant and beautiful of these is the 'butterfly effect' – the notion that movements in the air caused by a butterfly's wings, transmitted and amplified within the atmosphere, can trigger a hurricane half a world away... Huge and unpredictable consequences arising from tiny starting-points.

This is not to say that the situation will happen, merely that it *can*. The principle itself is built into the 'rightness' of the world. *Of course* what we do, or fail to do, can echo on through the years and change the general direction of our lives. 'Right beginnings' are essential.

But when does a beginning occur? We exist right now, at this moment, embedded in the rich field of our lives. We are indeed the product of all the accumulated moments through which we've lived... But the rest of our time can and will be influenced not just by what we've been, but what we *choose* to be now – and now – and now!

Every second is a new beginning, a right beginning, if we live deliberately. And so all of our practices from now on can be fruitful.

Today I consider the wealth of right beginnings that are open for me to use.

Eager to escape sorrow, men rush into sorrow; from desire of happiness, they blindly slay their own happiness…

Shantideva

⑥

There is a story of an ancient Emperor who, in middle life, married a beautiful young girl on whom he doted. She was, however, not a strong woman and died a few years later of an incurable illness.

The Emperor was devastated, his life wracked with sorrow. In his despair, he visited a sage and asked him how he could possibly rid himself of this heart-sickness.

The sage said, rather unhelpfully, that time heals all things … and on no account should His Mightiness waste time thinking of blue monkeys. The Emperor was, quite naturally, puzzled at this, but the sage would say no more and so the Emperor had no choice but to take his advice.

He found himself curious about these blue monkeys and so consulted every scholar, priest, philosopher and mystic in the empire. Nobody could help him. So the Emperor cast farther afield for his answers, even sending an expedition to the high mountains in the north, where the blue monkeys were rumoured to dwell. Alas, it returned empty-handed.

Months went by and the Emperor thought of little else but blue monkeys, until finally he realized they were dominating his life. He returned to the sage and begged to be rid of this plague.

'I can do that for you, Great One,' said the sage. 'But first you must see that the memory of your wife, as well as the lady herself, is now truly at peace…'

Today I realize more fully how my conscious mind works. Do I think of blue monkeys or worries?

*Freedom is not the liberty to do what you want, but the
ability to do what is required.*

Adapted by Stephen Cassettari

☉

We live in a world bound by endless rules, regulations, pre-
cepts, directions, orders, canons, standards, principles and laws
– sensible guidance to some, unendurably bureaucratic red
tape to others!

In these circumstances, we could be forgiven for wondering
whether freedom is anything other than a utopian ideal. None of
us will surely be free enough to do what we want, whenever we
want? Such individual liberty would grow into general anarchy.

A brief examination of the rules we must live by reveals
that many of them are, purely and simply, built into the fabric
of the natural world. We are bound by gravity, we are bound by
genetics – and we are bound by the political, religious and judi-
cial laws of civilization. Unlike natural laws, they are a necessary compromise.

But often the greatest constraints we place upon ourselves
come from within. These are the barriers which can prevent us
from seeing the world from another's point of view; or, indeed,
prevent us from seeing *our* individual circumstances improved
by our own efforts. These are the barriers of low self-esteem,
worry, envy, regret… They deny us the freedom to be ourselves,
to think, feel and act in a way that expresses our uniqueness
and the joy we derive from that uniqueness.

These are the barriers stifling our ability to fulfil our own
sense of purpose.

**Today, I reflect on ways of attaining the most
important freedom of all.**

In order to discover anything, you must be looking for something.

Attrib. Harvey Neville

✆

The story is told of the German chemist Friedrich A. Kekulé, who for many years had been working on the problem of how carbon and hydrogen atoms combined to form the benzene molecule. During the course of his investigations he arranged the atoms in every way he could think of, but the resultant model could never explain the full range of behaviour of the chemical.

Then, in 1865, he happened to be riding in a horse-drawn carriage which was making its way slowly through the streets of Ghent, in Belgium. Kekulé fell into a light doze...

Some accounts say that he dreamed of snakes writhing on the floor, others that he saw the chains of atoms comprising the benzene molecules twisting and turning in front of him. But whichever is true, one of the coiling forms suddenly looped itself round to form a circle. Kekulé startled awake, *knowing* without any shadow of a doubt that the benzene molecule existed in the shape of a ring. Subsequent experiments proved him right.

The point to be made is that Kekulé's inspiration did not come 'out of the blue', the gift of some mysterious omniscient Muse. A significant proportion of his life had been spent preparing the ground, making it fertile, so that the seed of enquiry might grow, flourish and bear a fruitful solution. Kekulé, like millions of others, discovered because he was searching...

Today I consider what it is I am looking for – and thereby increase my chances of finding it.

Is your cucumber bitter? Throw it away. Are there briars in your path? Turn aside. That is enough. Do not dwell on the thought, 'Why have such things been brought into the world?'

Marcus Aurelius

☙

Our language is filled with the terminology of war, the syntax of strife. Nature is 'red in tooth and claw' and only 'the fittest survive' in the 'hostile environment' of 'market forces' and 'the competitive world of business'. Such images accumulate to form a perception that the world is a cold, hard, cruel place where we must be strong, indeed ruthless, to endure. Our whole educational system is built not around the celebration of achievement on an individual level but upon competition and invidious comparison. Success in such a system is defined as being 'better' than somebody else. Thus it is a pedagogy of failure, of demoralizing élitism and waste.

Right from our earliest days, we are conditioned to do battle.

Yet who is your enemy? Another rat in the race? Anybody else who stands in your way? The vicissitudes of misfortune? The limitations you were born with? Can it be that you are your *own worst enemy*?

The consequences of the battlefield-of-life scenario can be devastating, insofar as we are made to judge success and failure on someone else's terms. To cultivate true well-being, it is necessary to redefine success in a way which is meaningful and useful to ourselves, then to look anew at how that success may be brought about.

Today I wonder whether I need to battle through the briars in my path.

The smile on your face is sight enough.

Jalaluddin Rūmi

◎

When are we ever satisfied? When do we know we have 'made it'? There is a world of difference between *not* knowing and thinking that we are never satisfied, that there is always another rung on the ladder.

Satisfaction seems to be one side of an insidious coin. Dissatisfaction is its opposite face. There is nothing in between. If we are not satisfied, then we must be dissatisfied. True enough, there are degrees of each – so we feel less dissatisfied having bought a pound of rotten plums than a car that breaks down on the drive home from the garage. And a day's fruitful work may be satisfying, but a lifetime's achievement generates a glow of satisfaction on a different scale entirely.

Damage is done when the notion of 'being satisfied' attaches to petty things (rather than simply small things). There is danger in being dissatisfied with the house you've got because your friend has a house that's bigger. And what *hurt* can come from the thought that your colleague's partner is younger/ more attractive/more influential (etc., etc.) than your own...

In a culture that endlessly encourages dissatisfaction with what we have and tempts us to want more and more, we would be wise to redefine the source and nature of our satisfaction, and look again, not merely at what we want, but what we already have.

Today the smile on your face is sight enough.

Whatever you do is evil for somebody.
That is one of the ironies of the whole creation.

Joseph Campbell

❻

In cultivating your lawn you kill some weeds. In eating your dinner you are most likely contributing to industries that, directly or not, have led to the destruction of natural habitats. In driving your car you deplete natural resources and add to the world's weight of pollution. Look around your house and see how many items were probably made by the exploited labour force of an 'emerging economy'…

Whatever we do is evil for somebody:

> Because we are all connected, embedded in the one
> holographic reality where small actions send ripples out in
> all directions.
> And because evil is part of the fabric of the world, woven in
> on a fundamental level, perhaps for purposes beyond our
> present understanding – but at least so that by its presence,
> we may know the nature of goodness.

Today I face the reality of evil and contemplate its purpose. As the worshipper walks to the church, small creatures die beneath his heels.

Thou breakest the heads of dragons in the waters.

Psalm 74

❻

Dragons and dragon-slaying myths date back to the earliest days of written story and probably long before that. They are to be found in many cultures and in a diversity of forms through the ages. There is a direct line of descent from the destruction of the dragon Tiamat by Marduk in the Babylonian epic to officer Ripley overcoming the alien in Ridley Scott's movie of that name.

Two points should be made here.

The first is that the general assumption exists, and has long existed, that the hero embodying pure goodness actually *slays* the dragon, the embodiment of all that is evil. However, many authorities point out that thousands of symbolic representations of the myth show the two combatants, dragon and hero, locked in perpetual combat. Evil is never entirely obliterated, while good cannot be completely vanquished. It takes but a small leap of the imagination to see this icon in the twined teardrop symbol of the Tao, an expression of the Yin/Yang nature of the universe. 'For the moon, there is the cloud...'

The second point is that mythology is of necessity a profound and living influence, continually evolving to be stated anew with each generation. We need myths. They express for us fundamental wisdoms and rich spiritual and psychological truths. To focus solely on the surface features of material reality is to ignore and deny the deeply beneficial power of myths, which portray in stylistic but thoroughly human terms ways toward a more meaningful and fulfilling existence.

Today I look for my dragons.

This world is nothing but a dance of shadows,
A line drawn between darkness and light,
Joy and oppression, time and eternity.

Fakhruddin Araqi

⑥

We are subjective beings. The world isn't what we see, but what we *think* we see. And the way we see it determines the degree of happiness we enjoy each day.

Despite these individual perceptions, it's generally true that people define reality for themselves solely in terms of physical things: objects that they would like to possess, the appearance of their own bodies, and so on. They make a huge investment of time and emotional energy wanting things, regretting they don't have certain things, coveting things other people own, enjoying brief satisfaction or happiness when things come their way... But once those objects wear out or are superseded by later models, the old cycle of dissatisfaction reasserts itself.

It is not wrong to want things or to own them. Physical reality is still reality, albeit just one aspect of a greater whole. As physical beings we will always relish tasty food, savour pleasant aromas, appreciate beautiful sights. But sensory experience on this level is not the be-all and end-all of existence. The quality of our emotional lives and the degree of spiritual awareness to which we can aspire enhance the physical world, just as our perception of what's 'out there' helps determine the nature of our inner self.

What life means to us is fundamental to its quality.

Today I reaffirm the importance of my inner world and the nature of my outer perceptions.

Who is dumb?
One who does not speak kind words when they are needed.

Shankaracharya

❻

Are you your own severest critic? Or do you flatter yourself to an exaggerated degree, to keep the ego inflated?

Our conscious mind maintains a constant mental dialogue throughout our waking hours, both with itself and of necessity with aspects of the subconscious. Although we may hardly be aware of what's being said (and it is a profound paradox and mystery as to how the conscious mind can fail to be aware of its own activities!), the messages are not meaningless, nor do they go unheeded.

Self-image is connected intimately with self-esteem. Both of these may or may not be fully grounded in our material circumstances. It is not inevitable that if someone isn't physically attractive, they will have a low self-opinion. Similarly, if a person has become extremely rich, it does not follow that they will be extremely happy or fulfilled.

We can make more effective use of our mental voice by firstly becoming aware of it and then by directing what it has to say. If a useful aphorism is to 'live deliberately', then an important element of that is to *think* deliberately. This of course is the antithesis of the mental habits that allow worry to flourish like mould in a forgotten corner.

Self-awareness is neither self-consciousness, nor false flattery nor pride. It is directing the light of consciousness back onto ourselves and thus is often an illuminating experience.

Today I will not be dumb to myself, or deaf, or blind...

Shut out the dead yesterdays, the unborn tomorrows.
Sir William Osler

⑥

Yesterday is not dead, of course, and tomorrow has already been born – in the limitless world of our imaginations. One of the automatic functions of the conscious mind is to review the past and anticipate the future in order to refine our picture of reality and thereby more fully inform our chosen course of action. And although we 'know' that imagined scenarios might never have happened, or might never occur, recent research using Positron Emission Tomography (PET) scanning has discovered that the activity of the brain in processing information remains remarkably consistent, *whether the information is imagined or 'real'*.

Be that as it may, in a very practical sense the 'past is past and the future neuter'. Neither can actually hurt us, though by constantly allowing our attention to turn to what is done or what might be, we load ourselves up with worries which, in the here and now, are quite without foundation.

Dealing with the past and future on the subconscious level requires particular psychotherapeutic or hypnotherapeutic techniques. On the conscious level, all it takes is the gentle discipline of increased self-awareness and our old friend, deliberate action. By a repeated act of will – and subsequent behaviour based on that act – it is indeed possible to close the book of the past and not be tempted to open pages that lie ahead in the unfinished story of our lives.

Living in today, I live *for* today.

Life is in the living – in the tissue of every day and hour.
Robert Louis Stevenson

❻

Today is another day, unique in the long succession of days that make up a human life, infinitesimal when set against the unimaginable framework of eternity.

And yes, indeed, our days can be problem-ridden, each problem bringing with it a burden of worry. But to know that a problem is a *perception* is already to have divested ourselves of some of its weight. To leave that problem behind at the end of a day (even if we need to tackle it anew tomorrow) lightens it even further. To put it in perspective and set it against the much greater framework of our entire existence reduces it to manageable and quite harmless dimensions. It becomes what it needs to be for it to be dealt with effectively.

Problems left unchecked flower in the mind. They are like shadows cast large on the screen of uncertainty – huge menacing things that are often out of all proportion to their cause. They can seem the biggest elements – the *only* elements – in our lives. And yet, properly regarded, they are diminished, and we are free to invest our time and energy in *living*, rather than in profitless agonizing.

Life is all we have. Let's live it actively!

I see that the tissue of every day and hour constitutes the body of my existence.

There are not two sides to an argument [when] there is no argument.

Paul Hawken

❻

The logical, reasoning part of the mind sneers perhaps at the childish obviousness of this quotation. Of course there are not two sides to an argument if there is no argument in the first place!

But that same mental voice, the cynic, the analyst, allows arguments to develop out of nothing and grow into huge structures of thought which can ruin friendships and haunt the corridors of the imagination for days and weeks, even years.

I am put in mind of an argument I had with a room-mate at college, a frighteningly long time ago, when we were green undergraduate students, each eager to be 'one up' on the other. One of our modular courses was philosophy ('But why?' you may ask) and we had been introduced to the concept held by the Ancient Greeks that the circle was the perfect shape.

Luckily the students' union bar opened before we came to blows and we reconciled our differences over a beer. For many years I looked back almost with shame at this ridiculous episode, but only more recently have I realized that our stance was *automatically* one of contention – we saw no other path, however 'rational' and 'philosophical' our argument was initially intended to be.

But there are other ways, including the gentle way of not arguing in the first place, turning aside from the brambles in your path...

Today, if an argument comes along, I turn aside. Thus, my antagonist does not win and I am not defeated.

I do not know what I may appear to the world; but to myself
I seem to have been only like a boy playing on the sea-shore,
and diverting myself, in now and then finding a smoother
pebble or a prettier shell than ordinary, while the great ocean
of truth lay undiscovered before me.

Sir Isaac Newton

☙

We have always existed on the shoreline of that great ocean of truth, a shoreline that marks the familiar boundary between the outer ocean of the cosmos and the inner ocean of the self.

So far, in the entire history of human evolution and development, we have known but the tiniest fraction of what there is to be known. And while mankind's acquisition of knowledge progresses at an exponential rate, it is still true that 'the brightest light casts the blackest shadows'. In a very fundamental sense, our species may always live in relative ignorance of the universe in which we are embedded.

Newton stood, as he said, 'on the shoulders of giants' to make his contribution to science possible. But the crucial nature of that contribution can never be doubted, even though it is now being superseded by more sophisticated perspectives.

Most of us as children loved to beachcomb, lost in the simple wonder of personal discovery. That innocence and joy may be obscured in us today. But other, deeper and more marvellous oceans beckon now, washing up their treasures to be found. Do we trouble ourselves, in the busy-ness of our day-to-day lives, to look?

Today I divert myself and play for a while on the seashore.

The effort to understand the universe is one of the very few things that lifts human life a little above the level of farce, and gives it some of the grace of tragedy.

Steven Weinberg

As far as we know we constitute the only species on the planet capable of making the effort to understand the universe. And in that gift of self-awareness and abstract thought there does indeed lie tragedy, wonder, terror, farce...

What we are not yet able to prove conclusively is whether the ability is the result of a random tumble of chemical reactions over geological time or a fundamental element written into the blueprint of the cosmic architecture. Perhaps amongst the busy daily details of living it doesn't even matter to most people.

But the facility itself is crucial, for in making an effort to understand the universe, we reach a more complete understanding of ourselves. And of course the converse is equally true – to understand ourselves is to know our place in the greater picture.

We can make this effort modestly, on our own level, this simple, vital act of asking 'Why?' And must take the answer as proof of our purpose.

Today I ask the most vital human question.

What shall we tell you?
Tales, marvellous tales of ships and stars…

James Elroy Flecker

6

All of us live rich lives of fantasy and make-believe; to such an extent, indeed, that the writer Colin Wilson asserts that we exist for 90 per cent of the time inside our own heads!

Fantasy serves many purposes. One largely unwanted and impractical purpose is to create the mental structures we call 'problems'. The very name prompts the subconscious to feed the conscious mind with (usually worst-case) scenarios of what might happen. This is accompanied by the simultaneous unpleasant emotional reaction we know all too well – the physical consequences of the mental act of worrying.

And yet, in most cases, for most of the time, 'problems' are simply thoughts in the imagination, without, necessarily, any firm basis in external reality.

Make a habit, instead, of using fantasy for the practical purpose of unashamed escapism. As children we enjoyed being carried away into worlds of make-believe. Why not as adults let us occasionally put aside the analytical, reality-testing portion of our minds and allow ourselves to be carried away into storybook worlds once again. While you're there – if not believing it, then suspending your disbelief – you will reap all the physical benefits as surely as if you had made the journey in actuality.

Today I let fantasy work in my favour.

God does not play at dice.

Albert Einstein

⑥

Whatever our view of God, it cannot be denied that as a species we have the capacity at least to be aware of a spiritual component to our complex natures. Intellectually we can reflect upon what might be called 'the soul'; and indeed, as always with our thoughts, this admission may carry with it a powerful emotional charge, allowing a more profound and less cerebral exploration of the nature of the soul.

Spirituality determines cosmology. Any blunt denial of a *universal* spirit is not sufficient even to satisfy the strictures and limitations of the sceptical conscious mind: absence of proof is not proof of absence. As thinking beings, we should, as a necessary first step, allow our minds to open and wonder whether they will subsequently be filled with light.

Einstein felt that a universal God would not have created a probabilistic universe. Certain knowledge is certain to exist and, if we take an optimistic stance, is certain to be found.

But there must be many paths. And for those still searching, this thought: the universe is either accidental or designed.

If you feel it is a random and spontaneous occurrence, then 'Patience, and shuffle the cards.'

But if it's designed, then it is designed down to the minutest detail. Thus, everything has purpose and even the smallest particle of dust burgeons with meaning.

Today I reach out to touch the subtle possibility of Spirit.

Do you remember when you were first a child?
Nothing in the world seemed strange to you?
You perceived, for the first time, shapes already familiar,
And seeing, you know that you had always known
The lichen on the rock, fern leaves, the flowers of thyme…

Kathleen Raine

⑥

Millions of people throughout the world are convinced they have been here before. The certainty of reincarnation forms a basic element of many religions.

And the phenomenon of 'familiarity at first seeing' is a real one, manifesting itself as a sense of rightness and belonging, a deep subliminal understanding that you have a place here … and perhaps that, somehow, 'the universe knew you were coming'.

It is all too easy for adults to dismiss this out of hand as an infantile misperception, a mistake based on ignorance and inexperience. But such a cynical view confuses 'childish' and 'childlike', and denies deeper wisdoms which we may all carry with us into the world and, if we are fortunate, carry out of it as well.

Present cares and grown-up concerns frequently blot out the fragile, gentle memories of childhood. But nothing is ever lost. What we are now is the result of an unbroken chain of moments from those early days when the world seemed puddle-wonderful, when we didn't simply accept its familiar richness and wonder – *we knew it without a doubt.*

To put ourselves back in touch with those times enhances the coherence of our lives. And, just maybe, it might allow us to discover what we have really known all along…

Today, in a quiet time, I let the tide of memory wash through me – a refreshing, cleansing experience.

Time is a great teacher, but unfortunately it kills all its pupils.

Hector Berlioz

⑥

The suggestion has already been made that great teaching is a co-operative affair between teacher and pupil. As learners we cannot afford to sit back passively and wait for insight, inspiration or wisdom to happen by…

What we do with our time is of paramount importance in determining what time does with us – both eventually and on a moment-by-moment basis. These days people talk almost glibly about 'the quality of life'. It has become a fashionable phrase. And it is usually linked with material wealth and status. But the dynamic of life is time, its limited supply, and the use we make of it. Time well spent means time well used.

So pause today and consider whether the things that worry you constitute time well spent. Are you failing to benefit from experiences replayed in your mind again and again? And are those experiences real – or scenarios set sometime in a hypothetical future which may or may not come to pass?

Yes, time kills us all in the end. But we can do it to ourselves very effectively if our attitude to life is one of killing time.

Today I reflect on my 'savings account' of time and how best I can spend it.

Not keep a journal! How are your absent cousins to
understand the tenor of life in Bath without one?

Jane Austen

⑥

You probably don't live in Bath and you may not even have any absent cousins, but Jane Austen's wonderfully genteel exclamation of surprise underlies an important general principle. Keeping a journal has many useful and therapeutic functions. In a very real way, by writing down our problems, we 'get them off our chest' and diminish them; and by writing down our joys, successes and triumphs, we remember them and celebrate them anew.

Glancing back through a journal may reveal to us that a problem which worried us six months ago is now hardly a memory – and we may not even understand the reference we made to 'the awful thing plaguing my mind' this time last year...

A journal is a repository of experiences, impressions, scraps and fragments to be treasured; words, sentences, whole paragraphs or chapters, or simply tiny punctuation marks in the story of our lives. A journal is as individual and unique as its creator. We can use it to understand ourselves more fully and to help express our individuality – our utterly singular perspective – to anyone we care to admit into our secret and sacred domain.

Today I record something of myself, for these hours will never come again.

There is only one health, but diseases are many. Likewise, there seems to be one fundamental force that heals, although the myriad schools of medicine all have their favourite ways of cajoling it into action.

Dr Robert Becker

⑥

Attitudes to health are similar in many ways to attitudes to life itself. When we fall ill, do we simply regard it as 'bad luck', 'one of those things? Do we feel that we have any say in or control over a disease? Do we lie back passively and let the experts run through the process of trying to find the bad or broken bit and fix it?

When we are healthy, do we celebrate that health? Do we relish our feeling of wellness and seek to maintain it in our thoughts, emotions and behaviour? What do we think to the idea that health and well-being stem from our active participation *at all levels* in the presentation and progress of our lives? Have we ever considered that both health and disease are meaningful things – that exist for a reason? And that that reason can be found?

There is a swelling tide of thought that each of us is the embodiment of a force, a life force, that permeates and drives forward the whole span and range of creation. It is the difference between significance and meaninglessness, design and causelessness, purpose and accident.

To be aware of it, and then to utilize it, makes all the difference.

Today I celebrate health – whether I am ill or not – to restore, maintain and improve the life force inside me.

Health has to be earned.

Harvey Diamond

⑥

To take health for granted is another example of the same mechanical thinking that creates, maintains and empowers worry. Taking anything for granted is essentially passive, an unthinking and unaware phenomenon. It is like not noticing the ticking of a clock until it stops – or, indeed, realizing how useful that clock was until it is broken.

Health is a force, an energy within us that needs to be attended to as we might nurture a fire to keep ourselves warm. In the same way as we would nourish those flames, so we should seek to sustain ourselves in body, mind and spirit, so we may grow and blaze in our lifetime.

Having said that, there's no need to be overly punctilious about active health – certainly we should not worry too much about whether we're eating the right foods or taking enough exercise! That would be in itself counterproductive. But of course, neither is health something we should regard as a passing or minor concern.

Today I realize that earning health leads to time spent in happiness and fulfilment.

Life is too short for any distant aim,
And cold the dull reward of future fame.

Mary Wortley Montagu

⑥

Much is written about the benefits of living in the here-and-now: the joy of experiencing *this* breath, *this* moment – not just then, not soon, but *now*!

Training yourself to live fully in the instant, developing, perhaps by meditation, that skill of becoming acutely aware, at will, of the moment's heartbeat, can bring enormous rewards.

But it is not the mind's natural state, or, in the spin and hurry of today's complex world, entirely appropriate. We have evolved an imagination and a certain degree of control over it. Sometimes it becomes a very real matter of survival to look back or to anticipate possibilities. At the very least this ability stands us in good stead more often than it plagues us with worries over the dead past or the fantasy of the future.

It is all a matter of balance and control. Never has it been a question of either/or. Living constantly in the moment with no regard for the meaning of other moments is quite useless and counterproductive. It leads to an *inability* to enjoy the present second because we have not prepared for it, or to failing to take pride and pleasure from our past achievements just because they are over and done with. The skills of grasping the 'now' and of fond reminiscence and forward thinking can all be useful instruments in our mental toolkit. But they need to be kept sharp – and used as often as possible.

Today I polish the useful instrument of my mind.

What's a person's age? We must hurry more, that's all;
Cram in a day what our youth took a year to hold.

Robert Browning

⑥

I don't think I've ever been an advocate of hurry or of cramming experience into any given span of time – which seems to me to have an air of desperation about it.

What I do find inspirational in Browning's words is the idea that life can be lived more fully. But to me it's a question of quality, not quantity. How much more satisfying to savour a fine wine, sip by sip, than to guzzle it! And to take time to appreciate the scent of a rose is no less an exquisite experience – and may be more so – than to stand in a flower-grower's greenhouse and madly inhale!

Age itself can bring a growing awareness that time is precious. But we needn't live a lifetime to reach this profound understanding. It is first grasped intellectually and then realized more subtly but more powerfully through experience. Our sensitivity to that experience is what counts: our ability to learn from what happens.

Likewise, only by allowing our experiences to unfold naturally and fully in their own time, do we come to see – and hear and smell and touch and taste – that to hurry and cram in later life is merely hollow mimicry of youth's wild flight towards the future.

What's a person's age? Everything they have done: everything they have left to do – in its own time...

Life is a revolt against the statistical rules of physics.
                                        Albert Szent-Gyorgyi

⑥

These words carry many meanings – from the notion that the appearance of life itself in the universe was never statistically likely to the idea that life as a burgeoning force constantly seeks to surprise what the ongoing rules of physics predict.

On an individual level, our own lives can be vehicles running contrary to the *statistical* rules governing the machinery of the world. Statistics deals with probability by looking back at what has been in order to project onto the screen of the future the chances of something similar happening. But the unpredictable nature of life in all its colour and complexity means that what is likely is never inevitable, and that any individual can, through accident, judgement or design, prove to be an exception to the rule.

'Likelihood' is sometimes a handy tool, but there is a difference between likelihood and possibility; and a world of difference between possibility and potential.

By using imagination, determination and faith, you can avoid being a number in a general equation. Whatever may occur *statistically* might never, in fact, happen to you at all. Revolt against the trend and take joy in it.

Today I feel alive. Today I feel exceptional!

The first day a guest, the second day a guest, the third day a calamity.

Indian proverb

❻

Worry is a guest that has stayed for too long. Indeed, as I think about it, worry was never a guest but a squatter. It moves in uninvited and by its presence claims the right to stay. It is unwelcome, unwanted, burdensome. And the towering irony of it all is that it creeps into our lives while we're still living there!

In short, this is a calamity.

If worry were a real person squatting somewhere that was rightfully ours, in a treasured and private place close to our hearts, we would surely take extreme and sustained measures to get that person evicted. No effort would be too great to restore order and balance, quietude and light to our property. We would seek help wherever we could, do whatever was necessary, be unrelenting in claiming back what was fundamentally and unarguably ours.

And yet worry squats on and on and on in our minds, unchallenged.

Why should it?

Go in there and kick worry out! Take extreme measures – take any measures you know will succeed!

Today I begin to reclaim what is rightfully mine – peace of mind, tranquillity, joy.

As I was saying the other day…

Luis Ponce de León
(Spanish monk, on continuing with a lecture
interrupted five years earlier, by his imprisonment)

◎

This must serve as a supreme example of not dwelling on the past and of a determination not to let the natural tendency of the mind hold sway, either by harbouring regret and bitterness or by apportioning blame. It is also a wonderful statement on one man's priorities in life – his wish to be getting on with the business that interests and fulfils him, rather than let a disruption *continue* to disrupt, once the actual cause has gone away.

Of course, this incident and Luis Ponce de León's reaction to it lie perhaps towards the extremes of human potential. Most of us would be traumatized and damaged even by the prospect of five years' imprisonment, let alone by the incarceration itself. We are not made of steel and can be hurt…

But the importance of this example lies in its general principle. By overcoming smaller foes, we learn how better to deal with the main enemy, the *habit* of worry itself.

The gentle discipline of picking up where we left off, once crises or difficulties have subsided, also encourages us to reflect on our priorities – unlike worry, which laces each wish with envy and threads every missed opportunity with regret. By laying down the burden of misfortune, we lighten our hearts and thus can walk with renewed vigour towards the true purpose of our lives.

Today I turn myself in the right direction. Today I choose happiness.

The pearl is lovelier than the most brilliant of crystalline gems, because it is made through the suffering of a living creature…

H. G. Wells

⑥

Long ago in northern India, a young prince married a girl he treasured more than anything else in the world. For a short time their love flourished and their time together was sublime – until the princess died of an insect sting one day while out riding. The young prince was plunged into the blackest despair.

But presently, he seemed to step away from a dreadful brink. He declared that he would erect a monument around the simple stone sarcophagus in which his love had been laid, a monument that would be known as 'The Pearl of Love'.

So began what became a lifelong project for the prince, so that year by year more magnificent rooms and chambers were built around the original mausoleum.

At last the prince, now a bent and decrepit old man, gazed upon his handiwork and felt satisfied. Though not quite satisfied. Because, as he wandered through the serene vastness of his achievement, he noticed an imbalance, a blemish, a flaw that lay at the centre of his Pearl of Love. A rough-hewn stone box had been left behind by a careless team of builders and the prince found that the longer he stared at this strange, ugly, quite purposeless object, the more it offended his eyes.

So he called his chief architect and, with his voice echoing through the vaults and galleries of the vast sepulchre, commanded him to have it taken away and buried.

Today I write down five lessons I have learned from this story…

Any time that is not spent on love is wasted.

Torquato Tasso

❡

It may seem at first glance that this snippet of wisdom stands in direct contradiction to the lessons of 'The Pearl of Love'. But further quiet reflection reveals that there are many aspects of love, and that, ultimately, the prince in the story harboured a love that was anchored in the past and unhealthily self-involved. Love of one person by another cannot surely be measured by material opulence or expressed merely by grandeur? Neither is true love just the *memory* of love, tainted by what can so easily become a selfish and indulgent grief upon the loss of the beloved.

Love is strengthened through time, but expresses itself moment by moment: its power and purpose exist now. Its power does not depend upon grand or dramatic demonstrations of proof. A word, a smile, some small, sensitive act or gesture – these are all that are necessary for love not only to survive, but to prevail.

In this sense, any time that is not spent on love is wasted. And, as importantly, any time not spent on love is time not spent on nourishing worry's greatest opponent.

Today, if only in a small way, I show someone that I love them.

Procrastination is the art of keeping up with yesterday.

Don Marquis

☾

Some people will go to enormous lengths to avoid doing something they find embarrassing or difficult, tedious, unfamiliar, new.

The trouble is that many problems just don't go away by themselves. Those that do, of course, simply strengthen the habit of putting things off by creating the illusion that 'no action can be the right action'. Why do anything, if nothing needs to be done?

True enough, not to take action is occasionally the best response – but it should be one that is arrived at deliberately and positively; a decision that is reached through quiet reflection as to the most effective route from A to B.

And it is not always appropriate even then. Indeed, some problems get worse as time goes by, growing and flourishing by inaction.

As Don Marquis tells us with such perspicacity, procrastination is an art. Years can be spent in developing what begins as a simple knee-jerk response into an elaborate weave of mental and emotional reactions to any and every obstacle or predicament.

In procrastinating, we hold ourselves back. We may wish the problem had never happened. But it has. And the only way through to a trouble-free tomorrow is to tackle those troubles today.

Today I take time to dwell on my problems, for the sole purpose of solving them!

There is only one history of importance, and it is the history of what you once believed in and the history of what you came to believe in.

Kay Boyle

⊙

Our beliefs are the big engines that drive us through life. They are formed from our earliest days, carved by our own experiences, sculpted by the people who have authority and influence over us as children: our parents, teachers, TV icons and of course our peers. What we believe is created and fed by their words and actions.

And all that we've done and seen, heard, said, felt and thought is still alive in our heads, programming our minds. We are what we've been – and what we were is the result of what we *thought* happened to us...

And if certain beliefs are not helpful to us, if they result in an outlook that promotes worry and fear, then something needs to be done about it, and something *can* be done about it.

Early beliefs – so-called 'core beliefs' – are not locked away in a safe, forever out of reach. There are mental mechanisms for accessing them. Nor are current beliefs fixed or final. We are never a 'finished product'; the story isn't over until it's over.

We have the capacity, and can create the opportunity, to become much more fully the author of our own story. And we should start now, because the history of importance informs and directs what we are yet to become.

Today I understand that I am what I believe in. And now I begin to believe in myself.

Toto, I've a feeling we're not in Kansas any more.

Dorothy

◐

We change, but the world also changes around us; sometimes radically, sometimes in a way we do not like or of which we would not approve.

The future comes upon us anyway. Change drenches us like a ceaseless downpour. It will never stop, it can only increase. We must learn to adapt or to flounder. In adapting, we learn moreover to flourish.

Saying this, I am put in mind of my earliest attempts to write, nearly 30 years ago. I used a typewriter that was too heavy to lift. Working on it for more than an hour became physically exhausting, and the quality of the print was, by today's standards, atrocious. Now I enjoy the benefits of a PC that can format my page, link me up to an encyclopaedia, thesaurus and spellchecker; I am able to leap through the text and move huge chunks of it from place to place in seconds; I can shoot the finished work down the phoneline; and store it – hundreds of pages of it – on a slip of metal and plastic small enough to fit in my pocket.

But it's not just technology that's changed. I am now in my middle-age and life no longer seems endless. There is less of my precious time to squander. The future bears down upon me – but whether I see it as an oncoming express train or an unfolding vista of opportunity is an outlook wholly of my making.

I'm not in Kansas any more. And I'm going to enjoy some sightseeing.

Today I begin to see how I can change myself for the best in a changing world.

Fear seems to be an epidemic in our society. We fear beginnings, we fear endings. We fear changing, we fear 'staying stuck'. We fear success, we fear failure. We fear living, we fear dying…

Susan Jeffers

6

Fear and worry are old friends. They hang around like a couple of school bullies on a street corner and taunt us as we go by, hurling threats and abuse, seeking to humiliate us, belittle us, cause us to change direction and run the other way. They feed off our cowardice, our lack of confidence, all of our previous failures. They seem relentless, dauntless, immovable…

But unlike real bullies these two thugs in our heads can never follow up their threats. All they can do – but all they often *need* to do! – is watch us hurt ourselves.

So how can they be beaten? The title of Susan Jeffers' book, *Feel the Fear, and Do It Anyway*, indicates one of many methods. Why should fear automatically paralyse us? Is there not something deeper within all of us that we can use to kick the hell out of the two gutter ruffians and put an end to their antics for good?

Can we focus on the sheer pleasure of achievement once we've succeeded? Can we let pure anger at our own passive state power us into action? Can we take a small problem, a minor worry, and turn the tables by bullying *it* into submission? Can we go right up to our enemies and tell them with confidence and determination (feigned at first, but not later) that we've simply *had enough* of feeling this way?

Any and all of these!

Today I feel the fear and do it anyway. Today I take worry by the throat and kick it out the door.

Those who love us may well push us when we're ready to fly.
Marilyn Ferguson

⑥

Independence, self-confidence, inner determination, open-mindedness – these are useful qualities to possess and ones that bring great benefit. The fortunate among us acquire them early and 'naturally' as part of their upbringing.

The rest of us need to work at things a little…

But we do not need to work in isolation. Indeed, few of us do unless we make a deliberate effort to exclude loved ones, friends and acquaintances from our journey and our quest. Practically speaking, if the wish to learn and become stronger is there inside us, then that learning will happen anyway. Sometimes it is through the inevitable osmosis of ideas from the outside world, sometimes because of quantum leaps we ourselves make and often because other people recognize the goals we have set for ourselves and want to help us in achieving them.

It can be a hard road to walk. We may feel the fear and *not* do it anyway, knowing that we hold ourselves back, feeling ashamed or angry with ourselves… We *want* to make that leap. We *want* to fly free, beyond the limits we previously set for ourselves. But when the moment arrives, we find ourselves wanting.

And that's when someone who truly loves us, truly knows who we are and what we can become, speaks the words or performs the act that launches us.

Briefly we panic as we cling to the old ways.

But then we soar.

Today I am prepared to put my trust in those who love me.

To imagine is everything.

Anatole France

❻

I am constantly surprised by the number of people who tell me that they have 'no imagination' and almost as frequently astonished to hear the contrary – as when one lady with a migraine problem came to me for advice, having been told by her doctor that her problem was due to 'an over-active mind'! I asked her if that was a technical term and what her GP thought the cure might be. In this case, he had omitted to qualify his diagnosis.

I am also put in mind, in thinking on this meditation, of an occasion when I was invited into a school to talk about my books. The teacher who met me in the lobby explained that the children comprising my audience were 'difficult' and 'not particularly clever', and that I wasn't to expect much of a response. Before introducing me, he yelled very loudly at the kids to put an end to their excited but relatively subdued chatter, then went on to explain that I was a 'special' person, a 'gifted' person, because I wrote stories. So they'd better treat me with respect!

My loathing for this individual almost put an end to my talk right then. But I forged ahead, asking how many of the kids had ever wished they could fly. All of them, of course. I then told a story about a boy who'd done just that – and as the wish came into his mind, so he rose up and up and up…

The gaze of everyone in the audience lifted up towards the ceiling. With the exception of the one other adult in the room.

Imagination is a wonderful gift that nurtures us in many ways throughout our lives.

Today I resolve to give my imagination free rein.

*I suddenly understand that it is most certainly necessary
to seek, to ask the question; rather than pushing away the
answer by dashing after it, one must ask and listen at the
same time…*

Reshad Feild

❻

When we look out into the world, we see various individuals
and institutions madly scrabbling for answers: big companies
desperate to get the edge on their competitors; research organi-
zations frantically updating what they know; electronics giants
energetically bringing out the latest model of this or that
machine as swiftly as possible…

And of course it would be foolish to deny that such vigour
has 'bootstrapped' our knowledge of medicine and technology
– of the physical world – immensely, bringing many benefits.
But it would be equally foolish to conclude that looking outwards for answers is the only way of asking; or that answers
come in direct proportion to the energy expended in finding
them.

The wisdom of many cultures throughout the ages informs
us that the universe within is as complex and wonderful as that
without. Each of us experiences life at the interface between the
two. The power and scale, the sheer *noise* of modern civilization
can cause us to forget that the inner world lies just a leap of the
imagination away. And it can also drown out the answers it
offers forth, if we are not listening quietly to ourselves.

**Today I ask and listen at the same time. I am
attentive to my own answers.**

Our lives cry out for intrinsic meaning.

Malcolm Boyd

❧

What we mean is what we *are*. This cannot be emphasized or restated often enough. Our lives can only be fulfilling if they are meaningful, and those meanings need to be deep-seated, derived from our own experiences and our reflections upon them.

Meanings are the answers we have sought within ourselves, in quietude, with humility, through imagination.

Our meanings define us and the shape of the world in our eyes. Such definition is not to be found in the *accoutrements* of our outward identity: the clothes we wear, the car we drive. Nor are we always clear in our own minds as to what we mean to ourselves. Who is this 'I' that happens to like Oriental food and crime thriller novels and cats and cool autumn evenings? What else is there that makes me *me?*

That is the fundamental question, the lifelong quest, the ultimate meaning.

Because in seeking itself we find meaning in everything around us. Simply and honestly to ask 'Who am I?' prompts us to look everywhere for clues – outwardly, to be sure, but if we are sensitive and wise, inwardly as well.

And where the answers meet, that's where we find and represent ourselves.

Today I find intrinsic meaning in *wondering*. My cry is answered.

*With freedom of choice and with honour, as though the
maker and moulder of thyself, thou mayest fashion thyself in
whatever shape thou shalt prefer.*

Pico della Mirandola

⊚

Worry makes us think that things can never change – except,
perhaps, to get worse.

Say we have a debt, we can't afford to pay it off, result =
worry. End of equation. Or is it? Perhaps one step we might
take is to examine more carefully *why* we can't afford to repay
the debt. It may be that by looking anew or thinking in a different way, we can redefine the problem so that it isn't insoluble
after all. And whether we can repay it or not, why should the
inevitable end product be worry? Does worry help us to repay
that debt? Does worry allow us even to begin thinking with
clarity or acting with determination so that our chances of solving the problem are optimized?

Not a bit of it. By worrying – by *automatically* worrying –
we have denied ourselves any freedom of choice. While we
worry, we can't solve the problem or enjoy the other aspects of
our life which, practically speaking, might not be linked with
the problem at all. We have nailed ourselves down so that we
are helpless.

And yet one of the secrets of our success as a species has
been our ability to adapt. 'Adapt and survive' has long been a
cornerstone of evolutionary theory.

Well, let's take that idea and apply it in other ways, in new
contexts.

**Today my task is to realize I have freedom of choice,
once I have decided that is so!**

All my possessions for one moment of time.
Elizabeth I of England on her deathbed

⑥

Do you ever contemplate the moment of your own death?

I do not mean, do you worry every time you board a plane or cross a busy street? I do not mean, do you lie awake at night wondering if you have cancer or a brain tumour? I do not mean thinking yourself into a state of morbid melancholy... I do mean, do you ever, in imagination, put yourself ahead in time to the point at which your Earthly life concludes – and use that experience to cast light back into your present moment?

We live at the cutting edge of our own mortality second by second, day by day, and death carves a keen appreciation of life in our hearts, if we allow it.

Though life may seem drab and monotonous, we are always entering new territory – the landscape of now, and now, and *now*. These are the moments we have. That's all. When they're all done, will we be able to say that we have used them wisely or profitably? Indeed yes, if we can say in sincerity that we have lived them as fully as we were able to.

Sitting quietly, doing nothing, take yourself ahead to the hour and the minute it's so very easy to hide away. Be extravagant – be 80 years old, 90 years, with teeth, hair, clear sight and thoughts and a smile on your face...

Now look back at the life you have yet to enjoy; at all of those precious moments. Elizabeth would have given everything for one of them. Don't give yours away for nothing.

Today I look at the span of my life and draw strength from it.

It is so easy to take breathing for granted. Breath is a fully automatic process, beginning at birth and continuing without interruption until the day we die…

Michael Sky

&

The weaponry we can use against worry is powerful and diverse. Focusing on a single moment, say, then sitting back to watch the ceaseless, seamless flow of moments that make up our lives can be an experience of great meaning and importance.

That same armoury can also be used for peaceful means – not just in the war against worry.

Choose your time and place. Make it pleasant. Arrange, if you can, not to be disturbed or distracted. This is an opportunity you are creating for yourself. Make the most of it.

Take a good, deep, leisurely breath. Feel the air flowing cool through your nostrils or spilling over your lips. Take pleasure in the expansion of your lungs and ribcage, in that exquisite instant of holding in the breath, to draw from it the last iota of invigorating energy…

And then, on the outbreath, experience that wonderful easing down into a deeper state of relaxation and calm. Exhale the useless gases, the toxins, any stresses and strains you may have (whether you're consciously aware of them or not). Have done with that breath.

It's another moment. Breathe again.

Unforced, conscious breathing is a valuable tool. Through patience and quiet dedication, we can improve its quality immeasurably. Read Michael Sky's book *Breathing: Expanding your power and energy* to learn more.

Today I rediscover the profound and simple benefits of breathing.

Autumn – even
birds and clouds
look old.

Bashō

ⓖ

Breathing can be more than just a habit – and should be, if we are to gain the maximum amount of pleasure from our lives. Yes of course we do this by dreaming big and acting with determination and courage to realize those dreams... But pleasure also comes in small but significant ways, encapsulated in tiny experiences.

The year moves on. The season will change and shift towards the next. Use what is here now for your benefit.

Set aside some time and go to a park or out in the country. Use your breathing skills to *capture* this moment. You are a part of this picture, embedded in this day. What do you smell? There's no need to analyse it, just appreciate it. Draw it into yourself and make it part of you.

Now what do you see? Hear? Feel? Aromas, colours, textures, sounds... What a special time this is. What an acute and exquisite sensation, to be a thread in this weave of reality!

**Today I am not too busy for the world. Today
I savour it.**

*We all inhabit a rich, diverse and vivid fantasy world... Just
pause for a moment and reflect on the chain of associations
that have surfaced freely during the past few minutes...*
                    Eric Hall, Carol Hall and Alison Leech

(6)

Just as we can raise our awareness of the outside world as it
passes inexorably by, so we can look inwards and listen to the
quiet voices and see the subtle pictures rising from the deeper
levels of the mind.

One of the functions of those deeper levels, as the authors
above explain in their book *Scripted Fantasy in the Classroom*, is
to make meanings, to weave the threads of our experience in all
their astonishing variety into a coherent and significant picture
of reality.

We let the subconscious get on with it and rarely, if ever,
give it a thought, just as actors during a play pay no heed to the
work that's going on behind the scenes.

And, to extend the analogy, in tranquil solitude, the actor
which is your conscious mind, your will-power, your sense of
identity, can talk more freely with the stage hands in the background. You can give them instructions, offer advice and suggestions; listen to *their* suggestions, ideas and complaints. In
short, you can improve and exploit your mental self-dialogue
for a range of beneficial purposes.

To begin, when you go out for your walk and smell, see, feel
and hear the world in its uniqueness, remember the good feelings that experience generates, put them back into your subconscious and recreate them in a mind-picture any time you need to.

**Today I make use of my rich, diverse and vivid
fantasy world.**

Light, as Sir Isaac Newton demonstrated three hundred years ago, is compound. What we call 'white' light is really a blend of all the colours of the rainbow…

From *A Young Person's Guide to Science*

֍

We learn in high school about light and the electromagnetic spectrum. But we are not taught about the spectrum of the mind and how that determines the reality we perceive as fundamentally as does light itself.

At one end of the mental spectrum lies what is often inaccurately called 'normal waking consciousness'. For our purposes it can be taken to mean that mental condition wherein we're alert and clearly aware of the outside world. We employ normal waking consciousness during the hours when we're not asleep. But it isn't constant, by any means…

At the far end of the spectrum lie deep unconsciousness and sleep. Here, the conscious mind is 'turned off' and we lose all awareness of ourselves and external reality. The mind is preoccupied with, and within, itself at the very deepest levels.

Somewhere between the two extremes we find daydream, reverie, the state we know as 'hypnosis'. Here the conscious mind is not turned off, but turned down, aware enough of itself to frame thoughts that can be passed back to the workers behind the scenes, yet subdued enough to catch the gentle but busy drift of information rising from below.

This two-way traffic of thought-impressions can be exploited for many beneficial purposes. Increasing awareness of the nature of the mind, if only in these simple terms, can lead to enhanced understanding and greater control in your life.

Today I see the colours of my mind more clearly.

Nasrudin was carrying home some liver which he had just bought. In his other hand was a recipe for liver pie, given to him by a friend. Suddenly a buzzard swooped down and carried off the liver.

'You fool!' shouted Nasrudin. 'You may have taken the meat – but I still have the recipe!'

Idries Shah

⑥

The recipe for happiness and success is useless without the ingredients.

But since we are *all* interested in happiness, and many of us in success, it is worth asking just what those ingredients are. Perhaps the first and automatic answer would be money, freedom, a big house, a partner, youth, health, vigour, longevity… And so the conscious mind goes on, adding rare and exotic spices to a dish that seems increasingly unlikely to be cooked.

Reflecting further on this, we soon realize that a staple though varied diet more easily achievable. This is not to say that we need to put up with a 'poor man's' happiness or any kind of hollow success. But it seems clear that by letting the imagination leap without consideration to the outward symbols of happiness, we are not only yearning for things which might not make *us* happy, but are accepting someone else's recipe.

By defining and then working towards our own honest and thoughtful dream of happiness, we come to see that the recipe and the ingredients amount to one and the same thing.

And the place of worry in all of this? It is the buzzard, feeding on the carcass of hope that has been allowed to die.

Today I reflect on my recipe for happiness and success.

We shall not cease from exploration
And the end of all our exploring
Will be to arrive where we started
And know the place for the first time.

T. S. Eliot

⑥

Life as a journey, life as a book in-the-making – these are two of the most common and most powerful analogies we use in trying to create for ourselves an overall impression of the nature and course of our own existence.

We see immediately how apt and how useful they are, because they allow us to realize that we can, for example, take time to appreciate the byroads and panoramas during our journey, or go back and look again at past pages of the book of our life...

But Eliot's words do more than supply a handy metaphor. They also embody and eloquently convey to us an *attitude*. We do not get the most from the journey if we fail to explore along the way. And the joy of a book is lessened if we sit passively and just let the words go by. How much more fulfilling to recall earlier scenes or to anticipate with excitement the action of later chapters.

Yet for all this exploration, we arrive where we started – in the present moment, inside the body with which we were born.

Is this is ultimate irony of being? Is this simply the cruel trap of human, mortal existence?

Know the place for the first time and you will know the value of exploration.

How do I see my life today? How do I see it *anew*, today?

Things have not only to be seen to be believed, but also have to be believed to be seen.

Stan Gooch

❻

We are good at creating illusions, past masters of seeing not what's there, but what we *think* is there. Our lives can be, and often are, controlled and dominated by a picture of the world that has far more to do with fantasy than reality. And this happens at all levels of our thinking, conscious and subconscious both.

At the same time, and by the same token, we frequently *fail* to perceive what is in front of our eyes, clouded as our vision can be by misconceptions and prejudice. Sometimes this is our fault, insofar as we have allowed our thinking to run on mechanically without being examined, challenged or tested.

We can improve ourselves by cultivating an open-mindedness to the world. This does not mean becoming gullible, but simply allowing our experience to supply and sustain a number of different interpretations, so allowing us to pick the one which is most beneficial to our progress.

Similarly, simultaneously, we can cultivate an open-mindedness to ourselves, look anew at the course of our thinking, at the strength and structure of our beliefs. These are not carved in stone, but woven into the fabric of our imaginations. Thus, they are always amenable to change. And with deliberation, that change will be for the better.

Today I look again at my beliefs, in anticipation of the new things I will then be able to see.

What is the ultimate truth about ourselves?
… There is one elementary, inescapable answer – we are
that which asks the question.

Sir Arthur Eddington

⑥

There are questions and there are Questions.

Worry at its worst takes from us the inclination, or even the capability, to ask any questions. Either that, or the worried questions we ask are rhetorical, narrow or closed completely: 'Why me?' 'Why did this have to happen now?' 'What's the point of bothering when *this* is how I end up?'

Questions like these have limited use, not least because they are undirected. But there are no answers at all without questions – and no right answers without right enquiry.

We are surrounded these days by a rich network of expertise, advice and guidance. And yet we may worry alone, trapped within the confined space of our despondency or despair. Careful questions, carefully targeted, will produce practical and effective answers to specific problems.

We also question ourselves and our own attitudes. Our remarkable success as a species, our outward urge to become something *more*, owes much to our questioning nature. Questions explore possibilities and test potential, draw meaning from experience and distil wisdom from random circumstance. If properly used, they are meaning-making instruments of immense power and flexibility.

And if you ask yourself, 'Surely I couldn't achieve something like that?', follow it up with the question: *'Why not?'*

Today I understand I am that which asks the Question.

*I keep wanting to go back to the analogy of fishing for facts.
I can just see somebody asking with great frustration: 'Yes,
but which facts do you fish for? There's got to be more to it
than that?' But the answer is that if you know which facts
you're fishing for, you're no longer fishing. You've caught
them.*

Robert M. Pirsig

◉

Another analogy, another way of seeing. The very act and
process of *seeking* is as important as anything you might discover at the end of the day. The explorer of life, the searcher after
themselves, embodies an attitude and an outlook, a style of living that is positive and creative, invigorating, healthy.

Worry closes doors and splashes grey rain across the windows. It keeps you inside, disinclined to go out for any reason,
even that of wanting desperately to get away from this place.
Any searching the worried person does happens inside that
drab room, looking again and again at the same things and seeing nothing new. It is an emptiness, quite futile.

Fishermen love to catch fish. But equally they love to sit on
the riverbank and let the world go by with the ease and fluidity
of the water itself. They don't trouble or fuss. They use what
skill they have to land the fish when it bites, but understand all
the while that the fish may not take the bait at all. Even so, the
day will not have been wasted.

And even when the fish has been caught, the fisherman
goes right on fishing…

**Today I fish for its own sake, in anticipation, but
without disappointment.**

The fun is in the trip, not the destination.

Robert Bloch

◎

Robert Bloch's parable *The Hell-Bound Train* tells the story of Martin, a young man who fell on hard times and became a lonely drifter, wandering along the railway line one cold night.

The first train by stopped beside him and the strange-looking conductor stepped down. The conductor gave Martin a splendid pocket watch which he could stop whenever he wished then time itself would stop and Martin could spend eternity within the moment of his greatest happiness.

Martin was by no means happy, so he smartened himself up, got a lowly job with a big company and, through diligence, loyalty and sheer effort, worked his way up to become its president.

Years passed. The vicissitudes of fortune took their toll on Martin's company. Share prices fell. Martin was sacked from the board. His children moved away to live their own lives. His wife ran away with a much younger man...

Elderly, broken, disappointed, his health failing, Martin found himself walking again by the railway. Even as he thought back to the night of his dangerous bargain, the train roared out of the darkness and came to a stop beside him.

Inside the first carriage, a party was in progress. All of the other poor souls who had fallen into the conductor's insidious trap were spending their final few hours having a great time. Wine was flowing freely. The carriage was filled with laughter...

Martin smiled. Before the conductor could stop him, he took out his pocket-watch and firmly pressed the winder.

If I had such a watch, would I press the winder today? Tomorrow? Sometime? Never?

...we invoke you beings of the future times, you who are waiting to be born. We cannot say your names, for you have none yet that we can know. Yet it is for you that we work to preserve this beautiful planet...

Pat Fleming and Joanna Macy

⑥

There is a fundamental difference between worry and *concern*.

Worry is an endless spiral down into helplessness and hopelessness or, at the very least, a debilitating emotional millstone. Concern is a positive and sensitizing force. It puts our own problems into perspective by setting them against the greater difficulties and dilemmas of others: a community, a nation, a planet. Not only that, but we are never alone in our concerns, as we frequently are with our worries.

In *Thinking Like a Mountain*, Pat Fleming, Joanna Macy and others outline intellectually, emotionally and spiritually the requirements which will take us towards a 'Council of All Beings'. Their concerns are world-wide and yet take account of the smallest living creatures. They never suggest that our own personal worries are groundless or illusory, but by taking heed of what they say, we may come to realize just how often they are.

Concern liberates us into the world. It offers opportunity and choice of action. It colours our existence and injects purpose into our being here. It is upward-looking, optimistic, empowering. And it is always possible – eminently possible – to diminish the deadening ache of worry with a healthy concern for the wider problems of the planet.

Today I begin to turn worry into concern.

After the final no *there comes a* yes,
And on that yes *the future of the world depends.*

Wallace Stevens

⑥

Worry automatically says *no*. It is a mechanical thing, a self-fuelling habit, a narrowing channel of thought that looks inward and downward at the worst that could possibly happen.

As soon as worry says *no*, tell yourself *yes*. Flip the coin instantly, making the mental 'after-image' a positive one. And do this every time, so that even if at first you don't believe it, the coin-flip trick will become a reflex action, so that the deeper levels of your mind will be fed constantly and cumulatively with affirmations, with determined resolutions not to be dominated by the small, mean thoughts that worry generates.

This technique deals with the surface features of worry, the conscious and obvious outcomes of the habit. Over time, positive thinking will penetrate, soaking down towards your subconscious attitudes and perspectives...

But even before it happens, go right to the heart of the problem. Go to that final *no* and look beyond it. Ask yourself what is the worst that could possibly happen? Focus on the notion of *could*, not *will* or *must*.

Can you survive that possible dark eventuality? Can you prepare and then prevail? How tenable does *no* seem now?

These techniques do not amount to kidding yourself that things can get better. They define, create and then celebrate an attitude that *knows* things will get better, knows that behind the final *no* is a *yes* – on which the future of your world depends.

Today I deny the *no* of worry and look beyond to *yes*!

It is necessary, therefore it is possible.

⑥

These words summarize beautifully the powerful act of looking beyond the close horizons of worry, denying the *no*, generating as a living force the potential of *yes*. For what is more necessary, indeed vital, to the quality of our lives than to have done with the endless nagging mental toothache that worry brings?

The conscious mind is the seat of our reasoning ability, the focus of the analytical logics we hold so dear in our present society. Yet it is wisely called 'the monkey mind', scampering here, there and everywhere yet going nowhere at all, chattering ceaselessly, very often just to make a noise.

The monkey mind will find it easy to rationalize away the *non sequitur* of Borghese's words, arguing that common sense tells us that something might be necessary yet impossible!

But it's the conscious mind that ignites the spark of worry and then lets the flames burn down to the deeper levels of the imagination. And where is the common sense in that?

'It is necessary, therefore it is possible' disdains the fragile rationales of common sense and sends the monkeys scattering. It defines an attitude, builds it like bedrock in the mind and thus creates a basis for action of enormous strength and endurance.

And in the case of eliminating the worry habit – it is vital, therefore it is inevitable.

Today I go deeper than logic, combining imagination with determination.

We underestimate ourselves. I emphasise self.
We tend to confuse it with the narrow ego.

Arne Naess

⑥

'The narrow ego' is as real or as illusory as we choose to make it – except that usually we, ourselves, don't actually choose and just as frequently it is 'made' from the outside, by other people, either directly or as an indirect consequence of what we see and hear.

The first thing to realize is that 'ego' is just a convenient tag, no more real than any other idea in our heads. It is a force within us and a latency too – only a *part* of what we are as entities. And yet, like one voice raised loudly in a room full of quiet conversations, the ego wants to be noticed, wants to be liked and pays no heed if it can help it to the rest of the personality.

It underestimates our greater, deeper selves, because it carries a sense of self-importance around like a banner, looking to its own limited resources to deal with any situation. Like a brash boor at a party, it hogs the limelight. But it is no *raconteur*. It has a limited repertoire of stories to tell, and it tells them again and again. It laughs at its own jokes. It feels hurt when people stop listening or remain unimpressed. It cannot understand why it cannot go from strength to strength, from success to success. So it worries, never tapping the power of which it is a part...

In sleep the narrow ego switches off. So now, in peace and tranquillity, turn it down. Let it settle itself comfortably and, with effortless attention, listen to what else you have to offer yourself.

Today I stop underestimating myself.

*I love this bird. When I see the arc of her flight, I fly with her,
enter her with my mind, leave myself, die for an instant, live
in the body of this bird whom I cannot live without…*

Susan Griffin

☙

Who is the 'I' that loves the bird? Not the narrow ego, which
loves itself, which loves the things our society persuades it
should be loved. The ego cannot fly with the bird, becoming so
completely involved with its skyborne life, because it is already
far too *self*-involved and in any case would reason away the
value of 'being a bird' as of limited usefulness and importance.

As children, before the meanings of the world had been
defined for us by grown-ups who 'knew better', before the narrow ego was as prominent or as sophisticated as it is now, we
would fly with the bird every day, stalk with the cat, glow with
the sun and rise with the moon. We would enter the make-
believe world of our games and there *make our beliefs*, rehearsing the routines and rituals of life, to be sure, but also testing
what was possible, both within and without.

The assumption is made far too easily, far too thoughtless-
ly, that this act of complete imaginative involvement is a childish thing, and that, if utilized in adulthood, would amount to
gullibility or detachment from reality.

But no. The confining barriers of what we think we can do
and be are the only outcome of the narrow ego's efforts. By flying with the bird we are not being childish, but child-like. It is a
powerful act, a liberating act, one that connects us more fully
and more truly with who we really are and why we are here.

**Today I live in the body of this bird, whom I cannot
Live without.**

Every day, in every way, I am getting better and better.

Emile Coué

⑥

How many millions of people must have stood in front of the bathroom mirror each morning and reiterated Coué's famous maxim, or something very like it, to themselves, that is, to their ego-selves.

And how many millions must have given up after a few days, weeks or months, when they found it wasn't working.

Why not? The ego, housed in the conscious part of the mind, tests the reality it has created for itself against the reality defined by the society around us. In making the affirmation, the ego will look *outside* to verify that it's working.

If that feedback does not appear, the ego begins to doubt. Doubt starts small, but grows fast, like a scrap of bindweed that all too soon chokes up the flowerbed. Then, when the affirmation is repeated, it is filtered through the doubting, even cynical, conscious mind and loses some of its force. This process continues until the affirmation becomes a neutral thing, carrying no weight of influence at all. And then it tips over into the negative, reconfirming every time it is spoken that it *isn't* working, that you're *not* getting better every day, in every way.

The answer? Not to abandon the maxim (although it is rather vague and woolly to have much power), but to turn down the doubting conscious mind and accept the words uncritically, so that they take hold in the imagination. Then, look *within* for signs of their power.

Today, as I might fly with the bird, so I fly within myself.

It is in intentionality and will that the human being
experiences his identity. 'I' is the 'I' of 'I can'. What happens
in human experience is 'I conceive – I can – I will – I am…'

Rollo May

⑥

Intentionality and will are driven by imagination and belief. If our intentions are merely intellectual constructs, then they can easily be dismantled by *other* intellectual constructs – the doubt, cynicisms and reasons-not-to-do of the ego/consciousness.

We limit ourselves constantly by adhering to the Cartesian idea of 'I think, therefore I am' and its corollary: 'I am, therefore I can … can't I?' Identity in its truest, deepest sense does not emerge from intellectualization. The leap from thought to identity is a simplistic and self-limiting one.

Behind the thought there needs to be a weight of belief, a power of imagination grounded in smaller, previous experiences that brought success and achievement.

At this point the conscious mind might argue (with itself!) that 'I haven't enjoyed any success or achievements on which to *base* my belief…'

Well, sit quietly and think back. Everyone has succeeded at something – at the very least to survive to this moment!

From here entertain the notion that progress is possible. The will to change is the tiny motor that kickstarts the big engine. But to get it firing on all cylinders, we need the intentionality of the imagination.

Today I see that 'I can' and 'I will' are the essential experiences of my identity.

Nationalism, racism, classism, sexism; all arise as consciousness of unity is lost. People take sides and favour this versus that.

John Heider

◉

The narrow ego takes sides and favours this versus that. It favours success against failure, wealth against poverty, youth against age and thousands of other mistakenly-perceived either/or situations. When the 'I' considers wealth, then it yearns for more of it, dreads less of it and rarely if ever feels fortunate in what it actually has right now. Similarly, it favours youth by envying it, anticipates age by fearing it and fails to celebrate its own experience of being young or contemplate the quiet wisdoms the experience of the years brings. It sees the world in terms of opposites without ever appreciating that such opposites are mutually necessary for the continuance of the whole.

The irony of all of this is that the narrow ego takes sides against itself and against the greater Self of which it is but a component. Each of us is all that we've ever been, everything that we have yet to do. By following the restricted diktat of the ego, we do not fully exploit what we have achieved and never lift ourselves to look beyond the horizon of what's possible.

In short, we do not allow ourselves to be a unity. And because this is so on an individual level, so it occurs on a larger scale throughout the world.

Today I stop taking sides and look at the whole picture.

What a strange machine man is! You fill him with bread, wine, fish and radishes, and out of him come sighs, laughter and dreams.

Nikos Kazantzakis

(b)

If there were no 'ghost in the machine', there would *be* no sighs, laughter or dreams, for there would be no point in them. If our only purpose as physical beings in a physical world were to survive, then we would merely pass on our genetic information and, having fulfilled our simple, mechanical function, become meaningless.

And yet, we are packed with meaning. Even worry means something – although we often misinterpret its message and fail to act upon its wisdom. Further, we should consider what place imagination, and altruism, spirituality and an appreciation of beauty have to creatures that are nothing more than husks protecting the seed of genetic information.

If meaning exists, then it exists above and beyond us. Thus, there is not just individual meaning, but universal, all-encompassing Meaning. We are a part of it. Our triumph is to attempt to discover as best we can *what* part that might be.

Our sighs, laughter and dreams bespeak our deep selves and our embeddedness in the greater Whole. What better use is there for bread, wine, fish and radishes than to bring them into being?

Today, at all levels, I contemplate the meaning of my presence here.

The Second World is the true centre of life... It is where anything can happen, for all things are possible there. It is a world of perhaps and why not...

Nancy Wood

⑥

It is worth remembering that asking 'Why not?' is as valuable and as potentially rewarding as asking 'Why?' These questions represent the two sides of the same coin – and yet while they are intimately connected, they are also forever apart. Asking why is never quite the same as asking why not.

And we can ask in these two unique and powerful ways both outwardly and inwardly. In the 'real' world of bricks and glass and steel we may be given standard answers based upon other people's expectations – and therefore limitations – 'If you can't measure it, I'm not interested' being just one kind of example.

By asking inwardly 'Why?' and 'Why not?' we explore the Second World Nancy Wood has referred to: the world of ourselves; the world where anything can happen but rarely does, because we don't *imagine it can.*

We all know the difference between fact and pure fantasy; we all know that much of what we imagine couldn't possibly happen in reality. But many of us have lost the distinction between actuality and potentiality, the distinction between what is manifest and what lies latent.

We are no more than what we think, feel and do. We are no less than what we *believe* we can think, feel and do.

Today I explore a little more fully the world of perhaps and why not...

Sail forth – steer for the deep waters only,
Reckless, O Soul, exploring, I with thee,
 and thou with me,
For we are bound where mariner has not yet
 dared to go,
And we will risk the ship, ourselves and all.

Walt Whitman

❂

We worry about problems, but worry is *itself* a problem. It inhibits clear thinking; it drains us of energy; it upsets our sleep and our digestion; it can, and frequently does, lead to a chronic deterioration of health and the quality of life. It can make us irritable, bitter, regretful, pessimistic, depressed...

What a price to pay for something that serves no useful function!

Worry is something wholly inside ourselves. Whatever the *cause* of the worry (which indeed often comes from outside), the reaction it provokes happens within. And whereas certain external problems are best dealt with bit by bit, a careful and deliberate step at a time, the problem of worrying requires much more drastic action.

So as far as worry is concerned, you must go where you have never dared to go before – deep inside yourself, wherein lie the means to revitalize and empower. It is a necessary journey and may be uncomfortable, leading to a destination you may never have anticipated, leading to an answer that is entirely new.

But how much does worry hurt you right now?

How radical are you prepared to get to defeat it?

Today I set sail and steer for deeper waters...

Love of others and love of ourselves are not alternatives.
Genuine love is an expression of productiveness and implies
care, respect, responsibility and knowledge…

Erich Fromm

🌀

The concept of love, it could be argued, is nothing more than the product of a highly evolved intelligence – simply a useful tag with which to identify a complex of otherwise blind behaviour. And, since we stem from such 'lower' forms of life, then why should we be fundamentally different?

Such an argument, created of course by the rationalizing conscious mind, fails to recognize the essential nature of love as a force which drives the individual and the species far more powerfully, far more effectively, than simple survival strategies. Indeed, territoriality and fierce protectiveness of family and pack are divisive and detrimental in a shrinking world, leading inevitably, and with increasing frequency, to conflict.

The idea of evolution is astonishingly elegant and successful in explaining a diverse range of phenomena in the natural world. It should not be disdained, but *extended*, through daring leaps of the imagination, to accommodate the no-less-real phenomenon of genuine love. As Fromm asserts, '[Love] is an active striving for the growth and happiness of the loved person,' whether that is another, yourself or both.

There is no more successful strategy than the cultivation and expression of love.

Today I feel the force of the idea that the universe evolves towards a state of genuine love.

Come back with me into a story we all share, a story whose rhythm beats in us still... There is a great yearning and great need to own that story – to break out of our isolation as persons and as a species and recover ... our larger identity. The challenge to do that now and burst out of the separate prison cells of our contrivings is perhaps the most wonderful aspect of our being alive today.

Joanna Macy

⑥

Beneath and beyond the routines and rituals of our day-to-day life, our 'surface' life, there beats the deeper, essential rhythms of which Joanna Macy speaks. They are varied and they are subtle, but their power has brought us all to where we are today – and will take us on over the barely glimpsed horizons of the future towards our unimaginable destiny.

We are all tied to the pulsebeat of life, all a part of the inter-connectedness of living things across space and through time. We exist as an inseparable element of the greater universe, utterly compliant with its laws, eloquently carved in accordance with its nature. We are composed of materials formed from past generations of stars, only to be rendered down to dust to feed the cycle of new life coming after.

We can do nothing *but* live to the rhythms that control us in every way, at every level of our being.

Our task is to become more sensitive to the dance. Our triumph and achievement is to become informed by it.

Today I look in seven directions – up, down, left, right, inwards, outwards ... and the seventh – the better to see the rhythms that guide my existence.

We have undersold the value of human relationships, and
the complexity of nature.

Marilyn Ferguson

⊚

We undersell much in our lives, including ourselves and our achievements.

In fact, the very language in which the notion is couched acknowledges the forces of commercialism controlling the shape and progress of our society. Such forces, and that notion, have more to do with cost than with worth. The dollar value of happiness is inestimable; indeed, the very idea embodies a fundamental contradiction in terms.

Money brings worries. Yet because of the conditioning process of a society attuned to the rise and fall of share prices, awed by the icon of wealth, we equate all that we do – and all that we fail to do – with the thickness of our wallet at the end.

It would, of course, be naïve – and ultimately highly detrimental – to ignore the power of commerce in our lives. We cannot exist without money. But that existence would be diminished, or even rendered impossible, without happiness.

The greatest happiness is to be found within relationships nurtured by care, respect and responsibility. And when it is found, it will demand commitment, but no cost. You get it for free.

Today I stop underselling myself.

To be sure of hitting the target, shoot first, and whatever you hit, call it the target.

Ashleigh Brilliant

⑥

It is easy to arrange *not* to fail through inaction. I want to attain a goal, but because of the fear of failing, I set my sights lower, hold back, turn away, don't bother at all. So in this respect I have not failed – but in no sense of the word have I succeeded, except in reinforcing the habit of deferral and self-defeat.

It might seem at first glance that if you shoot and call whatever you hit the 'target', then you are deluding yourself with a hollow sham of success. If anything can be the target, why bother with targets? And if that's the case, why bother to shoot anyway?

This is to miss the point (if I may continue with the archery analogy!) No one at the outset can expect to hit the bullseye – or even the target itself sometimes. But that is no failure. It does not diminish the attempt and indeed helps to hone the skill, so that later shots will fly more surely to their mark.

It is the attitude of trying that lies at the heart of the matter: the wish to succeed and the knowledge that all effort builds towards success – and thus is success in itself.

Shoot first, do what you fear to do and whatever you hit, add it to your list of minor triumphs.

Today I do not hold back or turn away. I aim at my goal in the spirit of success.

The hitter and the hit are no longer two opposing objects,
but are one reality.

Eugen Herrigel

❻

When we take aim, we do not test the target, but ourselves. To miss is not to fail. Failure comes in missing the opportunity of trying to succeed.

Life is full of targets: large and small, near and far. Saying 'Good morning' to a shop assistant is a major target for someone lacking in confidence or self-esteem. Paying off a sizeable debt is no less of a challenge for someone without the necessary money to hand. There are a hundred others we could think of in the next half hour.

But the point about targets is that they are best hit one at a time, after having chosen, aimed, then calmed the body and the mind in preparation for loosing off the arrow.

Worry isolates and separates us from our targets, distances us from them and feeds us self-doubt and repeated scenarios of failure. We come to see them as something quite apart from ourselves, and thus the act of hitting them also becomes unfamiliar and untenable in our minds.

Shoot first! For the whole world can be your target. No one can fail to hit the world with their presence. And in the attempt comes the understanding that you were never in truth divided. Archer and arrow and target are all one reality, each existing solely and fully for the other.

Today I do not oppose, and am not opposed, by the object of my aim.

It is very difficult to swim upstream. You need company and rights-of-passage from your fellow travellers.

Jillie Collings

⑥

For all that analogies can be helpful to us, they can also be invidious. Do we really feel that we are 'swimming upstream', fighting against the tide (of opinion, social acceptability, habit, worry, whatever)? Or are we helplessly being carried away *down*stream, swept along like a leaf by events over which we have no control, unable to determine or change our direction?

Either or both of these images, lodged in the mind and running like a tedious tape-loop through the day, could produce negative effects. In fact, they *will* produce negative effects unless we invest a little time to sit quietly and watch them, before deciding that the time for change has come and then acting upon that decision calmly, modestly, but with growing confidence as we see that we are achieving our short-term goals. Once this process begins then the waters of the stream don't seem so deep or their currents quite so dangerous. And, like all swimmers, we strengthen ourselves by practice.

This is something we need to do for ourselves. But when we encounter fellow travellers who too have struggled to stay afloat, they are as glad of our company as we are of theirs.

As to 'rights of passage', our fundamental right as living beings is to *live* and to *be*. And that right we can only grant fully to ourselves.

Today I plan my next move and take the plunge!

Those who subscribe to the 'New Age' philosophy of a changing world view ... believe that there is a different way of being which is life-enhancing and empowering; that we have far more potential than we are realizing; and that only in changing ourselves can society as a whole be transformed.

Eileen Campbell and J. H. Brennan

⑥

The growth of the so-called 'Human Potential Movement' over the past 25 to 30 years has been astonishing; and it is accelerating. There are many books which trace this growth, not least of which is Campbell and Brennan's *Dictionary of Mind, Body and Spirit* and *The New Age*, edited by William Bloom.

The underlying philosophy of New Age thinking urges us to step out, explore, meet up with fellow travellers and, through the synergistic power of our collective direction, cause a general shift in which we as a species regard ourselves and the finite world in which we live.

The practicality of the concept on an individual level is that it provides a potent new outlook. As Marcel Proust has said, 'Voyages of discovery are not made by going to new places, but by seeing with new eyes.'

Our aim might not be to change society at all. But there can be no doubt that fulfilling personal potential is the aim of many people, perhaps most. To realize that ways to achieve it exist and to form a coherent foundation for action are inspiring – and may even be transformational.

Today I open myself to the excitement of a new way of being.

A too-strict regimen is a wearisome malady.

Doris Grant

(☉)

Doris Grant, a nutritionist, is here talking about the regimen of dieting. But the principle of stricture is an important one on a much broader front. Working against worry is to be encouraged and celebrated, but continually to be back-checking, wondering if things are working, becoming a little anxious, perhaps, that insufficient progress towards happiness isn't being made can *add* to the burden of worry and can hinder the change for the better which is our aim.

We are 'soft machines', too complex to be broken down into our constituent bits and put together again and be made whole. And there are ghosts in our machines – mental, emotional, spiritual influences which are subtle and sophisticated beyond any concept of software the Cartesian philosophers would reduce us to.

All of this makes each one of us unique – both in ourselves and in the time and space we occupy. There is no formula which determines how quickly we learn or what use we might subsequently make of that learning. So to impose such a formula, a regimen of improvement, upon ourselves is simply to set another limit. By defining exactly how and when, what and why we want to change, we narrow the horizons of that change and make the journey of reaching it more difficult.

Today I will allow myself a little leeway – some extra freedom to enjoy where I'm going.

A tiger does not recall whether it is the thirteenth animal that has got away from it that day, but we do: we link the memory of our past failures with present situations, and worse, with future expectations…

Quoted by Jillie Collings

☉

We are in many ways victims of our own success as a species, retaining as we do a great number of the skills, abilities and more basic 'programs' which led to that success.

One of these is the well known 'fight or flight' reflex, a response governed by the hypothalamus. When triggered, it leads to an increased breathing rate, marked increase in blood-flow to the major muscle groups, sudden sweating, increased sympathetic nervous system activity, a slowing of the digestive processes, yet increased metabolism elsewhere in the body, all to prepare the body for the surge of energy required to fight or flee.

Once, long ago, this was the best way to survive. The decision to fight or run was probably made subconsciously and very quickly. And when the threat was over, we forgot it as the after-effects faded and vanished.

But we have changed, evolving a consciousness capable of remembering. Not only that, but the ancient fight or flight response itself is largely inappropriate in our modern world. So dangerous can this inappropriateness be that unchecked, it can lead to heart attacks, strokes and many more potentially fatal diseases. So we must adapt to survive.

Today I begin to reflect on change at all levels of my being, realizing that my choice is fight-or-flight or relax.

Everywhere I have sought Spring but found not Spring,
As my straw sandals trod the cloud-capped hills.
Back again, I playfully finger and sniff the plum-blossom,
And there, at the branch tip, is all the fullness of Spring!

Chinese poem, author unknown

☙

There is still a time to fight. There is still a time to run. But they few and far between now, so that mostly when we fight we just hurt ourselves and when we try to run we get nowhere.

Dr Herbert Benson in *The Relaxation Response* offers an alternative. His wisdom is to be found in many cultures, expressed in a diversity of ways. But all assert that the alternative response can be achieved through gentle determination and practice, practice, practice:

> Find a quiet environment, a place that is familiar to you,
> where you won't be disturbed, where you feel safe.
> Select a mental device – a word, a picture, a sound on which
> to focus.
> Assume a comfortable position.
> Adopt a passive attitude – not the passivity of helplessness
> or resignation, but of *empowerment*, an attitude that allows
> you to connect with the deeper levels of your mind.

In this state, using your mental device, 10 to 20 minutes of daily practice will bring about a *relaxation* response, and lead very quickly to enhanced peace and well-being.

Today I begin to train myself in the relaxation response.

People have used sounds ... naturally and therapeutically through the centuries. The origins of healing by sound and music can be traced into prehistory and beyond, into the realms of myth, religion and the memory of the soul.

Olivia Dewhurst Maddock

❀

We live in a world of indiscriminate sound, a world where silence and the peace that it can bring are rare indeed.

Many of the sounds that bombard us are constant and unrelenting, the polluting by-product of our functional, utilitarian society. Such sounds usually convey no information: they form part of the brutalizing backdrop of the urban world, desensitizing us, not just to themselves, but to the very notion of the healing, empowering properties of sound. They blunt our perceptions and dull our sensibilities, so that music becomes musak, and advertisers and programme-makers feel it necessary to machine-gun us with brief 'soundbytes' in the hope that some of them at least will strike home and force us to take notice.

And how we sometimes *yearn* to be away from it all, in the middle of nowhere, deep in the tranquillity of the countryside!

That's not always possible. Nor is it a practical solution on a day-to-day basis.

Let's, then, take sound and use it positively. Something as simple as quietly *and deliberately* listening to soothing music can be a first step, while Olivia Dewhurst Maddock's *The Book Of Sound Therapy* explores 100 other ways of harnessing the power of sound and our latent ability to wield its magic.

Today I become aware of sound and exercise my power of choice...

The Transcendental Meditation technique allows the mind to settle down to a less excited state. The person experiences quieter and quieter levels of thinking until s/he arrives at a state of complete mental stillness.

Peter Russell

⑥

The monkey-like chattering of the conscious mind is similar to the ceaseless onslaught of sound that reaches us from the wider world. It begins as we wake and lasts throughout the day. Its information content is limited; it gives us the same messages over and over again. The deeper self that lies behind the narrow ego stops paying attention and, as it were, lets the conscious mind 'get on with it', working its slow damage, its capabilities going to waste.

Transcendental Meditation is perhaps the most famous modern technique for utilizing the properties of sound to gain greater control of the conscious mind. Basically and simply, TM makes use of a personalized sound, a mantra, which is quietly and effortlessly repeated by the subject in order to achieve 'complete mental stillness'. Such a syllable of power provides a focus for concentration and 'damps down' the tendency of the monkey mind to leap away in all directions, especially since the mantra itself carries no information, or else is a simple invocation or affirmation that does not encourage conscious analysis.

The unhurried rhythm of a mantra further serves to slow the spinning flywheel of consciousness and is thus an ideal mental device for relaxation, meditation or prayer.

Today, sitting quietly, I let sounds flow through me, letting them come, letting them go again, untouched...

Hail to the Jewel in the Lotus.

Traditional Buddhist mantra

☉

Mantras are used in Oriental esoteric and mystical practice to quieten the mind.

Any sound which lacks thought-provoking connotation may be used, and to judge by the millions of meditators who use 'ready made' mantras in their practice the personalization of a mantra (as is used in TM) seems not to be necessary.

The most famous of Oriental mantras is *Aum mani padme hum* (Hail to the Jewel in the Lotus). This mantra, like many of the most popular and efficacious, 'swallows its tail', the final syllable blending smoothly into the first syllable of the next repetition.

Sit quietly where you will not be disturbed.

Say the mantra aloud for a few cycles, following this rhythm and pronunciation:

Aw-um mah-nee padmeh hummmmm um mah-nee padmeh hummmmm…

Steadily lower the volume of the voice until you can seamlessly continue the mantra within your mind.

Once the mental mantra is 'spinning' like a gyroscope, it will continue without effort, allowing you to sink deeply and satisfyingly into the unrippled waters of the mind.

To disengage from the mantra, slow it down and begin to speak it for a few cycles before stopping.

Today, harnessing the power of mantra, *I flow through sound…*

Most people, in time, learn to respond with fervour and obedience to a set of … abstractions which they feel provides them with an ideological identity. Quite arbitrarily, one's perception of what is 'true' is shaped by the symbols and symbol-manipulating institutions of the 'tribe'.

Neil Postman and Charles Weingartner

⑥

Today we are blitzed not only with sound, but also with visual imagery, presented to us either as a random kaleidoscope of colour and movement or else as slick designer packages engineered to manipulate our minds – at least to change our regular brand of washing powder!

It has been calculated that the average person living in the Middle Ages absorbed, in the entire span of their lives, as much information as you would find in the average daily tabloid newspaper. Our ordinary day contains many times that amount, most of it delivered to us visually via TV, computer screen, hoardings, posters, etc.

Of course, the coherence and meaning of all of this visual data bears little relation to its sheer quantity. Indeed, much of it is not intended to appeal to our intellect, but seeks instead to transmit an 'instant image' to which we will react on impulse. One unfortunate consequence for us is that this creates a false impression of what we need and want in life, much of which can only be purchased at your local superstore.

But still we can re-establish that most crucial of connections: awareness; understanding; control.

Today, by quieting the mind, I become more aware…

If the stars came out but once in a hundred years, how much more would we value the sky.

Emerson

⑥

What works for sound works equally well for light. Thus, by using light to calm and focus the mind, we immediately cut out the bulk of external distractions and quickly achieve a profound state of mental stillness and quietude:

Take a candle and light it, placing it several feet away from you.

Slow your breathing, taking long, deep, easy breaths (any good book on yoga or one of the many volumes on the art of breathing/rebirthing will give reliable guidance on breathing technique).

Fix your eyes on the flame and gaze at it steadily for a few minutes.

Now, note particularly the *shape* of the flame, its effortless *movement*, its subtle *colours*, spending a couple of minutes on each aspect.

Now observe the flame-in-its-entirety once more, not troubling to think about it or reflect upon it in any way.

Close your eyes and cup your palms over them. Focus on the after-image of the flame, trying to retain it while it fades. As it vanishes, replace it with a mental image of the flame, becoming aware of all its vital aspects: shape, colour, movement. Hold the image as long as you can without effort.

Briskly rub the palms together and again cup them over your eyes as you open them.

Today, with a simple flame, I begin to see the light.

Sometimes I just sits and thinks…
And sometimes I just sits.

From an Athena poster

⑥

It is easy to imagine that the most idyllic existence would consist of sitting on a palm-fringed beach of pure white sand under a dazzling blue sky, listening to the languid splashing of gentle waves; a cool drink in one hand, a bowl of exotic fruits within easy reach of the other.

And so it might be for the first day, and the second, perhaps the third, maybe the tenth… But all too soon a sense of lethargy would creep in, a dullness of thought. We would languish in an ocean of boredom, suffer the surfeit, cloyment and revolt of unending tedium. We would, in short, end up tearing our hair out in this tropical paradise.

Our minds and bodies are like an electrical wire, designed to carry an optimum current. For most people, the big problem is one of overload. There is too much current running through the wire, too much to do in too short a time, too many thoughts spinning around in circles, too much pressure, too much stress…

But insufficient current is just as debilitating. We *need* a certain positive tension in our lives. We need to feel the excitement of new challenges, the satisfaction of meeting them, the exuberance of careful decisions (whether reasoned or intuited) followed up with direct action. These things keep the wire humming, keep the mind/body system of the individual invigorated, fulfilled and essentially *alive*.

Today I throw problems aside in favour of challenges!

The spiritual and moral poverty of the western world is far
more difficult than the material poverty you find in India.

Mother Theresa

⑥

Given the complex seethe of contending forces within nations
and between nations across the face of the globe, it must be an
enormously difficult task to strike a balance between the material and the spiritual. We see societies rich in one but not the other, to the despair of many – to the detriment of all.

This same imbalance can and does exist also within the
individual. A person, too, is a complexity of forces, impulses,
drives, fears – 'a bundle of contradictions'. And yet, unlike
nations in opposition because of deep-rooted differences of
perception and belief, the supposedly conflicting aspects that
make up a human being are all striving towards the continued
survival of the whole. We are essentially, *fundamentally*, holistic
creatures – whether the conscious aspect of our minds realizes
it or not!

And so the poverty-in-ourselves we might recognize and
lament exists not for want of resource, but due to a lack of
awareness. Once awareness has been achieved, directions
become apparent. Deliberate action drives us forward to consequent understanding and greater control of our own life-path.
Thus, we achieve the balance, the completeness, of fulfilment,
finding ourselves rich in the most important ways of all.

Today I reflect on the notion that moral and spiritual
poverty is easier to rectify than material poverty –
and brings a greater reward.

And now the river is rich. A deep choir…
Now the river is poor. No song, just a thin, mad whisper…

Ted Hughes

⑥

We all have our times of poverty and wealth, both materially and in the more essential sense of the ebb-and-flow of our energies, ideas and spirit. The vagaries of life and the subtlety and complexity of our own minds conspire to create constant movement as we pass through the labyrinth of life.

Whether this is a 'good' or 'bad' thing is of no consequence, because the situation is unalterable. The only thing beyond change *is* change. That is the nature of the beast. Yet while it cannot be tamed, it can be understood and in that understanding we also come to know ourselves.

We are rich, we are poor, we are rich again. Above all, we are not product, but process. We are not an object, like scales, tipped one way or the other by the vicissitudes of circumstance. Rather, we are like the waters of the river, a swirl of movement in a greater flow and an inseparable part of the whole.

So whether our conscious mind harmonies like a deep choir or tests us with its thin, mad whisper, above and beyond all this we realize we are always the river, ever moving, inevitably drawn towards our destiny.

Today, rich or poor, I am the river.

I'm not afraid to fail, providing I fail honourably.

David Puttnam

&

It is a common myth that failure equals weakness. Not so. The real weakness is not trying in the first place.

We all fear failure, of course – but we fear more the *thought* of failure. That phantom which lodges in the conscious mind, that perception, that image of what failure will be like for us, is nothing more than a mental construct. It may, or it may not, be based upon the experience of failure we might have suffered in the past. But can we extrapolate in this way, in this instance, from what has been?

Life brings new challenges, large and small. The world changes, we change – and yet by avoiding challenge because we fear failure, we create for ourselves a kind of static state of inaction. We turn away from trying, enduring all the regrets or disappointments that might bring, and life passes us by. We harden ourselves to an absence of success and sit like a stone in a stream, while the vital waters swirl past.

It would be naïve and misleading to say that effort equals success. But what effort does bring is an increased chance of success each time we try. We succeed sometimes; we strengthen ourselves to deal with failure as it arrives; we come to understand that to fail does not make us a failure...

We realize at last that anything less than effort is unhappiness by default.

Today I try – and either succeed or fail, honourably.

If you knew that in one year you would die suddenly, would you change anything about the way you are now living?

Gregory Stock

6

Gregory Stock's *The Book of Questions* presents the reader with over 200 moral and ethical dilemmas. They are mind games which challenge us to face ourselves and take a closer look at who we really are. Some of them are utterly fantastical ('Would you want to slow your rate of ageing to enable you to live for 2,000 years?'), some of them are a little bizarre yet wryly amusing ('Can you urinate in front of another person?'), some of them are sobering ('Is there something you've dreamed of doing for a long time? Why haven't you done it?')

All of them help reinforce a vital habit we can establish for our own benefit and well-being: that of testing what we believe, evaluating what drives us, confronting what constrains us in a state of disappointment or frustration or fear.

Worry fails to ask such questions. It persuades us that it already knows the answers and tends to predict the worst. What questions do emerge through worry are rhetorical, circular, empty, narrowing.

Set yourself the task of asking at least one big, important, open question a day. Pay attention to the answers you get – from your conscious mind, from your mind's deeper layers, from your body. How do you *feel* about these answers? What other questions do they inspire?

Today I ask myself: 'Is there something I've dreamed of doing for a long time? Why haven't I done it?'

I've been overweight since I was four. I don't want to overinflate my role or my job, but isn't there more to me than what I weigh?

Jack Nicholson

⑥

Look in the mirror. Is there anything you see that you don't like? If yes, can you do anything about it? If yes, why not do something about it now?

If you can't do anything about it, then firstly, think again. Most problems are solvable if you look at them in the right way, because the difference between a problem and a challenge is usually one of *definition*.

If after that you still can't do anything about it, then do something about it by co-operating with the inevitable.

Sounds hard? Remember that in order to move on we either change our circumstances or we change ourselves. And if it should be that we can do nothing about the shape of our face, or that receding hairline, or the fact that time carries us steadily from the cradle to the grave, then we must learn that we are greater than these things – we are more than what we weigh.

Today I look beyond what yesterday I called a problem.

That there is a link between healthy expression of creativity and strength of the life force is becoming more and more clear; when the one flows, the other seems to be stimulated.

Jillie Collings

(b)

Life itself is an opportunity to be creative. And we can be creative in endless ways, at all levels of our being, though it's not just a question of 'can'. Each and every one of us *must* express ourselves creatively in some way, if we are to maximize the power of the life force which runs through us (whatever we take that 'life force' to be).

Being creative on a regular basis is like using tools from a toolkit. We might use just one to fulfil our purpose or all of them, heartened by the knowledge that such usage keeps their points and blades and surfaces both sharpened and polished. In which case, what a tragedy it is to let the tools of our minds and bodies lie rusting through lack of effort – or worse, through lack of care.

The 'healthy expression of creativity' can be anything from cross-stitch to hillwalking, from an act of kindness to writing a novel. For creativity *is* action, *is* effort, *is*, therefore, fulfilment by virtue of the attempt.

In the midst of creative expression, we touch the heart and purpose of life. And however modest our endeavours, however humble our outcomes, that heart remains constant, there for all of us to share.

Today I strengthen the life force in me through an act of creative expression.

I have a body but I am not my body,
I have emotions but I am not my emotions.
I have a job but I am not my job.

Roberto Assagioli

⑥

Roberto Assagioli is the founder of the Psychosynthesis movement, whose aim is to synthesize or bring together the different
and contradictory aspects of the psyche.

In daily life, we may not allow the energy of creative
expression to flow freely at all levels of our being, in which case
the whole person – our being – is not adequately nourished and
able to develop fully. This 'one-sidedness' leads to an imbalance
in our sense of identity, a narrowing or distortion in our concept
of who we think we are. If, then, events deprive us of all or part
of the aspect(s) with which we have identified, we feel dispos-
sessed and crippled on a physical, mental or spiritual level.

As Assagioli maintains, 'Often a crisis in life deprives a
person of the function with which he has identified: an athlete's
body is maimed; a lover's beloved departs with a wandering
poet; a dedicated worker must retire. Then the process of
disidentification is forced on one and a solution can only come
by a process of death and rebirth in which the person enters a
broader identity.'

'There is more to me than what I weigh' is another way of
reaffirming the fact that we are more than the sum of our parts.
Such affirmations, practised with gentle discipline and care-
for-self, strengthen who we are at every level and make us
resilient in the face of challenge or adversity.

**Today I begin to become aware of my whole self, my
entire being.**

The over-emphasis of the thinking function has devalued its polar-opposite of feeling [with the result that] a build-up of emotional drive is expressed torrent-like, in what few channels are left in modern society…

Anonymous

⑥

These words, quoted in Jillie Collings' book *Life Forces*, express the view of an eminent psychologist who wished to remain anonymous because he works with politicians. His feeling is that the emotional/intuitive aspects of our being are ignored, disdained or actively suppressed in light of the value placed on rationality and logic – in short, on the 'cerebral' thinking skills of the conscious mind. Thus, we do not nurture the very important qualities of family love, sympathy for our fellows and caring within our community.

This one-sidedness creates an imbalance in society and in the individual. But emotion is energy, so the suppression of that energy causes not a dissipation, but an accumulation of emotional pressure that can – and does – lead to uncontrolled and often violent outbursts.

The solution is not legislation and the imposition of ever-tighter social controls, but an awareness of the nature of the problem and the dissemination of techniques to rebalance all aspects of the individuals who comprise a society. Person-centred action, and person-initiated action, is the answer. This is something each one of us can do for the benefit of all. And we can start today.

Today, sitting quietly, I sense the energy of my feelings running through me.

We instinctively put our arms around a frightened child, a
grief-stricken neighbour, holding a hand in sympathy,
soothing a troubled brow or stroking a feverish cheek...

Allegra Taylor

⑥

Spiritual healer Allegra Taylor maintains that healing is an extension of that instinct and something which, 'in our most sensitive moments', we all use naturally.

That qualifier is important, because just as an over-emphasis of the thinking function has dampened our capacity for feeling, so our increasing reliance on technology deprives us of the opportunity to soothe and heal through contact.

It is an old argument, but still largely a valid one, that technology *per se* is a neutral phenomenon, but can be used for good or evil. However true that may be, there are consequences attached to the proliferation of technology which we as individuals may not be able to control, because they percolate down through society almost subliminally, beneath the threshold of our awareness.

Stand back and see how technology distances us from each other – isolated in our cars, talking to cashiers through reinforced plate glass, serving ourselves at petrol stations and in supermarkets, watching the world via TV and radio and the Internet.

I am no technophobe and I don't see why we shouldn't derive benefits both from what science can bring us *as well as* the gifts and capabilities we have always possessed, and which still lie latent inside us.

**Today I contemplate the thought that in reaching out
to others, I more truly reach myself.**

I think it would be a good idea.

> Mahatma Gandhi (on being asked
> what he thought of Western civilization)

（6）

Modern Western civilization has been spectacularly successful in certain ways – look around and list them! – but in other areas it remains woefully inadequate. Every answer we uncover throws up more questions; every problem we solve produces a new generation of problems.

These answers, these solutions, as well as the new questions and problems they spawn, exist within the self-defining framework of our society. The canvas on which society paints itself is bounded by its own perception of what is desirable, necessary and true. We are inevitably limited by what we believe to be possible.

But we are not hermetically sealed inside this picture, by any means. All areas of our world view, our cosmic view, undergo 'paradigm shifts' from time to time, sudden quantum leaps of understanding which lift us out of old ways, broadening horizons and offering tantalizing new directions to our gaze.

This is happening on the level of the individual also, where daily hundreds or thousands of people find important enlightenments, new ways of seeing, new foundations for meaning.

The road may be long and hard, for each of us, for all of us, but at the end of it we will truly have arrived at a state that we can, undeniably, call civilization.

Today I continue with my own personal process of civilization.

...you must begin by knowing that you have already arrived.

Richard Bach

⑥

The very act of desiring change initiates change. By beginning the process of deepening self-awareness, so making accessible a wider range of mental skills and emotional and spiritual potentials, we increase our self-understanding and extend the control we have over our lives.

But the temptation is always there to wonder how much is left to be done before that change is complete. How much longer do I need to meditate, to set short-term goals, to reach 'my deeper levels', to cultivate a balance between intuition and reasoning...?

And following hard on the heels of that may come a sense of frustration that things are not happening quickly enough. I've been diligently working against worry for six months now, but am I any happier? The guy next-door who just doesn't seem to give a damn is *much* happier than I am – and he doesn't even read books!

These are the thoughts of the conscious mind, the mind that sets limits, including time limits; that sees targets to be hit and scores to be beaten; that thinks in terms of a final, measurable outcome.

But we are here dealing with a more subtle and elegant phenomenon. By wanting to get there, you have already arrived. And yet, you will never reach the end of your quest – and rightly so, because the purpose of the journey is the journey itself.

Today I look again. Do I see that I've arrived?

The mind of the beginner is empty, free of the habits of the expert, ready to accept, to doubt, and open to all the possibilities.

Baker Roshi

⑥

A well known Zen story tells of the Japanese master Nan-in, who one day received a university professor. The professor had come to find out about Zen.

Nan-in served his guest some tea, pouring until the cup was filled – but then continuing to pour so that the tea spilled over the sides and across the table.

'It's overfull. No more will go in,' the professor pointed out.

'Like this cup,' Nan-in replied, 'you are full of your own opinions and speculations. How can I show you Zen, unless you first empty your cup?'

We might well ask, what does our cup contain that prevents more from being poured in? Our minds (and Baker Roshi is referring, I believe, to the *whole* mind) are filled with common sense, things that are 'obvious', past experiences from which we have 'learned our lessons' about life, beliefs, fears, prejudices, ambitions, dreams.

How can we empty that cup?

Zen has a way, but even the masters agree it is difficult to keep a 'beginner's mind'. We can look anew, see with fresh eyes, flow with the water instead of sinking with the stone, appreciate each day that 'I'm me, I'm now and that's all.'

But still, you know, it occurs to me to wonder whether by opening up to all the possibilities, am I emptying the cup or enlarging it?

Today I'm me, I'm now and that's all.

Christopher Robin is going.
At least I think he is.
Where?
Nobody knows.
I mean he goes
(To rhyme with 'knows')
Do we care?
(To rhyme with 'where')
We do
Very much.

A. A. Milne

⊚

I do not think that the Zen beginner's mind is the same as innocence. Innocence is increasingly overlaid with experience (albeit remaining an active force within us), whereas beginner's mind is recreated anew every instant. It is a sublime and subtle state that is generated by the very life energies which recreate our bodies on a moment-by-moment basis, our spirits soaking our every cell and atom.

In that sense, upon our arrival at each new second, we are beginners in the art of living in that second. We do not need to be gullible or naïve, or self-consciously astonished by the panorama of here/now. We are not playing at being steeped in life. This is no game or façade. We look around. We learn from it what we can. We move on.

And we may not know where we are going, but we know we are going.

Today I realize I haven't got a rhyme for that 'is' in the second line yet. Bother.

Life will only give you whatever you accept. If you accept being average and ordinary life will help you to stay that way.

Stephanie Spindler

⑥

Accepting the status quo maintains it, and that 'unchanged position' is, ironically, often one of dissatisfaction and worry, lethargy, apprehension, self-doubt or even despair.

The acceptance that Stephanie Spindler refers to, in her book *Learn to Live*, is the acceptance of habit. We accept in this way because we haven't seen what else is on offer, or because we've had our limits defined by other people and have never troubled or dared to question them.

But if we realize that change happens anyway, be it beyond current understanding, much as the bumblebee flies, we come to see that our status quo is an illusion. However, it takes energy to sustain that illusion – energy which could much more profitably be spent in burning it away like morning mist.

True acceptance, the acceptance of all that is possible, feeds us and nourishes our souls. It gives us energy instead of taking it away and that energy we can then use to give substance to our dreams.

Opportunities are out there. Break with habit and go look for them.

Today, in order to broaden my horizons, I hold my head higher.

There are no easy answers. Each of us must spend time
contemplating our life; must feel our own pain and make
our own decisions. Every day we stand at a crossroad. Every
day there are choices to be made. Our answers are within us.
We must learn to trust our inner guidance.

Elaine Stephens

🌀

Deliberate action means deliberate involvement. The aim of contemplation in any form is not to understand a distant abstract, not somehow to lift us out of life to some safe esoteric state. We contemplate in order to understand and we understand in order to live more successfully.

'Success' in this sense means tackling life's challenges; overcoming life's problems, large and small. We must not be afraid to 'get our hands dirty' by picking up the stuff of life and seeing what it's made of – and sometimes by grabbing a problem by the scruff of the neck and shaking a solution out of it!

Our answers are within us because our problems are too. The very word 'problem' identifies (and can exacerbate) an attitude by which we define life's meanings; and what life means to us, life *is* to us.

So we must choose, every day of our lives, which direction to take and not be afraid to change direction if that improves the quality of our journey. The inner guide will show us which way to go at the crossroad; forward, this way, that way… But never back.

**Today I contemplate that there may be no easy
answers. But there are always answers.**

In the infinity of life where I am, all is perfect, whole and complete. Each one of us, myself included, experiences the richness and fullness of life in ways that are meaningful to us. I now look at the past with love and choose to learn from my old experiences.

Louise L. Hay

⑥

The cynic inside us, the great doubter lodged in the conscious mind, might well regard this affirmation as so much wishful thinking, an insubstantial tissue of idealism with no strength in the cold, hard world of reality.

But what lies deeper than the doubter? Is it there? Have you found it yet? Have you *looked* for it yet?

If we possessed nothing but consciousness, rationality, the clear-sightedness of logical thought, we would go far indeed. We could arrive at each crossroad having anticipated our decision, worked out which way to proceed, and then stride forward, confident in our efficient common-sense approach to all of life's difficulties.

Or could we? There are no easy answers to a troubled relationship, the chance of a major career change, a nagging dissatisfaction with our lifestyle, regrets, worries, apprehension of what might be just over the horizon...

The very part of our mind that logically paves the way into the future for us also doubts its own direction. We need another navigator, one with a sense of direction (not necessarily a 'common' sense), one with a sense of fun and assurance that the guidance it offers improves with each and every experience we encounter.

Today I find my way in the infinity of life.

Perfection: An imaginary state or quality distinguished from the actual by an element known as excellence; an attribute of the cynic.

Ambrose Bierce

ⓖ

Ambrose Bierce must count among the nineteenth century's greatest cynics. The acidity of his wit and the scalpel-sharpness of his commentary upon the human condition make for some amusing, but often very uncomfortable, reading.

We might, for our own enlightenment, wonder whether we align ourselves with Bierce's view or with that of Louise Hay. The cornerstone of the affirmations in her book *You Can Heal Your Life* lies in the assertion that 'in the infinity of life where I am, all is perfect, whole and complete…'

How can these two opposing viewpoints ever be reconciled? Who is right?

Whoever does the looking.

Our outlook shows us the landscape of life, the territory of the future and the past. The unique and personal window through which we look is built not only upon what we've experienced, but also upon what we *think* we've experienced. Perfection is a perspective – but it is also an absolute and therefore contentious.

My own favourite commentary on perfection comes from R. S. Thomas's wonderful poem 'The View from the Window':

All through history the great brush has not rested
Nor the paint dried; yet what eye
Looking coolly, or, as we now,
Through the tears' lenses, ever saw
This work and it was not finished?

Cowards die many times before their deaths,
The valiant never taste of death but once.

Shakespeare

ⓖ

Worry makes cowards of us all. It forces us to turn away from acting upon a problem – or indeed, may even create the illusion that the problem doesn't exist in the first place. Worry pushes us back into ourselves, reinforces the impression that the worst will happen, that we can't cope, that we are helpless in the flow of circumstances which carries us inexorably towards unhappiness.

We never look coolly when we worry.

There are no easy answers. Certainly to worry is no answer at all. A solution may be difficult to achieve, but as President Kennedy said when committing America to putting a man on the moon within a decade, 'We do this not because it is easy, but because it is hard.' Such a stirring pledge of commitment can be nothing less than inspirational.

And yet what better commitment can be made than to ourselves? We are valuable; we are precious. We deserve the best, especially from ourselves – because it is each one of us who can most surely give us that best, whatever it may be.

But we'll have to fight for it.

Today I gather the courage to do what I fear to do and to be valiant in life.

In our time a secret manifesto is being written. Its language is a longing we see in one another's eyes. It is the longing to know our authentic vocation in the world, to find the work and the way of being that belong to each of us… I speak of the declaration of our right to self-discovery.

Theodore Roszak

⑥

Mundane existence can wear us down; problems can buffet us from all directions like gusts in a gale. We look back at what we have not achieved, anticipate with foreboding whatever difficulties and dilemmas the future might bring. In our darkest moments, we may think, 'What's the point of any of it?'

We are human and such dark nights of the soul happen for many of us. But the 'secret manifesto' of which Roszak speaks is being written anyway, despite the worried mind's chant of 'I'm tired, I give up.' At bottom, when we feel we can go no lower, we discover something more, something beneath and beyond the depression, disbelief, uncertainty and feeling of worthlessness. There comes – some say inevitably – a breakthrough to a fresh understanding. And where there is understanding, there is strength.

We are not here to be ground down by failure. Our place and purpose do not lie in mediocrity and stasis. Whatever our authentic vocation may be, we owe it to ourselves to search for it and have the courage born of self-commitment to continue with that search until it is rewarded.

Today I assert my right to self-discovery.

We are awakening to ourselves as individual beings with an inner rulership... People don't want to feel stuck, they want to be able to change.

M. C. Richards

⑥

In her book *The Crossing Point*, M. C. Richards goes on to assert that 'People are hungering and thirsting after experience that feels true to them on the inside, after so much hard work mapping the outer spaces of the physical world.'

It is a profound irony that such a profusion of knowledge of 'the outer spaces' has been accompanied by so many people losing their way within. We have scanned the universe across the spectrum of radiations, photographed the misty dance of atoms, evoked powerful pictures of how the world must have been throughout the ages of geologic time – and for the price of a CD or a coffee-table book we can have such knowledge glossily presented to us at our fingertips.

But what do we know of ourselves that is comparable in scope or majesty to what the stars tell us or the messages that spinning molecules speak?

The mapping of the outer spaces is largely a job for experts based in universities or big corporations. But the exploration inside, for which we hunger and thirst, must be carried out by each one of us. Each of us must go forward, driven by curiosity and that sense of 'authentic vocation', entrusted to the inner guide, sustained by the promise of the way of being which marks the end of our search, and the beginning of our fulfilment.

At that point, as Richards says, 'Freedom sings within us, as well as outside us...'

Today I obey the authority of my inner rulership.

Our health and sanity require that we learn to live lives that are genuinely creative.

Frederic Flach

ⓖ

Creativity does not come from outside. There is no Muse looking over our shoulder, providing any easy answers on which direction we ought to take, which opportunities are worth pursuing, which pitfalls we might encounter just around the next corner. If anything resembling a Muse exists at all, then it is the 'inner rulership' we provide for ourselves, that still, small voice of calm which speaks in the language of emotions and intuition, whose wisdom we receive as a sense of 'rightness-of-action' against a background of optimism and quiet self-assurance.

To be creative is a natural ability, but rarely an easy one to practise. And because it comes from the deeper levels of our being, its wisdom is not always recognized by the logical, rational conscious mind – or, when it is recognized, it may be ignored or disdained, or regarded as too radical or costly to act upon.

Creativity is the antithesis of habit. It thrives on novelty and diversity. It loves challenge. To live a genuinely creative life means to do the same and the 'cost' of any drastic divergence from the norm is simply the conscious mind's way of revealing its own limitations.

Today I wonder what I need to do to preserve my health and sanity.

We are torn between what others want from us and what we want for ourselves.

Marilyn Ferguson

(b)

We have already looked at 'wants' and 'needs', and that distinction might be worth bearing in mind here. As a first step in identifying what we want/need for ourselves, it is worth writing down what *others* want from us – indeed, demand from us in all kinds of ways:

Draw some concentric circles on a large sheet of paper. Reserve the innermost circle for yourself. Moving outwards, write, *partner, family, friends, work colleagues, acquaintances*. Then vaguer and more abstract categories such as *work, leisure, community, country,* etc.

Now continue from the outermost circle, moving inwards. Think about what your country wants from you, your community, your acquaintances, your colleagues at work, and so on.

Persevere until your list is as complete as you can make it. Now bring to mind what separates *want* from *need*. Needs should always take priority, so underline them.

Finally, look at what *you* need. Ask yourself to what extent you can fulfil your needs and those of the people who matter. Where do you need to arrange a workable compromise? Where do the real conflicts occur? Can a compromise be arranged here? If no, look again.

Today I look at myself and my loved ones, and realize that what we most need is each other.

The image by which the flesh lives is the ultimate ruling necessity.

James Hillman

⑥

Our reality is composed of imagery. Collectively we spend billions of pounds a year on creating a self-image and making sure it is the 'right' image for us to project into the world. Self-image and self-esteem are obviously closely connected and largely dependent upon one another.

That makes us vulnerable. Partly it is because we can be exploited by others working to persuade us that our image needs to change with the seasons, like fashion, and that what would do last year will be totally inadequate for the year to come. But, more critically, we are also vulnerable within ourselves if we equate our 'surface image', our public face, with who we feel we really are. Because then, we are open to manipulation, and to the doubt and cynicism of the conscious mind, which is easily persuaded that we need *this*, should buy *that*, should change in *these* ways...

My reading of James Hillman's words is that he is not referring to this outer façade, the 'I' which can be changed like a sweater. Rather, he is talking about a deeper sense of self, a truer self, that essential core which is the inner ruler of our lives. Only by increasing our awareness of this fundamental self do we deepen our understanding of who we are and thus maximize the potential by which the flesh lives.

Today I look towards the heart of who I am, that ultimate ruling necessity.

We have evolved a culture interested only in the obvious, the tangible and the usable.

William Bloom

⑥

The wonderful irony of this assertion is that to acquire an understanding of who we truly are is the most 'usable' and useful step we can take in fulfilling our potential in life. The deep sadness implicit in William Bloom's words is that 'the obvious and tangible' offer a steady supply of easy answers, and what is 'usable' can also be abused or used to the point of destruction.

The culture which has 'evolved' to this state now carries a huge momentum that drives it forward into the future. Indeed, it is by far the most effortless thing to be carried along in the slipstream of the way things are – 'That's the reality of the situation' being one of the neat little catch-all phrases of the moment.

But the reality of the situation is that each of us, as individuals, need not be interested only in 'the obvious'. We can extend our definition of what is 'usable' to include things which are usable in different ways (ways other than the obvious!)

A culture should exist through its people, should be defined and sustained by what people need and not what they are told they should want. To be offered the obvious and be made to feel better for having bought it is not to live a genuinely creative life but to move like a puppet through an ad-man's designer world, dazzled and blinded by his TV-dinner dreams.

Today I look inside for the less obvious; for what I really need.

When a small child ... I thought that success spelled happiness. I was wrong. Happiness is like a butterfly which appears and delights us for one brief moment, but soon flits away.

Anna Pavlova

❻

Most people's conception of success is of the obvious. It is what is tangible and usable – but in greater quantities than we have now.

Such a narrow definition anchored in the outside world is largely beyond our control – or at least, at the mercy of the slings and arrows of outrageous fortune. Such success rarely equates with happiness, even if it is achieved, as Anna Pavlova found. To be successful on our own terms, according to our own definition, might bring less ephemeral happiness; but even then, it is happiness based on a target, the outcome of a preplanned aim, the end of a journey of effort...

The implication is that by redefining success we can more easily achieve and sustain success. And by broadening our concept of happiness, we come to see that happiness can be the natural and continual outcome of all that we do – of the journey as well as of the destination.

This is not to live by an illusion. Changing your perspective does not mean pulling the wool over your eyes. Indeed, we may well ask if the way we live now constitutes 'the reality of the situation'.

To be happy as a consequence of living is the most lasting and satisfying form of success. It is to look beyond the butterfly and see the summer.

Being alive today, I find success in happiness.

All generalizations are dangerous. Even this one.

Alexandre Dumas

⑥

Ironically, to generalize is to narrow our perspective. And to say 'When I'm successful I'll be happy' is perhaps one of the most damaging generalizations of all.

Generalizing is a mental habit, a kind of misplaced syllogism in our thinking that gives little, but takes much. To say: 'I don't do well at interviews. This is an interview. Therefore I won't do well,' is as absurd as asserting: 'All dogs are animals. This is an animal. Therefore it must be a dog.' The difficulty is that while we can easily see the logical inconsistency of the second statement, we often blind ourselves to the illogicality of the first.

Thus generalizations coupled with negative mechanical thinking create a vicious feedback loop that is potentially highly destructive. To be genuinely creative, we must particularize – and the very act of seeing the unique, the individual, the particular, in all that we do enhances in us the creative power we all possess.

Begin now. Change your mind by changing the way you look at things. Say, 'I did not do well at my last … interviews. What can I learn from those experiences to help me in my next interview?'

Or if that's hard, get some practice by saying, 'All dogs are animals. This is an animal. But in this case it's a …'

Then look more closely and decide why it is a unique member of its species.

Today, and from now on, I become more aware of the unique, the individual, the particular.

There is no force so great as an idea whose time has come.

S. Best and C. Smith

⑥

Best and Smith are referring to 'the spirit of the times', a favourable period when the efforts of many individuals, through fortuitous circumstances, come together to create a beneficial leap forward – in science, technology or some other important field of endeavour. They sum up this phenomenon through the German word *Zeitgeist*, a force expressed by Dr Julian Kenyon in *21st Century Medicine* as 'a major shift of consciousness'. He likens it to the astonishing progress made in many areas during the Renaissance. More thinkers are aware of the spirit of the times than can pinpoint its causes, though all seem to agree that it is powerful, all-pervading and startlingly positive.

What emerges directly from the quote above is that ideas are potent, and that potency affects both the conceiver of the idea and other individuals by an osmotic process of communication throughout society.

Furthermore, the power of an idea culminates at a certain point, when 'its time has come' – when, driven by a sense of rightness, we act upon what we have conceived, despite what surface logics or the negative spirallings of worry might tell us to the contrary.

Best and Smith imbue *Zeitgeist* with a certain independence: it happens anyway. But how much more effective is that energy if we are aware of it and eager to exploit its potential?

Today I watch for opportunities cresting like breakers on the shore – and I surf!

An expert is someone who has made all the mistakes which can be made in a very narrow field.

Niels Bohr

🌀

I find this a wonderfully optimistic statement, in that Niels Bohr links expertise with error; indeed, suggests that we cannot achieve that state of knowledgeable experience *unless* we have learned to differentiate between what works and what does not. How can we possibly find the right direction unless we have wandered along at least a few blind alleys first?

All of us who have worried have become experts in it over the years. But worry itself is cunning: it is a distorting lens which hides from us the lessons it is teaching. It causes us to see an opportunity as a risk and a challenge as a problem. It denies us our rightful status as 'expert' by making us feel inadequate, helpless, frightened and enervated. It denies us the sense of optimistic endeavour with which a scientist like Bohr will explore the universe, eager for success but remaining undaunted in the face of a temporary setback, hungry to learn more, to hone that expertise which drives him on towards more skilful learning.

We learn best from worry by recognizing its limitations. It is itself a failed experiment. We tried it, but it doesn't work – it doesn't help us to solve any problems or move us closer to where we want to be. And what do scientists do with an experiment that fails?

They mark it down to experience and move on.

Today I celebrate my expertise: I discard worry and look elsewhere for solutions.

Home is a place where, when you go there, they have to take you in.

Robert Frost

⑥

If you have a home, in this true sense of the word, recognize it, realize it and set it as a huge *plus* against the many petty *minuses* that worry brings along. Those who have homes are luckier than most of them realize.

But we can also use this statement metaphorically to change the way we are inside – for our ultimate home, our primal shelter against the sometimes inclement climate of life, lies deep within our own hearts and minds. It should be a place where, when we go there, we are welcomed and nourished, allowed to rest and gather our energies before stepping outside once more.

How often does this happen? How many of us, because we have not invested much time or effort or care in *making* our homes, are strangers to ourselves? How many of us have somewhere to go inside ourselves for essential shelter?

When we take a close look at ourselves, who do we see? Is our automatic reaction one of self-denigration or doubt? Do we put ourselves down because of the way we look or because of other supposed failings in our character? Do we let these negative, often quite automatic thoughts blind us to the positive aspects of ourselves?

When we go home, we are cherished despite our failings and limitations. We are loved for ourselves. If others are capable of extending that love to us, can we not cultivate it in ourselves, for ourselves – beginning right now?

Today I go home and I am welcomed inside.

The pain passes. The beauty remains.

Pierre-Auguste Renoir

❻

The great artist was talking about endurance, continuing to paint while crippled with the agony of arthritis. There was something within him that went deeper than pain, something which saw through the negative to the greater positive beyond. The creation of beauty was for Renoir the ultimate purpose and achievement of his life.

The man's talent was undoubtedly exceptional, but his ability to endure is common to millions. He was a human being, no more, who had found something which gave a fundamental meaning to his existence. In his case it was the creation of fine paintings and through them the communication of beauty, but for us the aim can be a far more modest one. It need not lead to lasting fame and adulation. We do not have to live up to anybody's expectations but our own. Nor, indeed, are we required to please anyone except those we love and ourselves.

The vital first step is to see *and feel* that there is something beyond our daily perceptions which is worth enduring for. And it needs to be beyond price, else we be tempted to think that the cost is too great in achieving it.

I am not talking about something that lies far in the future. I am not talking about some cosy retirement home in the country, where we can sit out in the sunshine and drowse away our declining years. What's worth enduring for might be here now, but for recognizing it and reaching out to it.

To find it is a fine achievement in itself.

Today I ask, 'What remains once the pain has passed?'

The object of art is to give life a shape.

Jean Anouilh

⑥

Human beings express their most profound and finest feelings through the creation and appreciation of art. It defines our highest thoughts and embodies our deepest purposes. It symbolizes all that we are and aspire to be. It is an essential statement of our fundamental humanity.

Because of this, life itself is an art: *being here* an act that is genuinely creative – at least in its potential, if not for all of us yet in its execution. We are living portraits, self-created, proclaiming 'I am here. I am me.' What else matters but this?

I am put in mind of a poem by Jacques Prévert called 'The Dunce'. This boy has been made a fool and a laughingstock by his teacher and classmates, and is left far behind in their talk of times and places, numbers and words:

> All the problems are posed
> sudden laughter seizes him.

It is the laughter of self-realization.

The dunce endures the pain of the teacher's threats and the jeers of infant prodigies, and:

> with chalk of every colour
> on the blackboard of misfortune
> he draws the face of happiness.

Great art indeed.

Today I see giving life a shape the finest art of all.

There are no new truths, but only truths that have not been recognized by those who have perceived them without noticing.

Mary McCarthy

❀

The secret of drawing the face of happiness on the blackboard of misfortune is only a secret because we have not told ourselves the answer.

A large part of the problem is this ongoing lack of recognition of who and what we are. Each of us is a limited creature. We are here, warts and all, and we either work with that in our favour or suffer the purposeless pain of wishing we were someone else, somewhere else, somewhen else. Such wishing conceals old truths behind equally ancient lies.

To be happy is to be what we are. And to be what we are – *what we truly and fully can be* – is to be happy. Jacques Prévert's dunce is happy, not despite what he is, but because of what he is. He is a dunce by someone else's definition, but a genius in living his life to its limits. The sudden laughter that seizes him is the laughter of self-recognition, not the bitter laughter of envy or self-disparagement or despair.

Deep down, many of us know who we are; we know the answer to our own question. On the surface we deny what we know, or fear to initiate the changes which will bring that self-truth to light and express our essential selves in all aspects of what we do in our lives.

Today I look again at the face of happiness, scrawled simply on the blackboard of misfortune. What old truth do I recognize there?

We could never learn to be brave and patient if there were only joy in the world.

Helen Keller

(6)

I count myself lucky that I have never needed to be as brave and patient as Helen Keller had to be. Some qualities are undoubtedly forged from adversity, but we are tempted to hope, in secret moments of fear, that life might pass by without such distress, even if it means that these qualities forever lie dormant…

However, there is comfort and inspiration to be gained from Helen Keller's words, which point out a simple but basic truth. We live in a Yin-Yang world, as two-sided as a coin. And in this real world, George does not slay the dragon. They are forever locked in combat, an eternal struggle wherein each exists for the other and because of the other.

It is therefore a futile aim, and the most naïve kind of wishful thinking, to hope for a world filled only with joy and with light. There is little chance that any of us can banish adversity from our lives – but every chance that we can use it to strengthen ourselves, come through it and use it to experience the joy that lies beyond more acutely.

Today I do not run from problems or deny them.
Today I tackle them and triumph.

The only place where success comes before work is in a dictionary.

Vidal Sassoon

⑥

The conscious mind leaps quickly to qualify sentiments like these, pointing out that the rich and the famous can *afford* to tell the rest of us how hard they struggled for their fortune. Anyway, the work these people do is varied and interesting and increasingly under their control. It must be fun to make millions that way!

Such thinking greases the slope towards envy and dissatisfaction, and to be disparaging in this way helps no one. Reading the biographies and autobiographies of successful people will dispel many myths, and can be a source of inspiration to the rest of us in our own endeavours to succeed.

But we must also remain aware of what *we* mean by 'success'. Have we succeeded if we amass a fortune? And how large a fortune might that be? And what else would we want, apart from a sheer quantity of money? Happiness and satisfaction, a sense of fulfilment in life? This, trite but true to say, goes beyond simple monetary wealth.

And since we are making distinctions, we should do so too with regard to 'work'. Our daily occupations may bring us a wage, but little else. So what might our life's work be? What is our vocation? If it's there, can it be achieved? And if so, however modestly, is that not in itself a very important measure of success?

Today I consider the difference between making a living and making a life.

Instead of wanting to look at the back of the moon, remote from our lives, we can try to look at the back of our own minds.

J. B. Priestley

☾

Priestley was talking literally here about the moon, his tone one of anger and frustration, perhaps even despair, that Western culture seemed desperately to be searching for its centre, expending vast energies in its hunger for completion, in reconciling its inner and outer existence. Like an engine in neutral, revving itself to destruction, it was going nowhere in finding fundamental answers.

Priestley urges us to stop disinheriting ourselves:

We can challenge the whole de-humanizing, depersonalizing process that is taking the symbolic richness, the dimension of depth out of men's lives, inducing the anaesthesia that demands violence, crudely horrible effects, to feel anything at all…

That challenge must be on an personal level, firstly transforming the individual, before its effects can be felt on the larger scale.

And it is ironic that the moon, for thousands of years before it became a 'real' target to hit, was the source of inspiration and enchantment and wonder for millions of people from all cultures throughout the world… More ironic still that the Apollo space programme, whose aim was to get there, was cancelled prematurely because its ratings dropped on network TV.

Today I reflect that I make my own meanings. I choose symbols which work for me and use them to inspire.

We meet as professionals … wise enough to know what works and is to be retained, yet humble enough to seek new solutions.

Beverley Galyean

(6)

Beverley Galyean, a consultant on 'confluent education' for Los Angeles city schools, is quoted in Marilyn Ferguson's excellent *The Aquarian Conspiracy.* Her point is that, in many different situations, people cling to the old ways of doing things, even if those ways are no longer effective, either wholly or in part.

Fear of abandoning even obsolete methods because they are 'the devil you know' is a powerful force against change. This is often coupled with the mistaken idea that change necessarily means letting go of *everything* with which you are familiar in favour of a totally new system.

A little quiet thought in respect of your own situation, however, will probably reveal that there are aspects of your life that work well for you, while others do not, and that there are ways in which these can be separated, so making room for changes and new directions.

Today, in wisdom and humility, I retain that which works for me even as I seek new solutions for that which doesn't.

Symmetry is rigid. Rigidity excludes life.

Christopher Day

☙

Christopher Day is an architect and a sculptor, and is here talking about the symmetry of buildings. But we also build walls and façades around ourselves which are made not of brick and glass but of habit and routine, apprehension, fear or rage.

The very fact that many of us long for change, yearn to be free of our self-imposed confinements, yet continue to follow the same old ways and routines, amply demonstrates Day's point. Symmetry is rigid. Our lives can be neat, tidy, organized and ordered – but crushingly dull.

Change is not an all-or-nothing situation, however. *Because* our lives are so ordered, we can introduce small changes, or a sprinkling of refreshingly different *dis*order, without upsetting the whole balance. This can be achieved without having to relinquish any of the comforting controls we cling to with such fervour.

The changes we choose might be precisely located in space and time: a few hours one day a week to meet new people or try a different activity; a visit to a place we've never seen before; a shopping trip where we deliberately try on new styles of clothes or sample an unusual cuisine… But make the list yourself, as a tantalizing precursor to the act of knocking those sharp edges off life's routines.

Today I 'think flexible' and celebrate life.

The skies are filled with great white geese migrating homeward after winter's southern sojourn. Are these wondrous beings thinking about which bearing to fly, or worrying about being off course? It is I, watching them, who hold such thoughts, not they. For they possess an instinctual knowing that I have long ago surrendered so as to develop the faculty with which I ponder their being 'on' or 'off' course. They are at one with the world in which they fly, and they do not wonder why.

Danaan Parry and Lila Forest

⑥

To wonder is to *know wonderment*, to be enchanted and uplifted by the phenomenon of life, to be awed by partaking in its dance. Surely what we as humans have surrendered, if anything, is an instinct that never once allowed us the capacity to be moved by music or inspired by the stars.

Do the geese ever take joy in their flight or ponder the nature of their destination?

Parry and Forest continue, 'Early in the development of humankind … we naturally and unconsciously lived each moment in harmony and balance.' Well, perhaps. But I am reminded of quite frequent archaeological finds of human remains where the bones have been twisted with arthritis, the skull shattered in battle, the teeth rotted by decay and disease. Harmony and balance might have been a rarer experience for our ancestors than for us.

If there is any design to life, then we have become what we are for a purpose – one that allows us to wonder.

Today my skies are filled with wonderment.

*...just at this time in our troubled world we stand on the
brink of maturity, in a position to recognize that we are
neither perfect nor omnipotent.*

Elisabet Sahtouris

❦

This comment is aimed at us as a *species*, but there is much that
each of us as individuals can learn from these sentiments.

We are neither perfect nor omnipotent, though how often
do we push ourselves to the point of exhaustion (or beyond),
either to please others with our 'efficiency' and diligence or
because we cultivate totally unrealistic self-expectations?

To operate at maximum capacity is not the same as making
optimum use of our abilities and resources. Driving a car flat-
out is not using its fuel most efficiently. Similarly, I feel, to
throw ourselves at an endless list of tasks with the sole intention of getting them all finished as quickly as possible leads to
rushed results and a serious drain on our energy and ability to
approach problems creatively.

There comes a point – at the brink of maturity – when we
must realize that we are not perfect and that attempting to push
ourselves beyond our natural limitations imposes a *further limitation* on what we can possibly achieve. Speed does not equal
efficiency: efficiency does not always equal effectiveness. To be
effective – which is to say, to produce a powerful effect – it is
necessary to work in balance both with our strengths and our
weaknesses.

**Today I assess more realistically what I am able to
achieve.**

No matter what you or I do, other people can cause problem after problem [but] I do not accept that we are losers who cannot cope adequately in this industrialised, urbanised, sanitised space age.

Manuel J. Smith

⑥

Manuel Smith's *When I Say No I Feel Guilty* is a bestseller and rightly so, being one of the most useful and empowering books I have ever read. Smith's central premise is: 'Not only is it natural to expect that we will have problems in living, it is also natural to expect that we all have the ability to cope adequately with those problems.'

Problems are often created and imposed upon us by other people – or rather, by our inability to prevent other people from loading that weight of trouble on our shoulders. We habitually and implicitly say 'yes' to problems, because many of us do not have the coping techniques to assert 'no'. And assertiveness is what Manuel Smith's book is all about.

Rather than attempt to summarize his explanations and techniques, I simply recommend you read the book as one of your short-term goals, meantime rehearsing in your mind your aim of acting upon what you learn. And it *is* possible to learn to say 'no' without guilt, since true guilt is the intention to cause harm, followed by the act of causing that harm. Few of us are that malicious in life.

Today I realize I have the right to judge my own behaviour, thoughts and emotions, and to take the responsibility for their initiation and consequences upon myself.

Pollution of the ethos (the spiritual environment of the community) is just as dangerous a threat to the survival of humanity as is the pollution of the physical environment.

Michael Bentine

⑥

Whether we realize it or not, we live within a complex *ethos* which we all help to create and suffer the consequences of. We cannot see the ethos as such, only its results, but undoubtedly it is as *real* as our everyday environment of houses, roads and shopping malls.

Michael Bentine, in his book *The Shy Person's Guide to Life*, is therefore talking about conservation in a very particular sense, urging us to be as committed to 'cleaning up the world of the ethos' as, hopefully, we are to cleaning up our physical environment. He encourages us to assert our right to live in a spiritual environment which is healthy, positive and caring, and suggests:

Always questioning the motives of someone who is
　spiritually destructive.
Never believing destructive criticism unless it embodies
　constructive alternatives.
Dealing resolutely with scolding or nagging.
Stamping out jealousy immediately.

Our spiritual world needs to be strong and clean if our physical environment is to flourish.

**Today I play my part in stopping 'mental vandalism'
in its tracks.**

Two may talk together under the same roof for many years yet never really meet; and two others at first speech are old friends.

Mary Catherwood

❻

There is often a difference between talking and communicating, and there are many qualities of silence.

These days, many business and salespeople pay high prices to attend training courses in 'power communication' through mechanisms like Neuro-Linguistic Programming. There they learn to 'read' eye movement and posture, and to pick up on subtle cues revealed by the voice, to 'pace and lead' the client almost subliminally along a certain path of persuasion and agreement. In less systematic and scientific days, we would have called such a complex of techniques charm or charisma. And we may still wonder if it can really be gleaned from a training manual.

However clever we may become in the techniques of communication, at the deepest heart of *true* communication lie sincerity and enthusiasm, genuine interest and love. Two people may talk together for years yet never communicate. But the real tragedy is if neither of them thinks or troubles to ask 'Why?'

Talking can be difficult for a person who is shy or lacking in confidence. Yet involved listening, driven by an honest interest in what the other is saying, forms a vital first step. Beyond that, asking a few friendly, open questions works wonders and helps build the common ground where people really meet.

Today I take a step in meeting people I may only previously have talked to.

Fate chooses your relations. You choose your friends.

Jacques Delille

❧

It depends, of course, on how you define 'a friend'. We live within a complex and multi-layered society, wherein most of us belong to many diverse groups, all of whom contain people we might consider to be our friends.

But it seems to me that a true friend is a rare and special person, and the relationship to which you both belong something that may reach back in some instances further than you can remember. In other cases, that warmth and familiarity, that closeness and camaraderie which characterize real friendship are present and welcomed 'at first speech'. It is hard to define, but easily recognized by everyone.

Choosing friends thus represents something of a dilemma, being often a social convenience, or an obligation, or sometimes a mistake. Avoiding negative persons, those that drain the energy of the spirit, is necessary for our well-being, however awkward achieving it might be. Beyond that, it becomes a matter of *realizing* who our true friends are, making the distinction and then allowing the synergy of the relationship to work its magic.

A friend of mine – in the deepest sense – gave me a book shortly before she died of cancer. Inside she wrote:

True friendship is a plant of slow growth, and must undergo and withstand the shocks of adversity before it is entitled to that appellation.

That plant of slow growth owes nothing to time, space or absence.

Today I make an investment in my true friends.

Our ability to be objective, to see ourselves as the 'I' or 'eye'
of our cosmos, as being independent of nature, has inflated
our egos – 'ego' being the Greek word for 'I'.

Elisabet Sahtouris

🌀

The 'I' of which Elisabet Sahtouris is speaking, in defining itself, limits itself. It is, essentially, a selfish aspect of the psyche, with a tendency to take rather than give and to give if there is something of equal or greater value that can be taken back. Ego-driven friendships (and we all suffer them!) are played out like games on the chessboard of social intercourse. They are all about losses and gains, point-scoring and the inflation of the 'I', which achieves its aim by diminishing others.

True friendship sends its roots to deeper levels and empowers us beyond the understanding of mundane logics. True friends give endlessly, but gain without limit. The 'I' within us ceases to be the point and pivot about which the universe turns – nor do we find our lives necessarily revolving around the person who is the subject of our friendship. There is nothing 'objective' about friendship. Indeed, it is the most subjective of phenomena, having a power that frequently moves it beyond the comprehension or control of our conscious, reasoning minds. And indeed, in a very important sense, true friendship *should be* 'unreasonable', since it is not something that can be sustained or enhanced by the limited self-definitions of the surface ego. Friends orbit together through a field of warmth, by which they are both nurtured. There is no 'object' to such a relationship, no final product or outcome, no end.

Today I see that the 'I / eye' of my cosmos is half closed.

Ah, Power that swirls us together
Grant us Bliss…

Gary Snyder

@

Gary Snyder's poem is to 'All Threatened Beings', but I take it as my inspiration in other senses also. It leads me to wonder what the 'Power' might be that 'swirls us together' – true friends; fortuitous circumstances; help when I need it most… At least, my ego, the 'I' of my cosmos, reflects on this question. Deeper down, I just accept it and draw comfort and warmth from the factless knowledge of its existence.

Recent scientific findings suggest that the universe is connected at deep levels in ways that were previously unsuspected before the advent of quantum physics. The cosmos is not made of separate particles which join and disassemble in compliance with simple mechanical laws. Rather, there exists a fundamental unity between everything that *is*, such that the fate of any 'component' cannot, in reality, be separated from the destinies of all others.

We are all 'swirled together' in ways we cannot imagine, which imparts to our actions an importance that goes beyond what we, as individual beings, want, need or intend. The deepest insights of modern science are defining us as part of a community which is greater than any of us can comprehend. Because of this, it is neither our technical know-how that will guide us, nor any intellectual conception of how or why we belong, rather it is by trusting to an all-embracing *sense* of community that we will find our way.

Today I find awe and delight in the Power that swirls me through life.

'If any one of them can explain it,' said Alice, 'I'll give him sixpence. I don't believe there's an atom of meaning in it.'
'If there's no meaning in it,' said the King, 'that saves a world of trouble, you know, as we needn't try to find any.'

Lewis Carroll

❻

We are makers of meaning. The 'I' of our cosmos *defines* that cosmos, both individually, through the way we feel our lives have progressed, and scientifically/collectively, through the questions we ask, based on what we have previously found to be true. Incidentally, and ironically, 'not to believe' implicitly imbues the world with as much meaning as unshakeable faith, albeit of a negative nature.

But there are ways and ways of finding meaning. Not to try in any sense leads to lethargy, apathy and purposelessness. Problems crash over us so that we are swept helplessly along in their wake, never realizing or exploiting the fact that a challenge is simply a problem invested with positive meaning.

On the other hand, to search too avidly or desperately for reasons, in order to 'put meaning into my life', can lead to a loss of sensitivity and independence, such that we may be attracted to any philosophy, creed or cult that seems at first glance to promise us the salvation of 'An Answer'.

However, if we accept (even with open-minded scepticism) that meaning is latent in all that happens, then whatever happens will become a source of learning. And how much easier answers are to find if we know they there in the first place!

Today I allow myself the possibility that there is meaning in every atom.

It is the theory that decides what we can observe.

Albert Einstein

❻

This is as true of theories of science and the universe as it is of theories of ourselves.

A theory is defined as a 'supposition explaining something, a speculative thought'. Properly speaking, theories only become physical laws or rules to live by once they have been verified by the balanced and open-minded accumulation of evidence supporting the original hypothesis. That evidence must be tested by experimentation, in an attempt to reproduce early results. In this way, science arrives at a useful working model of the world, one which has practical value on a day-to-day basis and stands as a solid foundation for further enquiry.

What, then, of ourselves? Do we assess what *we* are and what *we* do in as balanced and open-minded a way? Not nearly as often as we need to!

If we fail to achieve a particular aim, we take this all too frequently as an all-encompassing rule that we are failures. If, due to circumstances beyond our control, we find ourselves depressed or unhappy, then we feel that things must always be like this, that we will never be able to steer our lives in a more promising direction.

But such evidence of failure, unhappiness or whatever has not been put to the test; rather, it has been used – often without conscious reflection – to 'prove' a general observation, which further evidence and experimentation in the 'laboratory of life' would refute.

Today I begin to construct a more useful working model of the world and my place within it.

The situation is hopeless, but not serious.

Arabian proverb

⑥

A very useful mental technique is that of 'situational reconstruction'. It is, if you like, a 'video playback' of a problematic or stress-causing event. By sitting quietly and looking back at the details of such an event, further information about it might be gleaned. More than that, it is possible to imagine different outcomes – outcomes which may have made that situation better *or worse*. The next step, armed with this further evidence, is to visualize how you could perhaps have made the better outcome a reality. Thus you will likely realize that there were more options available to you at the time than you initially believed. Also, you can use this in future situations which seem to be heading in one bleak direction. Researcher Dr Suzanne Kobasa suggests, 'When you realize how much worse it could have been, you know you didn't mess it up as much as you might have.'

Another technique which Dr Kobasa and her colleague Dr Salvatore Maddi advocate is that of 'compensatory self-improvement', which can be employed whenever you encounter a situation that cannot be controlled or changed. They advise that when this happens, you must be realistic. If the situational reconstruction technique offers no answers, then 'that event is a given situation, and must be accepted as such'.

A *particular* situation does not, and should not, make a *general* statement about you. Examine the wider picture and *see* how improvements can be made elsewhere.

Today I understand that a situation can be hopeless, but not serious.

Language not only conveys information, but also expresses a world-view.

Paul Watzlawick

(b)

Recent research indicates that the human capacity for language is deep-wired into our brains. It is a fundamental ability that in a very profound sense makes us what we are.

Given that we employ language consciously (albeit with an occasional unintended 'Freudian slip'!), we might think that it is under our control. Well, yes and no.

The use of spoken language is analogous to that of *body* language. We might dress, or stand, or gesture to project a particular image of ourselves – although these overt signals might be belied by subtle cues of which we are entirely unaware. Similarly, although we 'know' what we are saying and what we intend to say, the unconscious use of metaphor or sensory-modality references offer clues to what we feel and believe deeper down. Our world-view is expressed through the window of our words.

To become ultra-sensitive to what we say serves no particularly useful purpose. Worrying about 'saying the wrong thing' in that sense is fruitless. What can be valuable from time to time is to observe how we use words, to examine without interference the 'subtext' that the way we say things reveals. Beyond that, by deliberate ploys to make the underlying content of our language more positive, we can use words to weave a stronger fabric of belief, intent and subsequent action.

Today I meditate on the view that 'Words are the physicians of a mind dis-eased.' (Aeschylus)

Create a 'coping dialogue' with yourself…
'Here I go again, already worrying about the future. Let me
just settle down to do my best.'
Sharon Faelton and David Diamond

⑥

Potentially we have a great deal of control over the way we talk to ourselves.

We have already touched upon the monkey-like or mechanical nature of the conscious mind – best exemplified perhaps in the way we sometimes find it hard to 'turn off' a catchy tune, even when we're irritated by it. More frequently, the bleak melody of worry runs in our minds as a kind of background noise to our lives. Here the irony is that we don't even *make* an effort to eliminate it, but just listen to that same old refrain of hopelessness and gloom.

But in the same way that we can learn to get rid of the wearisome pop song – perhaps by replacing it with another or focusing our thoughts on more important and immediate concerns – so by establishing a coping dialogue we can diminish and dispel the tedious repetitiveness of worry.

Master it in stages. Take 'time out' every day to give yourself a peptalk. Be upbeat, confident, determined. Kick worries out of play like footballs. Simply tell yourself with as much conviction as you can muster that you are going to take deliberate action to achieve what you can and refuse point-blank to be troubled by circumstances that are beyond your control.

Be firm in this time out investment. Gradually, the coping dialogue will become a stronger habit than the purposeless motif of your problems, allowing your mind to sing with confidence.

Today I talk to myself to stay sane!

Even if we can't define silence, we can recognize it. Gentle, unobstructive, calming, life-supporting, holy sounds allow us to be quiet within: sounds of the breath of air, the serene endlessness of water … but they are not eternal. Silence, tranquillity and the eternal have a lot to do with each other.

Christopher Day

⑥

Silence may be an absence of sounds, but once achieved it reveals other presences. We all know and appreciate the value, the refreshing nature, of some good, old-fashioned 'peace and quiet'. It may not be too easy to find these days, both because of the vast seethe of city life and because we have come to regard 'sitting quietly, doing nothing' as idle and unproductive. On the contrary, of course, simply to let the body rest and the mind drift softly through a calming silence charges the batteries and strengthens us to face the vicissitudes of a busy life once more.

Yet what we often think of as silence is not silence at all. We may drive out into the countryside and sit beneath a starry sky or enter an empty church where, at last, even the faintest echoes ebb away to nothingness... But if our mind is clouded with problems, wracked by worry, endlessly shifting from one difficulty to another, then silence is nothing but a surface feature of limited worth.

True silence exists within more crucially than without. And, like the external silence that we sometimes crave, if only as a contrast to the bustle and 'busy-ness' of life, while we may not achieve it completely, we can approach ever more closely that powerfully beneficial state.

Today I go in search of inner silence.

Watch for moments of stillness.
In a scene of beauty.
Or in a moment of surprise or shock.
Look up on a starry night.
Everything sits in space.
See the space between the furniture.
Listen for the silence in between the sounds.

Barry Long

⑥

Barry Long's teachings (as, for example, in his book *Meditation: A foundation course*) deal with subtleties, powerful subtleties. And yet they are subtleties merely because 'we have evolved a culture interested only in the obvious'.

It is so very easy to think that more-faster-bigger-brighter is better. This is tied in with the notion that to be effective we should be able to accomplish a greater amount in the same time (or less!) as we did before. We load our food and drink with additives and enhancers to boost the flavour or to reduce the preparation time because we have so much else to do. We trade in our modest colour TV for a larger widescreen format model with surroundsound and look forward to the day when we can also get 3D or maybe even virtual-reality quality movies…

Please don't feel that I'm simply being churlish about technological advances: word processing beats writing longhand outright! But we tend to allow them to lull us into thinking that there's only one way to go – more-faster-bigger-brighter.

Actually, we can enjoy the best of all worlds – excite ourselves with CD stereo and appreciate and use the power of the silences between.

Today I listen for the silence between the sounds.

A fairly large number of people have a private mythology about traffic lights. Reason may tell them that these lights are either set to turn from yellow to red to green with unchanging regularity, or are controlled by sensor loops embedded in the street surface. On the other hand, they are convinced that the lights are working against them, [changing to red] as they approach…

Paul Watzlawick

⑥

There are a multitude of examples in people's ordinary every-day lives where this very common phenomenon of 'selective attention' comes to the fore. The process is simple, understand-able, insidious and potentially very damaging.

Indeed there are times when traffic lights turn from green through amber to red as we approach. We notice it *and we note it*, especially if we're in a hurry or are late for an appointment, say. Days or weeks later, the same thing happens again, either at the same lights – leading us to invest those lights with this odd malicious property! – or at different ones – in which case we start to think it's something to do with us as individuals.

More often than not, we can shrug off the whole thing as being a silly superstition. But Paul Watzlawick cautions that selective attention can come to resemble a 'mini-psychosis', wherein the general picture of reality is increasingly distorted, usually to our detriment.

Does the universe conspire against me? Let me step back today and take a cool, calm, considered look.

If I don't know I know, I think I don't know.

Ronald D. Laing

🜋

Everything happens in a context, though because we experience the world 'in the first person', i.e. from the supremely subjective viewpoint of our own perceptions, we never see the whole picture. In other words, we don't see the wood for the few trees which surround us.

The positive side of this is that each of us possesses a unique perspective, which we can and should express to the world through creative actions – 'What I do is me, for that I came…'

The flipside of this state of affairs is that we exist in comparative ignorance, confronted by endless ambiguities, paradoxes, scraps and fragments, inaccuracies, errors, misperceptions and lies.

There may be no way out of this, unless by some magical process we can attain that mythical state of objectivity. But *at least* we can realize that the difficulties we see in our lives might well be due to our viewing the partial picture. And we need not make the mistake of arrogance in thinking that there is but one reality and ours is the one right way of regarding it.

Today I see my point of view as but one among millions.

Customers who think our waiters are rude should see the manager.

Source unknown

ⓑ

Not all ambiguity is as humorous as this. The British hypnotherapist David Lesser once recalled how he dreaded to go shopping with his mother, in case they should pass by the shop with 'Family Butcher' writ large above its doorway. The fear generated by taking on board the unhelpful and sinister meaning of this phrase, if left unrecognized and unresolved, could easily lead to difficulties in later life. Indeed, Lesser's method of treating most problems through hypnosis is to 'track back' to the information which first set a patient on the path to creating their problem and uncover how the mind misperceived that information initially.

Accessing the subconscious for such a purpose requires the outside agency of a therapist. But not all ambiguous information is 'laid down' in the mind early in life. As adults we may frequently and consciously assume that our understanding is the correct one, steadfastly refusing to see another's point of view and accepting a single interpretation of an event *because that's how we've always seen things.* This leads to narrow-mindedness, stubbornness and hostility – with all the attendant worries that these can bring.

There are no easy answers, but there are certainly a number of answers in most cases. By accepting this simple fact, we can save ourselves a great deal of subsequent pain.

Today, instead of refusing to give the benefit of the doubt, I'll try to minimize the doubt!

The causes of emotional problems are rarely 'all in the mind', but it is in the mind that anguish is felt when things go wrong.

Mary Manning

❦

Medical journalist and counsellor Mary Manning, who has herself experienced the dark days of emotional and mental problems, asserts: 'Thoughts are the implements through which anxiety, depression and morbid fears take hold and sap our initiative once we have allowed negative thinking free rein.' And we *do* allow the habit of negative thinking to flourish – although often by default.

The vital first step in reversing that trend is to assert our authority over ourselves. We are brought up to respect authority figures and accept the wisdom of their judgements, but hardly ever do we define ourselves as such a figure. This leads to problems when tough decisions need to be taken and the only person who can take them is you.

Mary Manning's book *Help Yourself to Mental Health* clearly maps the jungle and signposts many ways out of it:

Learn relaxation. Become more body-aware.
Get out and about. Break with stale routines.
Identify risk factors for worry and depression.
Deal with difficulties one at a time, decisively.
Learn a new skill, set yourself an upbeat, enjoyable challenge.
Seek out sources of laughter – but never be afraid to cry.
Allow yourself a daily dose of success.

Today I begin to beat anguish by realizing it *can be beaten.*

*I will go by what I know, not by how I feel. I will deal
with behaviour, not motives, and interpret what others say
in a calm and matter-of-fact way, instead of dramatizing
situations and attributing motives to them.*

From the GROW
Group's *Guidelines for Objective Thinking*

✆

GROW is an international mental health community with branches in Britain, the US, Australia, New Zealand and various European countries. Its advice might puzzle those who enjoy health, fitness and vitality in mind, body and spirit. Such people are confident in 'going with how they feel', in dealing with motives rather than behaviour, and will naturally interpret their experiences calmly and positively. For them, no 'special strategies' are needed to cope with life, other than simply to enjoy and prevail. That there *are* special strategies is a source of general comfort, however, to others – and the strategies are of great practical value in themselves.

GROW was founded in the 1960s by Father Cornelius Keogh, a Jesuit priest who had himself suffered a nervous breakdown. He realized the need for a 'non-denominational' self-help movement and incorporated some of the principles of Alcoholics Anonymous into the structure of the GROW groups he established.

Important components of group meetings include 'personal testimonies, discussion of members' problems and progress, discussion of readings from GROW literature and assigning practical tasks and out-of-group contact between members'.

**Today I learn, from examples like GROW, that
there's always somebody out there for me.**

Whoever in discussion adduces authority uses not intellect but memory.

Leonardo da Vinci

⑥

Authority, power and wealth are the big girders which support the world as we know it. Authority sometimes accrues to those with charisma. All too often it is 'built in' to the hierarchical structure of institutions, groups and society itself.

There is no doubt that we need authority and authority figures – who ideally base their decisions upon the consensus view of those who must live by the consequences of those decisions. But authority is neither always right, nor just, nor helpful. And while we may look up to the icons of authority, we should not be drawn into the trap of swallowing their received wisdom whole, pips and all, as an alternative to reaching an independent conclusion.

Beyond all the wise words of others, we each have to find our own direction in life and beat a path towards our destiny as we see it. We can of course call upon many sources of help and support on the way.

In striving to become 'the authority to ourselves' we should not always expect to be right, or just, or helpful. We are just ordinary people, living the best way we can. And in that objective lies both humility and a nobility hard to find anywhere else.

Today I understand I can make my own way to wisdom.

As these rare words come, one senses a sharpened feeling,
or a felt relief, a felt shift, usually before one can say what
the shift is. Sometimes such words are not in themselves
very impressive or novel, but just these words have an
experiential effect, and no others do.

Eugene Gendlin

(6)

The words Eugene Gendlin refers to are those spoken softly to ourselves, words generated by the mind's deeper levels, in response to a mental request for a fear to be confronted and beaten, or a difficulty to be resolved. Gendlin calls this powerful technique 'focusing'. It is a way of finding and exploiting the inner wisdom that we all possess, did we but know it.

Sitting quietly, unconcerned and undisturbed by anything going on around, fix the conscious mind gently upon a particular concern. Suggest to your deeper mind that the nature and origin of that concern should identify itself. In a very short time, just a minute or two in some cases, a word or phrase will come to mind and, if they are the right and appropriate words, the body will respond accordingly, as it always does upon information received and accepted as 'true'.

Marilyn Ferguson, in quoting Gendlin, cites the example of someone on a journey. On the way, that person realizes they have forgotten something and runs through the possibilities. When the item which *has* been forgotten comes to mind, there is an accompanying sense of rightness, coupled with a sense of relief – a shift, in other words, from frustration to certainty at having identified the thing that was the source of the trouble.

**Today, sitting quietly, I seek the rare words which
tell me where to go now.**

*A human being is only a reed, the weakest thing in nature –
but a reed that thinks.*

Blaise Pascal

⑥

There are many different ways to think. The spectrum of
thought that has at its extremes 'normal waking consciousness'
and the profoundest sleep imaginable merely represents one
aspect of this astonishing and still largely mysterious ability.

'Worry' is both the source and outcome of a kind of
'thoughtless thinking' that runs on by itself like an engine left
untended. It uses energy, makes a lot of noise, but goes
nowhere.

There is an old Chinese story about an Emperor who was
suffering a head cold. He consulted his retinue of royal physicians, who prescribed this medicine or that, but with little
effect, for the Emperor dwelt on nothing *but* the cold, nursing it
along as though it were the only thing worth thinking about.

Finally, he went to see an old quack doctor in a nearby vil-
lage. The medic pointed to a corner of his squalid little hut,
where there was an iron bed-frame chained to a system of pul-
leys. The Emperor lay on the frame, as he had been told to do,
and the old man winched him higher, higher, ever closer to the
ceiling.

'Will this cure my cold?' the Emperor wanted to know.

The quack doctor let go of the rope and the frame dropped
to the floor with a crash.

'No, your Mightiness,' he replied, 'but it will give you
something else to think about.'

**Today I turn a weakness into a strength and give
myself something else to think about.**

Without wind the grass does not move.

Chinese proverb

⑥

In a sense we can only 'give ourselves something to think about' by letting the world do it for us. Out there, beyond our skins, lies a universe of experience, opportunity and adventure. And we are lucky, because we can taste that experience in various ways, given the new technologies that allow us to communicate so quickly with so many of our fellow travellers.

The brain is an information processing system. It *loves* things to think about and exists primarily to put all this information together in a way that allows us not just to survive, but to flourish. Its entire energy is directed upward and outward, to the positive, to that which strengthens us and empowers us.

So, when we worry, we are thwarting a very natural tendency of the mind. Because worry is inward-looking, restrictive, self-reinforcing, it is like building a wall around the 'thinking reed' that is a human being. The wind of experience is blocked, the sense of rightness and completeness-in-life is lost, the conscious mind dwells upon an increasingly narrow focus of concern and is starved of the food of raw information on which it thrives.

I break down the wall, let the wind of change blow fresh and clean through my thoughts. Feel the grass move again!

Pinch yourself to know how others feel.

Japanese proverb

⑥

It is a novelist's cliché for a character to pinch themselves to check that they are awake. But the advice holds true even in 'real' life, when we are not conventionally asleep, for what is termed 'normal waking consciousness' can *become* a kind of sleep when worry turns every day into a nightmare.

Many writers and philosophers have put forward the view that even when we are generally happy, our senses can still be closed to the full wonders of the world and we remain blind and deaf to the vast potentials that lie latent within us. But at certain times a huge energy stirs; we find ourselves 'surprised by joy' and understand (without the need of logical proof) that 'spring morning consciousness' is just a perception.

That 'just', of course, is the pivot on which the quality of our lives are balanced. For how do we reach that state, take it under our control and make it the basis for our day-to-day existence?

Religions across the world and throughout history have indicated the path; so too have any number of secular philosophies. They are not hard to find, but may be hard to follow if the weight of habitual worry on your shoulders means that you never lift your head to look into the distance.

'Waking up' to possibility is a necessary precursor to any period of growth, any transition to a healthier state. So we pinch ourselves metaphorically, not just to see how others feel in a negative way, but to startle ourselves into an appreciation that life can and will be better.

Today I find a way to pinch myself awake!

There is no-one who will give you the keys to paradise. It is you, having shut the door on your fears which have hitherto ruled your life, who can open a new door.

Stephanie Spindler

❧

'What is paradise anyway?' we might think to ask. We tend to regard it as a place rather than a state, in the same way that people once treated thunder as a person rather than a process. And yet many still conceive of paradise in conventional terms, as some*where* to be, having 'got there from here'. Moreover, the insidious element of 'deferred gratification' often creeps into the equation, so that paradise becomes some kind of retirement home, a reward of peace and rest after a hard life of struggle.

This puts me in mind of a schoolteacher friend, who, 10 years off retirement, was already dreaming of the little house he planned to buy in the country, where he would spend his days just pottering in the garden and, for once, enjoying the luxury of a leisurely breakfast…

I do not disdain the dream, but I am appalled at what is likely to be a waste of those 10 intervening years, which for him will pass like the scenery we rarely notice as we travel on a speeding train to a destination we have already reached in our imagination.

The plain truth is, I assert, that the keys to paradise are thoughts and the doorways we seek are behaviour. Furthermore, any new door through which we step will not deliver us to a new place, but to a new state of feeling. And when it happens we will, in all senses of the word, 'look differently'.

Here, now, in my hand, are the keys to paradise.

Keep one foot in the grave
Obey your grandfather,
Chain yourself to the railings of his tomb,
Let him tap out his messages on the heel of your boot…

Bob Deveraux

⑥

If you are appalled, you are halfway to freedom! Some children are bound and gagged by the views and opinions of parents, relatives, 'elders and betters' of all kinds who never allow a young mind to hatch out into mature and independent thought. For some of us, this lasts throughout adulthood. The ties that bind keep our hands fixed behind our back, while the keys to paradise lie on that table, easily within arm's reach.

Writer Mark Tobey asks:

> What is the foe to our finding a voice of our own? I should say fear. Fears, governed by public opinion, by ideas of friends, by accepted patterns of traditional modes of thought… From where can release from all this rigidity of pattern come? To me, it must come from the Creative Life – that life which, drawing upon the vital forces within us … [is] the will to experience and order the phenomena about us.

One way of freeing ourselves from those fears is to give them a shape – *one that we define* – within our own minds. Break those chains, stamp on that crabbed and wicked old hand, turn and walk away from the graveyard of intimidation and deceit.

Today I break the chains that bind me to the past.

*I mistrust all systematisers and avoid them. A will to a
system is a lack of integrity.*

Nietzsche

☉

I once worked in a school where a 'systems man' was appoint-
ed as Deputy Head. His badges of office were a clipboard, two
colours of hi-liter pen and a watch that kept precise time. He
believed – alas, quite sincerely – that if you had a system in
place then chaos would automatically diminish.

There is an important difference between a useful organi-
zation of time, information or effort and a system (especially
imposed from without) that seeks to dominate our thoughts,
attitudes and behaviour. The most effective institutions do not
work because of rigid systems, but through the organic, fluid
synergy generated by interactions between people. You might
say that the healthiest institutions *are* the people of which they
are composed.

Similarly, to impose too inflexible a system upon ourselves
is tantamount to narrow-mindedness. It signals, as Nietzsche
so astutely observes, a lack of integrity – a fear, perhaps, of
being true to ourselves. Lives can be organized without being
systematized: potential is more fully realized by sometimes
striking out in a new direction, going against the rules and
common sense and what is expected. To live the Creative Life,
we need to cultivate flexibility within a structure of daily life –
with the built-in proviso that the structure is liable to be
changed if it fails to meet the full and beneficial requirements of
the individual.

Today I examine what I must do to be true to myself.

You teach best what you most need to learn.

Richard Bach

⑥

Perhaps you have experienced that very pleasant situation when, as you explain a particular point of view or idea to others, you suddenly come to understand it more clearly yourself? This, to be sure, is the mirror image of Richard Bach's elegant aphorism, since it is certainly true that we learn best what we most need to teach. And mirror-image it is, each side reflecting an important truth.

One of the reasons I wanted to write a book about worry was, in part, because I needed to learn about it. All through my life I had suffered from worry in a strange way – not by having a hard life or being directly exposed to worrying situations, but exactly the opposite. My parents were always trying to shield me from worry, shouldering on my behalf the problems of having too little money, or job insecurity, or family illness. I was protected from worry. And yet the stress of my parents' worrying communicated itself to me, so my anxiety seemed causeless and vague, a chronic unease.

So, when I decided to learn ways out of the worry trap, I learned with a vengeance. And that learning has never stopped, nor ever will.

Now I am neither complacent about 'knowing how to beat worry', nor take any happiness for granted. I have found these small wisdoms to be essential. And you will too, as the quality of your existence improves and you seek in your turn to 'teach best what you most need to learn'.

Today I define what I most need to learn.

Being and knowing are often quite separate. Nothing could be more admirable than when they coincide, but only too often they remain estranged.

Soetsu Yanagi

⑥

Knowing how to deal with worry is not the same as dealing with worry, just as you can be a bookseller without ever having read a single volume. The best learning, like the best teaching, is a consequence of 'the best doing'. Experience itself is the most effective vehicle to improved happiness and well-being. Any mere complex of techniques, no matter how cleverly systematized into an action plan, remains a mere theory unless, and until, we act deliberately and creatively to *embody* that thinking in the warp and weft of everyday life.

Yanagi illustrates his assertion by explaining: 'I know many famous art critics who have no feeling for beauty, and I cannot therefore respect their knowledge.'

Because knowledge is potential, but potential that is yet unfulfilled by inaction is like a wine corked in a bottle, unpoured and untasted… How can we therefore ever savour its vintage?

Knowledge and feeling must, then, work together. Logical, considered thought must be accompanied by the 'inner voice' that sings in the blood, that stirs the guts with excitement at what is yet to be achieved. When these things coincide, then we can indeed delight in the satisfaction of true self-respect.

Today, being and knowing come together for me in deliberate, creative action.

If you think along the lines of nature, then you think properly.

C. G. Jung

Modern living frequently forces us to adopt lifestyles quite contrary to the 'lines of nature'. Most fundamentally, as already mentioned, the ancient and natural 'fight or flight' response is in the majority of cases completely inappropriate to the situations we encounter.

But other aspects of our existence are also distorted by the pace and nature of daily life. The way we eat, the way we sleep, the style of our thinking, all of these are affected by the timetables of work and leisure to which we adhere.

Realistically, we may not be in a position to move across to a way of living that totally reflects our body's natural rhythms. But there is much we can do to arrange a workable compromise.

The ground rule is, simply: eat when you're hungry, drink when you're thirsty, rest when you're weary. And the corollary is: laugh when you're happy, cry when you're sorrowful – in short, allow your emotions to 'have their say'.

Any effort you invest in following this advice will bring benefits.

Today I begin to think along the lines of nature.

A creature without memory cannot discover the past: one without expectation cannot conceive a future.

George Santayana

◎

It has often been said, wisely or not, that the human capacity to imagine is what distinguishes us from all other animals. It is a huge and powerful ability, and yet all too frequently one that we allow to master us, rather than us being the masters of our own imaginations.

Our conscious minds have the capacity to remember – but also to regret. In trying to recall the past, we might remember only our impression of it. We also anticipate the future – but that expectation may be of unpleasant times ahead. And so we don't conceive of the future at all, but only of *a* future, based usually upon narrow impressions of what we think has been.

Thus, whatever has happened to us, the picture of our lives has been given colour and form by a single way of looking. And that perception can only ever be one of many possible alternatives.

We are indeed the product of all the seconds of all our years. But what we make of those seconds makes us. The future is bleak or bright not in reality, but merely in our minds. So in a very potent sense, what we conceive is what is and what will be.

Today I will rediscover my past and conceive a brighter future.

Laughter, genuine and helpless – and therefore of a kind
way beyond conscious control – could well [be a way to]
release the healing power of the Superself: just as release of
consciousness improved Timothy Gallwey's inner game
of tennis, and Eugen Herrigel's Zen-inspired learning
of archery.

Ian Wilson

⑥

There is no doubt that, whatever it's called, some great reservoir of energy and potential exists inside each and every one of us. It often emerges in a crisis situation or may manifest spontaneously as a peak experience when we find ourselves surprised by joy and a certainty that the universe is unfolding as it should.

For most of us, the force of the Superself is largely locked away. But there are innumerable keys which can open the door to the vault. Laughter is one of these, and a useful one too, because it is a habit that can be cultivated and used very swiftly and effectively to wipe out the polluting effects of worry.

Everyone has the capacity for laughter: there is the gentle laughter at seeing the antics of a young child; the wilder 'trigger-happy' laughter we often see at parties and other social gatherings; the uncontrolled outbursts of laughter as we listen to a skilled comedian… Any and all of these varieties should be welcomed.

Get into the laughter habit. It might seem strained and artificial at first, especially if worry's gloom is hanging over your head. But be reassured that a minute's genuine laughter clears away the damage of many hours of worry.

Today I look for laughter as a way of unlocking my Superself.

The greatest king must at last be put to bed with a shovel.

Russian proverb

⑥

We have all encountered the bullying teacher, the brash sales-man, the braggart, the swaggerer; the self-important person whose ego, pumped up like a balloon, conceals a hollowness within. And although we may recognize the empty vessel that's making all this noise for what it is, we can still be daunt-ed in any dealings we may have with such individuals.

Somehow, to think 'Well, they're an ordinary person, just like I am' doesn't do the trick. It never used to for me … until I happened to be chatting with a friend whom I took to be supremely confident, completely self-assured. He revealed as we talked that, in fact, he had always been shy and rather ner-vous, especially if he needed to deal with the kinds of people mentioned above. Even speaking to perfectly friendly, sincere folks caused him to go through agonies of awkwardness and self-doubt.

His trick was to focus on ways of seeing these men and women as *being* just ordinary and normal. He might, he told me, imagine what they would look like when they were chil-dren or visualize them as elderly. Another tactic was to picture strawberry jam or chocolate sauce around their mouths. In cer-tain cases, when confronted with unpleasantness or the intimi-dating behaviour we all detest, my friend would imagine his 'opponent' sitting on the toilet after two days' constipation.

The trick never failed – the balloon of self-importance was always deflated.

Today I realize that even the mightiest among us is put to bed at last with a shovel.

Acceptance of what has happened is the first step to overcoming the consequences of misfortune.

William James

✆

People often talk about 'the dead past', things that have 'been and gone', incidents that should be 'left to lie'. We are told not to 'rake over old ashes' because 'the past is past and what's done is done…'

But in a real sense the past is very much alive inside us. We are, at this present moment, the outcome of all that has ever happened to us – the consequence of all we did, or failed to do. The incalculable amount of information, taken in through our senses or generated by the mind itself, which has gone into creating the picture of reality by which we survive, is actively working within us, whether it was received two minutes ago or as we were born into the world.

What has happened can never be made to *un*happen. There are, however, techniques such as hypno- and psychotherapy which can allow us to reinterpret and resolve inner dilemmas caused by the events of the past.

There's also much that we can do for ourselves, at a conscious level. The best course is always to prepare as sensibly as we can for the future outcomes of that event, and, secure in those preparations, to get on with the business of *living* in this second – and this second – and this second…

We can never go back. We must go forward. To accept that what's done is done is a healthy stance to take.

Today I reflect on more words of William James: 'Be willing to have it so…'

I have loved the stars too dearly to be fearful of the night.

Source unknown

(6)

Nothing is ever perfect. The innocence of Eden has long since passed. The world is full of hurt and anguish, loneliness and pain. We work to strengthen ourselves against these storms; we empower ourselves to withstand the global hurricane of wasted life and the more minor but no less ferocious squalls of our own misfortune. We live the best way we can, only at last, like the greatest king, to be put to bed with a shovel.

Whether we turn our backs on the bleakness inherent in 'the outside world' or devote our lives to minimizing its damage, in however modest a way, we must still, all of us, keep a star to steer by firmly in our sight.

What we love dearly might be a person or a pastime, a quiet time of day, music, a picture, a prayer… Whatever our star may be, its presence is vital both to focus our positive energies and to help restore balance in a life that may sometimes seem to have tilted too far towards darkness.

So invest yourself gladly in those you love and what you most love to do…

**Today I understand that, however dark the night,
I can look up and glimpse the stars.**

When life performs at its best, it is most radiant and
accomplished.

Henryk Skolimowski

⑥

It seems to me that there are three ways of looking at this statement.

We can disagree entirely and continue to view life as a rather mundane panorama, a kind of dull but necessary train journey where the scenery moves but is unchanging.

We can agree, but make the assumption that 'life's best performance' is something that happens beyond our control – when it comes along it's great, but if only it would happen more often…

Or we can agree and presume that life at its best has a lot to do with ourselves as *participants* in life being at its best. This, I believe, to be the true and most valuable interpretation of Henryk Skolimowski's affirmation.

As we practise the art of caring for ourselves, in every sense of the word – as we become more sensitive to the way we feel and to whatever exists around us; as we develop and strengthen our repertoire of mental skills in order to deal more effectively with problems, dilemmas and difficulties – *then* we will find that our internal state has a positive and powerful effect in allowing life to perform at its best.

Today I am radiant and accomplished in my life.

To walk in beauty is not an easy task... You must be forever watchful and aware... It is a ceaselessly dynamic and balancing activity.

Henryk Skolimowski

☉

The ugliness of worry creates the burdensome image of ugliness in the world. In such a state, nothing seems 'radiant and accomplished'; all seems grey, drab, pointless and petty. Furthermore, there is nothing dynamic and passive about worrying. It is a condition that, left to itself, will not change, except, perhaps, to get worse. And the imbalance of such a condition is as obvious as it is unhealthy.

Skolimowski, in his exquisite book *Eco Yoga*, looks to the beauty of the natural world for inspiration and uses the power of that inspiration to create the dynamic of elegant awareness which restores the balance of life. Perceiving and celebrating beauty does not mean denying the pain and ugliness that exists, for the very presence of light makes us more acutely aware of the shadows. But *only* to languish amidst the gloom helps no one, because how can you make your way in the dark?

Awareness, understanding, control. These are the three irrevocable steps to walking in beauty. Beauty is already there, in the fall of a leaf, in a smile, in the stars, in a handful of whispered words expressing sincere love. Look for them today. See their light.

Today I regain my sense of balance.

*There's always something fascinating about a passing
freight train – the big, black engine with the ugly, bony
arm on its side, the string of box cars with sometimes a
munificent supply of tramps sitting on the top, the heavy oil
tanks, and bringing up in the rear, the stove-piped caboose.
One and all, from youth to old age, will stand and watch it
in silence and with interest.*

Sarah McShane

⑥

This description comes from a notebook written by Sarah McShane in 1935, entitled *Four Days in Glacier Park*. It is a wonderful example of the balanced, dynamic activity of walking in beauty. Sarah's perception does not deny the mechanical ugliness of the train, or entertain the naïve and romantic notion that 'travelling people' are sitting on top of the box cars. They are tramps and the train is just a train – but beautiful for all that, because its presence coincided with a moment in Sarah's life, a moment that was precious for her, because life itself, fragile and finite, is also precious.

Attentiveness and awareness are not intellectual exercises; nor do they happen in a vacuum. They need to be *driven* by fascination, by the same boundless curiosity that moves a child to look for creepy-crawlies under stone or to sit, chin in hand, exploring the drift-by of thoughts from an endless imagination. An interest in all that we as individuals do and think is the engine that powers us to seek. And in seeking, we find more than we ever thought possible.

**Today, though perhaps only metaphorically,
I go trainspotting!**

The business of art lies just in this – to make that
understood and felt which, in the form of an argument,
might be incomprehensible and inaccessible.

Tolstoy

❻

Paradoxically, worry is confrontational. Although its continuance is underpinned by negatives – can't, won't, don't, no, never, not – and its 'solution' is one of avoidance, it repeatedly confronts the perceived problem, much as you might bang your head against a brick wall. In that sense, worry is the mind arguing with itself.

But what debate and discussion are to argument, so the art of living is to worry. Although Tolstoy was referring to specific arts – writing, painting, musical composition – the truth of his assertion is as evident and as profound when we apply it to the business of dealing with today, tomorrow, and all the rest of our lives.

No one wins arguments. Usually opposing viewpoints simply become polarized, resentment becomes heightened, disrespect intensifies and solutions slip further away. The situation is no better with regard to the self-argument of worry, where the battle is internalized – except when we lash out, usually at those we love, because the pressure becomes too great to bear.

The art of living is to make felt and understood, in many subtle and sophisticated ways, what the world means to us, and what we, in turn, mean to the world.

**Today I go about my principal business in life,
which is life itself.**

Tell me more. Tell me all you can. I want to understand more about everything you feel and know, and all the changes inside and out of you. Let more come out.

Brenda Ueland

✿

Brenda Ueland's little book *If You Want to Write* is an inspiration. It is subtitled *Releasing your Creative Spirit*, and in that sense, and in the quality and nature of the advice she gives, it is much more than a manual on how to construct a short story or novel. It has the flavour of a book by Shakti Gawain or Dale Carnegie or Napoleon Hill or W. Clement Stone – the pages are bursting with both optimism and common sense, are alive with encouragement, and vibrant with the certainty that you *can* and you *will* achieve your aims – because you *must*.

All these authors are ordinary folks living the best way they can. But they are artists in the business of life, stylists in strategies for getting what they want, for squeezing every iota of enjoyment from each vital moment of the day.

When you read books like this, you sense the *imperative* of living. Life is not something to let slip by: it is not a leisurely stroll or a chore or an endless round of grey drudgery. It is both an opportunity and an experience to be exploited and savoured. It is like a good book, elegantly crafted, full of crises and dramas, triumphs and tragedies … and anything less would not leave us satisfied readers.

Today I demand of life:
'Tell me more. Tell me all you can!'

The writer has a feeling and utters it from his true self.
It is an infection. *And it is* immediate.

Brenda Ueland

❦

I could not resist quoting Brenda Ueland again, because what she has to say about writing is so apposite to the art of everyday living.

She in turn quotes Tolstoy and how he addressed the idea of 'interestingness' which, Ueland says, 'is the secret of enchantment and fascination'.

Things are not interesting of themselves. It is we who make the meanings that are translated as 'interesting' or 'dull', we who invest the world with its sparkle and vitality – which is why, I contend, people who are frequently bored are frequently boring.

It is an astonishing thing to me that in a world of such diversity and colour, boredom has any chance of survival. And yet it does, because so many folks gaze tiredly through the dusty windows of their worry and fail to see it. They have not yet taken the step of contacting their true selves, their inner selves, and using that empowering connection to find the source of fascination which informs and sustains all that they subsequently experience.

We do not need to write in order to utter the feeling from our true selves. Once that immediacy, that infection of creative living begins, then it will be apparent in every word and gesture, in every thought and action, in every moment.

Today I am infected with the enchantment of being alive.

> *When I see young painters compose and draw from*
> memory *and then haphazardly smear on whatever they*
> *like*, also from memory – *then keep it at a distance and put*
> *on a very mysterious, gloomy face to find out what in*
> *Heaven's name it may look like, and at last finally make*
> *something from it, always from* memory – *it sometimes*
> *disgusts me, and makes me think it all very tedious and dull.*
>
> Van Gogh (his italics)

☉

Life is a story being written, a picture being painted, a piece of music being composed… Which particular analogy you choose hardly matters, providing it is useful to your view.

The framework of our 'self-portrait' is limited firstly by the constraints of our imagination and then – often much more severely – by the perspective created by our own past perceptions and by the opinions of others (which may be, it goes without saying, unearned and unsolicited).

A vital step, therefore, in framing the boundaries of what's possible for ourselves is to understand that what we *were* is not what we *are*. We change through time. Circumstances alter us. Our own evolving attitudes and abilities alter us.

So we should also avoid the mistake of gaining a 'snapshot impression' of what we are from any particular event. As R. S. Thomas has already so eloquently made clear, 'The great brush has not rested… Yet what eye … ever saw this work and it was not finished?'

We cannot, in all honesty, sum our selves up from *memory*. Only by practising the art of creative living do we shine, in light of how we engage with life now.

Today I view my self-portrait anew.

Where there's smoke there's fire – but a pile of fresh manure will do just as well.

Roda Roda

✆

One of the great tragedies of some people's lives is that they become diminished by unfavourable memories of what they've done, or what has been done to them, or by the negative views of others – including, alas, so-called 'authority figures' who frequently need to belittle others in order to inflate their own egos.

The habit and attitude of 'thinking yourself small', then becoming a self-fulfilling prophecy, stems from taking as true what other people say, agreeing that 'where there's smoke, there must be fire'.

The philosopher and writer Paul Watzlawick identifies a sentence like this as a 'self-sealing premise', one that achieves the same effect whichever way you look at it. Thus, if you believe you're a failure, or that there's no way out of the problem, then you'll behave accordingly. Yet if someone reassures you that you *aren't* a failure, you'll likely think they're 'just saying that' to make you feel better, to cover up the sad truth of the matter.

The worry habit is one big self-sealing premise. It's at its most insidious and damaging when it disallows even the chance of change for the better; when apathy or cynicism become so deeply ingrained, the worrier won't even begin to admit that escape from worry's nightmarish trap is possible.

Today I consider that where there's smoke, there might be a pile of fresh manure instead.

Instead of dividing 'sick' people from those who are somehow defined as being 'well', Aaron Antonovsky believes that all of us exist on a continuum between what he calls 'health-ease' and 'dis-ease'...

Clive Wood

⑥

Worry pushes us steadily towards 'dis-ease'. Worrying about how well we are pushes us in the same direction, but more quickly. A huge and growing body of research is making links between our day-to-day state of mind and the ongoing state of our health. The old wisdom of 'how we think is how we feel' now exists within the ambit of scientific respectability.

A person enjoying life towards the 'upbeat end' of the health continuum is probably inhaling as many germs with every breath as someone lower down that spectrum. The difference between them is that the one who practises 'health-ease' is less likely to succumb to viruses and bacteria than the person whose tendency is towards dis-ease.

Obviously, general external factors play their part. Living in squalor or working in a polluted and unhealthy environment puts pressure on an individual's resources, so they may collapse more readily under the strain. And any illness suffered by someone whose 'self-portrait' incorporates the self-sealing premise of worry, apathy, failure, etc., will linger longer, or even become a chronic state forming a bleak backdrop to life.

Sleep, nutrition, exercise – all play a crucial role in general health and well-being. But 'thinking healthy' maximizes their beneficial effects and guides us inexorably towards the positive end of the health continuum.

Today I affirm my good health.

In finding resemblances between remote objects or ideas, metaphorical-analogical thinking opens new pathways of thought and thus of creative problem solving. If the unlike things are really alike in some ways, then perhaps they are so in others. That is the meaning of analogy...

Morton Hunt

⑥

We have already touched on this idea in looking at life as a story, a picture, a journey. Such an analogy helps to frame and define meanings in useful new ways, as well as offering fresh insights into hitherto unaccessed elements of our existence.

But smaller scale analogies can be just as productive, as Kurt Hanks and Jay Parry show in their book *Wake Up your Creative Genius*. 'Sometimes,' they assert, 'the insights for solving problems lie right under our noses... The pencil is an example of how object analogy works to produce creative thinking.'

They illustrate the point with a simple drawing of a pencil: it has an eraser attached by a pinched ring of gold metal, the brand name 'Superior' and the price stamped into the paint. Analogical thinking sees the six 'sides' of the pencil as 'six things to do: budget, be more assertive, start now...' etc. The pencil lead suggests, 'If I continue, I'll be worn down. If I press myself too hard, I'll break.' The brand name highlights feelings of superiority/inferiority which may exist in relationships. The eraser might give rise to the thought of 'rubbing out past mistakes or present problems'.

Today I 'pursue the thought and find new meanings, new understandings and, often, new solutions to old problems'. (Morton Hunt)

Looking at the negative space of the problem is like
that wonderful example from Sherlock Holmes when he
said, 'Did you notice anything about the dog barking in
the night?'
And Watson said, 'I didn't hear the dog bark.'
'Precisely,' said Holmes. 'It's the fact that the dog didn't
bark which is significant.'

Jonathan Miller

֍

Betty Edwards in her book *Drawing on the Artist Within* explains
that the Japanese don't see things as 'empty' but 'full of nothing' and believe 'emptiness' is as valuable as whatever exists
within or without it. She quotes Witter Bryner's poem 'The
Way of Life according to Lao Tzu', in which the vacancies
between the spokes comprise a wheel, the use of a clay pitcher
comes from the space inside and doors, windows and the
rooms inside a house are useful because of their 'emptiness':

> Thus we are helped by what is not
> To use what is.

Richard Pascale, in his article *Zen and the Art of Management*,
explains that Japanese executives operate within the 'empty
spaces' of business problems, in contrast to the Western practice of focusing on 'objects' or 'objectives'. For, by limiting possible solutions to 'objectives', any information that falls outside
these boundaries is not used.

**Today I don't just focus on the difficulty, but, by
looking at the spaces that are full of nothing all
around it, on the *context* of that difficulty also.**

There are truths but no Truth. I can perfectly well assert two
completely contradictory things, and be right in both cases.
One ought not to weigh one's insights against one another –
each is a life for itself.

Robert Musil

&

Embracing this idea has many benefits, not least of which is the evolving 'knack' of becoming sensitive to spaces which are not empty, but 'full of nothing', and using them to explore the contexts within which problems and other perceptions exist.

Furthermore, in this world of systematizers, line managers, hierarchies and specialisms, is it not refreshing, indeed empowering, to contemplate that the received wisdom of authority is often no more than a view and that we are no less an authority when it comes to painting the picture of our own lives?

Insightful thinking comes about more readily by accepting that there are many subjective 'truths' rather than one objective 'Truth', cast in stone. And because, amidst the ambiguity of life, we never know for sure just *how* many truths are possible and available, we feel the deep imperative to keep exploring, picking up hints and pointers and useful strategies on the way.

Adopting this mind-set, living in this way, with style and elegance and a burning fascination for reality to 'Tell me more!', we learn to deal with what is paradoxical and unclear, looking beyond the boundaries of problems to the spaces 'full of nothing' in which they exist. Thus fresh answers come to us from unexpected quarters – innovative and unorthodox solutions, each of which 'is a life for itself'.

**Today I look for truths, my way, in the spaces
between problems.**

*Every creative act involves a new innocence of perception,
liberated from the cataract of accepted belief.*

Arthur Koestler

⑥

Perhaps the ultimate 'new innocence of perception' takes us into religious realms, where you may or may not choose to venture. On a more secular level, it means allowing the mind to open to the *idea* of possibility, even before the search is made to find the *variety* of possibility that exists. Worry, as we have seen, tends to close the mind, to narrow it down fruitlessly on to the problem as it is perceived, on the object of the worry itself. Creative action does not bemoan the existence of a problem, or hide from it, or pretend it isn't there. It takes the problem, wonders what else it can more usefully be called, pulls it apart and, like a potter creating something new from a lump of clay, reconstitutes a solution from the 'raw material' which initially seemed as stubborn as stone.

A. F. Osborn, an American expert in the art of invention, suggested the following as part of his 'checklist of original thinking':

Are there other uses? Other modifications I can make?
What parameters can I usefully change?
What could be magnified? Multiplied? Strengthened?
How can I arrange things differently?
What could be reversed, transposed, combined, streamlined?
What are the bottlenecks, intersections, surprises, goals,
   inefficiencies, vital needs?

**Today, by asking practical questions, I move towards
a new innocence of perception.**

You have only to work up imagination to the state of vision and a thing is done.

William Blake

❦

Some people are lucky enough to be driven by a vision so powerful that it automatically sweeps all difficulties aside. The imperative to realize the dream is so great that from somewhere the resources are found to overcome what otherwise might seem to be insurmountable problems. And problems there are aplenty, no doubt – but because the vision beckons, they *must* be solved. And solved they invariably are.

Such is the potential of creative action and of the human spirit in its quest to find fulfilment.

Most of us will never know, perhaps, the extreme satisfaction of that 'state of vision' and will always smile wryly at Blake's use of the word 'only'. We might find challenge enough in living with imagination and with sufficient focus to keep more modest, less visionary, goals in sight.

But to *know* that such visionary states are possible is itself an inspiration and a comfort, and to aspire to work with imagination so that the tendency of life is upward and outward is likely to be enough to get us where we want to be – which is right here, right now, with a different view of the world in front of our eyes.

Today I am empowered by my imagination, inspired by the human capacity to envision.

Hasten slowly, and you will soon arrive.

Jetsun Milarepa

🌀

Most of us, probably, when we were younger, went through a phase of trying to cram as much as possible into our lives as a way to avoid being dragged down by drudgery into tedium. We mistook quantity for quality and 'turned up' life like a volume control – not realizing that sheer noise ruins every symphony.

Some people now, alas, find they have reduced the 'quantity' of life, but not improved its quality. The music is a dull drone and the silences between the notes (those spaces 'full of nothing') go unappreciated.

Yet others – an increasing number, I fear, in this age of leanness, meanness and improved efficiency – repeat the mistakes of youth and strive ever harder in their work towards a happiness which seems to come no nearer. The tragedy of mental and emotional burnout is a profound one, given the good folk who go down in the name of the icon of productivity … which is just another name for quantity, in most cases.

Festina lente, hasten slowly, is an ancient and useful jewel of wisdom. It implies the self-generated motivation to 'get there', but incorporates an attitude of care and consideration – for ourselves, for others who matter and for the journey as much as the destination. It understands that the music plays anyway, but the secret is to listen, to savour, to be transported.

Today, by hastening slowly, I know I will soon arrive.

Don't wallow in self-pity.
> From Atisha's *Seven Points of Mind-Training*

❦

Well, why not? People are younger, people are smarter, people are more attractive, people are richer, people are luckier than me. That's the reality of the situation and there's very little I can do about it, since I have no direct control over these people or what they do. To make matters worse, I am older than I was, my teeth are not in such good condition, my hair is thinning, I feel the cold more readily, I can't run as fast as I once did, I'm closer to the end of my life than I've ever been before, I'm not a millionaire, I don't have a huge house, my car needs servicing, I have indigestion from a meal I ate last night, a book deal I was hoping to swing has fallen through, I'm into my last pair of socks because all of the others are in the wash (and the pair I'm wearing has holes in the toes), over the past 10 years I've lost three members of my family, the old cat who's been my faithful companion for 18 years hasn't been feeling too good lately, the garden needs digging, my pile of paperwork is building up and I don't really have time to attend to it, a cheque I was expecting in the post this morning hasn't arrived and the cup of coffee I made for myself an hour ago has gone cold because I've been concentrating as I write this…

Does any of this apply to you?
Does all of this apply to you?
How do you feel about it?

Today I don't wallow in self-pity.

Samsara *is the tendency to find fault with others.*

Narapa

❻

It's easy to find fault with others. And the more we practise this little trick, the easier it becomes. We evolve into experts at fault-finding, past masters at spotting the flaws in people's appearance or personality or lifestyle. Our criticisms steadily grow more venomous, more bitter, more heartfelt … more painful to make, because deep down we see the sham of what we do. We understand, perhaps without ever openly admitting it, that we belittle others to inflate ourselves, we pick out the imperfections in those around us to camouflage our own defects and shortcomings. We indulge in backstabbing through uncertainty or envy or mere malice, because we hurt inside – and anyway, people do just the same to me, don't they?

Don't they?

The ultimate outcome of such a dog-eat-dog perception of the world is that we chase our own tails. The more hurtful we are about others, the more hurtful they are to us, and the more hurtful we are *to ourselves*. Because we find fault to hide faults, we are constantly reminded of those that exist inside. And the irony, the tragedy, of the whole sad episode is that we lift not a single finger to do anything about it.

Today I sweep *Samsara* out of my life.
I celebrate the positive.

We tend to build a false image of ourselves in order to comfort ourselves. This form of self-deception is very difficult to penetrate – which is why we need 'the mirror'.

Dharma-Arya Akong Rinpoche

☉

'The mirror' technique, practised diligently and honestly, reveals the inner self. Sit quietly and allow to rise whatever aspects of the personality are going to emerge. Dharma-Arya Akong Rinpoche points out that we should look calmly and uncritically at both the positive and negative aspects that appear: 'To see only the bad side is as harmful and fruitless as to see only the good one.' There is no white knight without the dragon; the two are in endless conflict, each existing for the other.

To deny the pettiness and ignorance and fear which may form a part of our psyche is to leave the dragon free to continue its work unseen, throwing our whole selves out of balance. But by appraising what we truly are, by reaching a new understanding through a heightened awareness of self, we enhance our capacity for self-control and can allow the negative forces within us to dissipate harmlessly – neither injuring others, nor destroying ourselves.

Dharma-Arya links the image of the mirror to that of the mask. He recognizes what the old saying asserts: 'We have as many faces as we have enemies and friends.'

Inner reflection brings these masks out of the prop cupboard and allows us to try them on for size, under controlled conditions. And when we see how wooden and unconvincing we are, then we recognize our true face in the world.

Today I look in the mirror, honestly and calmly.

The Lord may forgive us our sins, but our nervous system never does.

William James

⑥

Dale Carnegie quotes an interview he once conducted with the actress Merle Oberon, in which she relates the struggle she had trying to break into movies. 'After all,' she told herself, 'you have no experience, you've never acted at all – what have you to offer but a rather pretty face?'

> I went to the mirror. And when I looked in that mirror, I saw what worry was doing to my looks. I saw the anxious expression. So I said to myself: 'You've got to stop this at once! You can't afford to worry. The only thing you have to offer at all is your looks, and worry will ruin them!'

Thoughts – attitudes – behaviour. The effects of worry not only create a range of hideous masks, but send the poison of *Samsara* inwards to eat away at whatever strengths and qualities we may possess, but perhaps are not fully celebrating and exploiting.

Merle Oberon found her 'inner face' by realizing what ruinous effects worry was having on her physically – and by building up her positive qualities was able to achieve international success in her chosen field.

Look in the mirror – inwardly and outwardly – to check the effects of worry. And next time someone asks, 'What's eating you?', you'll understand the true horror and danger of what they've noticed.

Today I affirm my true self, because the mirror doesn't lie and the nervous system doesn't forgive.

Critic: A person who boasts himself hard to please because nobody tries to please him.

Ambrose Bierce

❧

The tendency to chronic or habitual criticism is *Samsara* in another form. Self-criticism is the most damaging kind of all: utterly negative, completely unproductive, totally insular and self-defeating.

To gain a healthier perspective on the whole subject of criticism, open the idea out – lay it bare and see what others have to say…

Some critics are emotionally dessicated, about as
attractive as a year-old peach in a single girl's refrigerator.
Mel Brooks

My job is to make people laugh.
The critics' job is to stop me.
Paul Hogan

Critics are fuelled by their own failed ambitions.
Robert Redford

To silence the critic inside us, it is not necessary to ladle out gratuitous praise or become in any way sycophantic. As ever, to strike a balance is the healthiest approach – recognizing weaknesses where they exist, repairing them where possible, celebrating strengths and achievements at every opportunity.

Today I am not hard to please, because I please myself.

In order to help all living beings in their seemingly unavoidable suffering, we put on the tender armour of compassion, not only for humans, but for all living entities, seen and unseen.

His Holiness the XVIth Gyalwa Karmapa

✆

It seems to me that compassion is the opposite of criticism. For when we criticize we tend towards pettiness, look to the negative, distance ourselves from the object of criticism. But through compassion we draw close to its subject, indeed to the point where we take that 'living entity' into ourselves, into our hearts, and there offer the comfort and help of one life touching another.

Compassion is a mutually strengthening force, totally positive and good, finding and defining joy and purpose in those it embraces. It seeks no reward, but invariably gathers the treasures of its simple existence back to itself. By giving, we grow.

Today I put on the 'tender armour' of compassion and by helping others in their suffering, I help myself in mine.

*The fairy tale is therapeutic because the patient finds his
own solutions, through contemplating what the story seems
to imply about him and his inner conflicts at this moment in
his life.*

Bruno Bettelheim

⑥

To a very large extent, we live a fairy-tale existence…

I do not mean that our lives are filled with helpless maid-
ens, glittering castles, evil wizards and fierce dragons (whom
we invariably, eventually, dispatch) or that they are easy, innocent and filled only with good things. 'Fairy-tale' is often interpreted this way, but it is a way which fails to grasp the potential
power of metaphor.

We don't live in the 'real' world, in the sense that we inhabit a universe of interpretations, which either we have made or
which have been made for us. The fundamental reason for finding meanings, at all levels, is simply to survive – and beyond
that, to flourish. And while we require *reasons* to accept what
we see, hear, say, do, etc; those reasons can sometimes be based
on a false premise, on a *misinterpretation* of information at a conscious or subconscious level.

Thus we find (or fail to find!) ourselves living under a
misapprehension. The deepest, most powerful mechanism for
change-through-reinterpretation is to reflect upon a narrative
which can sustain a breadth and depth of thematic complexity,
that can then be 'customized' by the individual, who takes from
it what benefits them the most.

In other words, a fairy-tale.

Today I consider the power of fairy-tale in my life.

Metaphors, in the form of fairytales, parables and anecdotes, are consciously and unconsciously used by therapists in order to assist a client in making the changes he wants to make...

David Gordon

❧

It is all too easy to dismiss fairy-tales, parables and anecdotes as flights of fancy, whimsical stories to entertain children. Yet right across the world people still use stories to worship local gods or laugh themselves to health or for a thousand and one purposes.

As individuals we are driven by the need both to express ourselves, to communicate what we know, feel and believe, and to explain to ourselves what the world means. The truth is out there and the imperative is to make sense of it.

Heinrich Zimmer has said of stories:

They are the everlasting oracles of life. They have to be questioned and consulted anew, in every age, each age approaching them with its own variety of ignorance and understanding, its own set of problems, and its own inevitable questions.

In other words, we each take the essential themes of life and embroider them into our own personal design. Traditional storytellers recognize a hierarchy of story types called 'The Ladder to the Moon', ranging from jokes, personal anecdotes and 'shaggy dog stories' through folk tales and historically-based legends to epics, sacred stories and creation myths. That ladder still links us to the cosmos.

Today I listen to the everlasting oracles of life.

*When presented with random dots on wallpaper, one
organizes them into figure and ground… When confronted
with diverse behavioral data – a strange noise at night, an
unusual facial expression, a senseless international incident
– one makes 'sense' out of it by fitting it into a familiar
explanatory framework.*

I. D. Yalom

⑥

In *Existential Psychotherapy* Irving Yalom explores the fundamental human need to organize, to make patterns out of the
'random dots' of life in general and our personal circumstances
in particular. Meaning, says Yalom, reduces anxiety and uncertainty, attributing to life at all levels a comfortable predictabili-
ty, a context wherein we feel a sense of belonging and of
attachment. Such a context may not always feel *safe*, but it's better than nothing.

Our personal belief system, set of values, self-identity and
participation in social norms and mores form the bedrock
which anchors us to the world, allowing further questions to be
asked and further possibilities to be explored.

Yalom points out that some philosophers distinguish
between *cosmic* meaning – 'What is the meaning of life?' – and
terrestrial meaning – 'What is the meaning of *my* life?' Both of
these imply purposefulness, at a universal and/or at an individual level.

It is the impulse to ask and the drive to seek that sets the
agenda of our lives.

Today I delight in 'joining the dots' of my life!

The map is not the territory. The menu is not the meal.

R. D. Laing

﴾

Or, as Postman and Weingartner say in *Teaching as a Subversive Activity*, 'The word is not the thing.' Laing goes on to assert:

> We live within, or can easily come to live within, a skein of words such that we see, as it were, other people's descriptions of the world, instead of describing what *we* see.

To describe what *we* see requires the clear vision that comes from open-mindedness, together with a recognition that life's stories – the ladder to the moon – are such that we can and we must engage with them constantly, taking from them what's of use to us as individuals. We are at our most powerful as storytellers when we tell these stories *to ourselves*, for, as the old saying goes, 'I am responsible for what I say, but not for what you hear.'

When you take responsibility for what you say and what you do as a consequence of your storying, then you create a strong and healthy sense of life purpose which can translate into the following activities (as identified by Irving Yalom):

Altruism – serving others, the act of giving for its own sake
Creativity – in living life fully, finding pleasure in new
    connections
Self-actualization – the increasingly powerful reaffirmation of
    your true potential

Today I stop reading the menu and start eating the meal.

*In order to know ourselves it is not enough to make an
inventory of the elements that form our conscious being.
An exploration of the vast regions of our unconscious
must also be undertaken.*

Roberto Assagioli

🌀

Assagioli is in agreement with R. D. Laing and the Gestalt psychologist Fritz Perls that this exploration can be made by an individual but, as Helen Graham states in her book *A Picture of Health*, it is 'a tremendous undertaking, long and arduous'. Perls feels strongly that 'awareness *per se* – by and of itself – can be curative'. But that awareness must not be simply of the conscious *by* the conscious.

As Laing observes:

> For as early as I can remember I never took myself to be what other people called me… That is, whatever, whoever I may be is not to be confused with the names people give to me, or how they describe me. I am not my name.

We are the only ones who can undertake the journey because the life we live *is itself* the journey. Yet, to hurl ourselves into the seethe of life merely to be defined by our experiences is too simplistic, because to experience a moment does not necessarily put that moment into context or allow it to carry significance and meaning for us…

**Today I act as the meaning-making interface
between the inner universe and the outer cosmos
and put my life into context.**

Most people are capable of looking at themselves, and assessing their state of physical and psychological health or wholeness… [Whether or not we enjoy doing so] will tend to determine the individual's ability to find solutions to the puzzles, more than any inherent capacity or lack of it…

Helen Graham

⑥

To a worrier, it seems almost perverse to suggest that an illness, a debt, a crumbling relationship should be the source of enjoyment. But of course, these things are not the source. The enjoyment originates in the pure and unequivocal state of *being*, that boundless awareness of living, that thirst and hunger for the world to 'Tell me more!' Anything which interrupts the flow of that living, anything which diminishes its zest, is to be resolved as swiftly and effectively as possible. That is the challenge, driven by the appetite for more life, the urge to continue with the journey on which we have embarked.

And as Assagioli says:

Between the starting point in the lowlands of our ordinary consciousness and the shining peaks of Self-realization there are intermediate phases, plateaux at various altitudes on which a man may rest or even make his abode, if his lack of strength precludes or his will does not choose a further ascent.

And, it seems to me, we embark upon this ascent because life, like Mount Everest, is there…

Today I take a new look at myself.

If you understand the situation you are in, and let the
situation you are in control your actions, then you learn
how to cope with life.

Fritz Perls

❨❩

An immediate reflex response to this assertion might be, 'But my problems in life *comprise* the situation which is controlling my actions – that's why I'm worried!'

Look again at what Perls is saying. His guidance is based on understanding the situation by *letting* the situation control your actions, in the same way that a consummate swimmer will use the currents or an exquisite flyer use the thermals to take them where they want to be. The real control lies with the swimmer and the flyer: they utilize the power of the water or air for their own purposes. The tides will never stop. The wind blows anyway.

Aside from this, to a worrier it's not the situation which controls their actions, but the worry itself. This creates a tediously familiar *perception* of the situation, leading to a self-conditioned response of inaction. Worriers don't act; they worry – and sink to the bottom, dropping to the lowest level of thinking, feeling and behaving.

Perls notes that when a need is genuinely satisfied, the reality of a situation changes. By cultivating that energy, that zest, for life, the need becomes one of fulfilling potential. Thus, the reality of the situation changes so that it acts as a signpost to move us positively and progressively onwards.

Today, I listen to the situation.

Here none think of wealth or fame,
All talk of right and wrong is quelled:
In autumn I rake the leaf-banked stream,
In spring attend the nightingale.

Daigu

⑥

Coping is great, but being able to achieve more than that would be better. But even when we operate to the limit of our capabilities, there will be some situations that we can only ever partially cope with, some problems/challenges that we can solve just to some extent. That is not failure – though even if we thought it were, we would undeniably have 'failed honourably'.

The hunger for life which takes us out into life – and which brings life flooding through every fibre of our being – leads us to do more than just 'cope' with whatever comes our way. Though we listen to situations and let them drift us towards a satisfactory resolution, the choice is ours to ring the changes and refresh ourselves by enjoying, for a while, a 'situationless' existence. We can do this through meditation in the conventional sense, by concentrating on a light, a sound, a scent… Or by actively carrying that meditation around with us, letting all thoughts of 'coping' and 'doing' and 'achieving' and 'fulfilling' become subdued, so that all we have left is *being*.

Today I rake the leaf-banked stream or attend the nightingale.

The greatest separation feat [of the individual from the organization] of all is when one gradually manages to free oneself of the grip of unconscious culture.

Edward Hall

'Unconscious culture' is not the same as 'the culture of the unconscious' – quite the reverse, in fact. Hall is here talking of the systematizers and systems so loathed and disdained by Nietzsche, and the powerful expectations those systems create.

The state of mind we can all suffer from when we are in the grip of unconscious culture is called a 'consensus trance' by David Feinstein and Stanley Krippner in their book *Personal Mythology: The psychology of your evolving self*. They define it as the mechanical, habitual routines of normal waking consciousness, 'a retreat', as Charles T. Tart says, 'from ordinary sensory/instinctual reality to abstractions about reality'.

Ordinary/instinctual reality is what we experience when we have achieved a clearer, more independent perception of who we are, coupled with the facility of 'listening to the situation' in a sensitive way.

Hall's answer to the breaking of the consensus trance is to seek exposure to other cultures, where we will begin to find that our prejudgements and knee-jerk expectations are disconcerted often, and systematically, by a different mode of thought.

Feinstein and Krippner propose embarking upon the kind of inner journey we have already discussed – not travelling to new lands, but seeing with new eyes.

Today I choose the culture of the unconscious in preference to the consensus trance of unconscious culture.

If we merely do what we like, and don't do what we don't like, our difficulties only increase and will recur again and again.

Dharma-Arya Akong Rinpoche

ⓑ

Escaping from the grip of unconscious culture does not presuppose some kind of personal programme of anarchy, a devil-may-care approach where we 'turn off, tune in and drop out'. To become, however unselfconsciously, a bohemian eccentric, a neo-hippie or a mystical seeker of the deepest secrets of Creation does not pay the bills and probably won't help much in the relationships that matter.

Doing what we like does not allow us to engage with experience and be receptive to what that experience has to offer, while not doing what we don't like simply boils down to the same kind of avoidance tactics which lead to an increasing dread of ever confronting any kind of challenge head on, face to face.

Our aim, in conquering worry and fulfilling the potential we possess, is to utilize whatever comes our way, in whatever way we can, for our optimum benefit and profit. Anything less is to give in to weakness which means, as Dharma-Arya Akong Rinpoche maintains, 'We just get weaker and weaker and less likely to rid ourselves of suffering in the longer term.'

Today I see that avoiding or escaping situations takes my mind off my problems without doing anything to solve them.

The mind of Man is capable of anything because everything is in it, all the past as well as all the future.

Joseph Conrad

☾

It is the unconsciousness of unconscious culture that is dangerous – the unconsidered assimilation of impressions by a kind of mental osmosis into the mind. If we subscribe at all to Conrad's optimistic view, then the tragedy is greater when we see how little some individuals achieve – because the past and the future which exist 'holographically' in their heads are composed of other people's ideas and predetermined expectations untested by open-minded involvement with the world.

There is nothing wrong *per se* with junk food (nutritional arguments aside), or with TV soap operas or quiz shows, supermarket muzak or glitzy advertisements. Where the harm comes is in the unchallenged acceptance of these things, which we put together into a picture-frame reality that we then call our 'culture', our 'society'. Because that frame is a barrier of sorts, a limiting factor which extends to and includes our 'cultural' attitudes and beliefs about deeper issues, people from other countries and cultures, women, education, politics, wealth, progress, etc.

We are indeed – within our human limitations – capable of anything.

Today I look at my capabilities from a perspective that is entirely my own.

It is wrong to think that the task of physics is to find out how nature is. Physics concerns what we can say about nature.

Niels Bohr

⑥

Finding out how something *is* implies a search for objective truth. Victorian science attempted to do just that, making its pronouncements on the basis that there was a certain amount of 'knowledge' to be uncovered about the universe and that the exploration to winkle out the last particle of data was well advanced. This belief was held so strongly that one professor at an Oxford college expressed the view that it would be pointless admitting new postgraduate students before long, because everything that *was* to be known would soon be known.

The new thinking has changed this, moving towards the more subjective and human perspective of 'finding out what we can say'. The implication is that reality is as much a part of our inner selves as the outer realm, and that our very presence affects the nature of whatever is out there, beyond our skins.

The paradox of this is that recent scientific evidence has, as it were, gone some way to verifying the objective truth of the subjective nature of the us/universe interface.

But on an individual, day-by-day level, Bohr's comment is equally pertinent. We explore life not to find out how it is, but to discover what we can say about it. Our 'commentary' amounts to what we believe. And what we believe colours what we can subsequently see.

Today I look again at what I can say about life.

*If I have exhausted the justification, I have reached bedrock
and my spade is turned. Then I am inclined to say, 'This is
simply what I do.'*

Wittgenstein

⑥

We may walk with our eyes closed in a 'consensus trance', but
most of us are not motiveless beings. We do things for reasons,
and so, ultimately, it is not our actions of which we need to be
aware, but the reasons behind them.

Reasons weave themselves through 'what we can say
about life' at all levels. A phobia, for instance, is a subconscious
response, manifested at a conscious and physical level, created
for a reason based on 'information received'. That information,
misinterpreted probably in childhood, has become a perception, creating a justification for the consequent behaviour. By
looking at it anew, a fresh and more beneficial perspective can
be created.

Conscious reasons-for-doing are no more and no less easy
to access. If we are not fully awake to ourselves, then justifica-
tions run unchallenged in the mind, manipulating what we do.

Beyond all this is the question: 'Do we ever reach the
bedrock?' Do we really exhaust justification and become rea-
sonless? If indeed we ever accept that 'this is simply what I do',
then we use the spade to break down the walls of morality and
sane human behaviour.

**Is justification ever exhausted, or simply
unperceived?**

Too long a sacrifice
Can make a stone of the heart.

W. B. Yeats

✿

Sometimes a sacrifice prevents us from 'saying what we can' about our lives. Too long a sacrifice leeches the act of all justification, so that we continue to go along with our partner's wishes, or devote ourselves to the kids, or fetch and carry for an elderly parent because it is 'simply what we do'. By that stage, the nobility of our gift of time has become the drudgery of a ritual, empty of warmth, its love diluted. Indeed, we may actively and venomously wish for a break in that cycle of sacrifice, so that we can be free of its burden without taking upon our shoulders the equally weighty burden of guilt. 'Let it end!' becomes the one passionate plea in our otherwise stony response to life.

Assertiveness skills highlight that to say 'no' is not merely selfish, but a move towards self-nourishment and regeneration. Workable compromises are usually possible, given the strength to insist upon them and the open-mindedness to engineer them.

When sacrifices decay to a state of begrudging routine, the time has come to transform what began as an act of kindness to another into an act of kindness to ourselves.

Do I now need to sacrifice the sacrifice, for my own sake?

*Life is a mirror. If you frown at it, it frowns back. If you
smile, it returns the greeting.*

W. M. Thackeray

⑥

This elegant little adage reads like homespun wisdom, or the
kind of epithet you might find in a fortune cookie or a Christ-
mas cracker. But it sums up simply in a powerful metaphor the
deep-rooted notion that we – our conscious egos – act as a
mediator between the depths of our mind and outside reality.

True enough, it's hard to smile if deep down we're hurt or
angry or just plain envious. And most certainly damage can be
done when we're buffeted by the storms of life, thrown from
pillar to post by unfortunate (and are we tempted to think
'unfair'?) circumstances.

This is the way of things. We're only human and it's hard to
take everything that comes our way as a valuable lesson. It's
equally hard to fully forgive past hostilities and pettiness. We
are never pure, because we can never be perfect.

But that mirror is ours, and we do ourselves a grave disser-
vice when it's dulled by habitual thinking and the unwanted
rituals of negative attitudes. The least we can do is to keep the
mirror polished, so that when we do smile, we shine.

Today I see that life is a mirror – my mirror, my life.

*I read not only for pleasure, but as a journeyman, and where
I see a good effect, I study it, and try to reproduce it.*

Lawrence Durrell

⑥

Much of our standard education consists of mimicry. We are
shown how something is done and we copy it. If we copy it
adequately, we are given good marks; if we fail to reproduce
the effect to our teachers' expectations, we are told to 'Try, try,
try again.'

It is well known that emulation is inevitable on the road to
originality. By listening to what others say, we find our unique
voice. Similarly, we come to understand the extent of our own
potential by studying the works and actions of people who
have fulfilled theirs.

Only by slavishly reproducing the particular style or
nature of another's achievements do we fail to create anything
new that is our own. But attempting to recreate 'a good effect' –
by imbuing it with individual meaning – is the obverse of
moral plagiarism: it is the recognition and effective adoption of
ways that *work*.

**Today I learn from the experts, on my way to
becoming an expert.**

If it be now, 'tis not to come; if it be not to come, it will be
now; if it be not now, yet it will come: the readiness is all.

Shakespeare

❻

To learn from the experts, we must first decide what an 'expert' is. By that I mean we need to define expertise for ourselves and not rely upon a prepackaged idea based on someone else's viewpoint. If we swallow whole, like a pill, what others think, then we are firmly in the grip of unconscious culture and not likely to derive maximum personal benefit from any 'good effects' we may encounter.

The readiness we cultivate in gathering wisdom, as it were from the trawl-net of our imagination, is no more than an open-mindedness to be taught. We should not anticipate how the teaching will come or what shape it will take, any more than we should form prejudgements about the nature of the teacher. Lessons may be understood long after they have officially been imparted; and seemingly insignificant fragments of trivia might eventually assume a crucial importance, when put together with other items subsequently.

The preparedness to see primes our ability to understand. Anticipation without prejudice informs our need to know.

Today I am ready to learn, however the learning may arrive.

If the only tool you have is a hammer, you tend to think of every problem as a nail.

Attrib. Lieutenant Charles Heal

⑥

This is equally true if you *think* the only tool you have is a hammer and, through habit, strike out at all difficulties that come your way. But not only might you find that your hammer is ineffective – in the worst case, you may not even recognize that what you are using isn't a hammer at all, but something far more dangerous you just happen to be holding to your head.

Let's take anger as an example. We can begin to see its inappropriateness as a problem-solving tool by applying the analogy above. Anger allows us to strike out, sometimes to 'batter down' an opponent by dint of the extremity of our emotion or the sheer noise we might make. Anger can usually let us dominate the object of that anger, but we do not dominate either the situation or the problem itself by its use.

Moreover, it's all too easy to hammer the wrong person. If we shout at our partner because of a bad day at work, we do nothing but compound the stress we already feel, as well as placing unnecessary and damaging pressure upon our relationship. Any temporary relief we enjoy from 'getting it off our chest' costs us dear in the longer term. It also strengthens our tendency to use the same technique if this or similar situations should arise in the future.

Today I look at the variety of my problems and begin selecting an appropriate tool for each.

*What we are gathering from our efforts … is the
knowledge that the mind is infinitely more subtle than
we had previously thought, and that everyone who has
what is ironically called a 'normal' mind has a much
larger ability and potential than we previously believed.*

Tony Buzan

⑥

Tony Buzan is the modern 'guru' of thinking skills. His books
Use your Head, *Make the Most of your Mind* and *The Brain User's
Guide* offer sound advice on a whole range of mental tools.

Perhaps Buzan's best known technique is 'mind-mapping'.
A word, phrase or sentence conveys an image which immediately creates associations in the mind. Some of those associations will be unique to the individual, while others illustrate
the 'multi-ordinate' properties of the language itself, i.e., that
words act as foci which 'spray out' meanings which, in turn,
create links or hooks for us to use.

Try the idea yourself. Take a word like 'run', write it down
in the centre of a sheet of paper, then begin making associations. You will probably be surprised by the ideas that surface.

Problems consist of information which can be explored and
evaluated using tools like this. But the benefits are even greater,
for as Buzan explains:

…researches showed that when people were encouraged
to develop a mental area they had previously considered
weak, this development, rather than detracting from other areas, seemed to produce a synergistic effect in which
all areas of mental performance improved.

Today I grasp a more realistic idea of my abilities.

Work hard and don't settle for lousy ideas… In order to go on, to hope, to believe that there is some chance of actually creating what we ideally visualise, we are obliged to feel that it is necessary to start … over again, every day, as it were from scratch.

Rollo May (adapted)

⑥

As already mentioned, in order to have good ideas, you've got to have *lots* of ideas. And, as Rollo May says, don't settle for lousy ones.

You can make this your chosen working method through life. For, in dealing with life's problems, we never come to an end of things or become so adept at dealing with crises, dilemmas and difficulties that the process becomes easy. Not even the most worry-free person in the world (whoever that may be) would find it a simple matter to sail blithely on through life. Because if, through whatever means, we come to see problems as challenges, then the very nature of a challenge suggests that an effort needs to be made to master it. This continues for as long as we live, because such challenges form the texture and substance of life.

It's not over 'til it's over.

Learning to live creatively means learning to see the whole of life as a challenge, not just some particular aspect of it. Designing a useful mind-set to deal with, say, career-related challenges will set the tone of the greater task of creative living; but one does not presuppose the other.

A cornerstone of such creativity is not to assume mastery or ever take it for granted. Because there's always tomorrow.

Today I start over again, from scratch.

The only thing that makes me do something is the feeling that it will be worse tomorrow if I [leave it]. It'll be worse tomorrow…

Mel Calman

(6)

The positive pressure (i.e., energy) of successfully overcoming challenges is one side of the coin. The flipside is the fear that lack of effort – not necessarily failure to succeed – will make it 'worse tomorrow'.

Optimism and confidence, like worry, require effort to maintain. That maintenance consists of becoming aware of difficulties, learning coping techniques to deal with them, creatively refining and adapting those techniques in light of experience gained – and then starting from scratch next day.

Not to strive, *not* to keep up the creative pressure, allows the fear of things being worse tomorrow to grow. We worry by default if we don't actively seek to sweep worry aside in our quest to succeed, in the same way that turning down the light replaces the brilliance with gloom.

Today I distinguish between the positive pressure of living creatively and the negative forces of worry.

When something's going well, I get a sense of elation, a feeling of being released in some way, finding powers I didn't know I had. I suppose that's why it's so awful when things go badly.

Michael Frayn

❊

The bootstrap effect of moving things on, of coping with change through innovation, is illustrated no better than here in Michael Frayn's comment. Applying ourselves creatively to deal with problems doesn't just bring the satisfaction of seeing problems solved, but also the effort itself is a joy, coupled with the fierce delight of 'finding powers I didn't know I had'.

And although, like Frayn, we might feel awful when *things* go badly, we strengthen ourselves with the knowledge that *we* aren't going badly. We do what we can, however we can, to rise to the challenge. The rising is all.

And in this universe of uncertainty and unpredictable circumstance, if the challenge defeats us we will at least have failed honourably and learned much to prepare ourselves for the challenges of tomorrow.

Today, in the face of challenge, I find powers I didn't know I had.

*[Creative people] need single-mindedness, stamina both
mental and physical, not getting diverted by transient
moods or fads or critics, sticking to what you know.*

Jean Muir

❻

Single-mindedness necessitates a clear vision which is flexible
enough to accommodate a range of possibilities and prepare for
them. It is not stubbornness or ego-centred selfishness, but
rather that positive pressure to move things on, with an idea of
where those things will lead.

It should not ever be thought that to be creative implies
becoming coldly efficient and somehow unemotional. A vital
aspect of living creatively is a new and essential sensitivity to
the world and to ourselves. The world is a rich source of material and experience; the mind the fearsome engine of innovation.

Certainly, as we change we will still have moods and fads,
and criticism might still hurt… But we will not be *diverted* by
these things. We will regard them as the clouds passing across
an essentially sunny sky, transient features which simply add
fleeting texture to our days.

And by 'sticking to what we know', we do not set barriers
precluding ourselves from knowing anything else. We move
outwards from what we know into new realms of understanding – broadening our horizons to bring a growing landscape of
experience within reach.

**Today I realize that living creatively is 'a continuous
process of making – fashioning'. (Jean Muir)**

Was this life? Was this the vital adventure to which I had looked forward so eagerly? Was this all life would ever mean to me – working at a job I despised, living with cockroaches, eating vile food – and with no hope for the future?'

Dale Carnegie

❻

What would you do under those circumstances…?

What are you going to do under *your* circumstances?

Carnegie asserts he had nothing to lose and everything to gain by quitting the job he despised and writing the books he had longed to write since his college days. As he says, he came to his Rubicon – 'to that moment of decision which faces most young people when they start out in life'.

You can reach your Rubicon at any time in life and deciding to cross it on a sink-or-swim basis is never any easier. For Carnegie, the basis on which he made his decision was clear-cut, practical and achievable. He was not interested in making a lot of money, but in making a lot of living. He was prepared to trade one off against the other, although, as his subsequent career demonstrates, wealth and fulfilment are not mutually exclusive.

That career of writing, teaching and lecturing spanned several decades and is itself a confirmation that Dale Carnegie acted not just out of desperation, but out of wisdom also. He assessed the situation, decided upon a course of action – and carried it forward.

Today, though I may not have reached my Rubicon, I consider how and why I must overcome the obstacles that stand in my way.

The maintenance of problems does not involve conscious malingering with its associated blame and guilt, but a myriad of habits and patterns which have become ingrained with time.

Dr Brian Roet

@

One sad fact of worry is that it may never lead us to realize we have 'reached our Rubicon'. We may wonder if this is all life has to offer us – but rather than being driven to act by our dissatisfaction, we suffer instead a low-level chronic malaise which we tolerate as a drab backdrop to existence, rather like a nagging toothache… Even when it increases to the point of agony, we convince ourselves that we don't need to go to the dentist, fearing a drastic remedy.

As far as the rest of our lives are concerned, we are our own dentist with the capacity to give ourselves the best advice and treatment of the highest quality.

Dr Roet in his book *All in the Mind? Think yourself better* believes that we all play a role in maintaining our troubles through 'habits and patterns'. Roet describes a 'course of treatment' that allows us to wake up to ourselves. We need to:

know what to do
know how to do it
have support and guidance during the process of change
make a commitment to provide the necessary effort
allow time for adjustment

Today I make a commitment to extract unhelpful patterns and habits.

That knowledge by which we attain liberation – that is real knowledge.

Ramdasa

ⓖ

Ramdasa, the famed guru of King Shivaji, makes the distinction between 'real knowledge' and knowledge of science, language, art, dancing, etc. These forms of knowledge, he says, 'are only a product of the mind'. The real knowledge of liberation is deeper, subtler, yet more profound. It addresses the spirit and its relationship to God (whatever it conceives God to be).

The guidance is also useful on a more prosaic level, because it behoves us to distinguish between types and quality of knowledge if we are to know, as Dr Roet advises, 'what to do and how to do it'.

'Knowing what to do' comes as a result of the internal process of converting information into knowledge. Information is raw material: it is 'knowledge-in-potential', waiting to be taken, assimilated and utilized as a basis for action. It is 'real' only in that it means something interesting, useful or significant for us as individuals. This idea has far-reaching implications for education generally, as well as for us in constructing the bridges and boats we may need to cross the Rubicon. The information we will use is as much about ourselves as about the 'patterns and habits' through which we maintain our problems.

So real knowledge and liberation from the waking sleep of an unfulfilling existence can operate on a secular level and succeed on that level – though if you have the spirit to be free, your task is that much easier.

Today I seek the real knowledge of my liberation.

The best way to dismantle a personality is to isolate it.

Diana, Princess of Wales

⑥

Any kind of isolation, if protracted, weakens the cohesion of a personality.

Problems often act as an isolating force, as it were 'locking us inside' with their source, causing us see the world through the distorting lens of worry, which blocks out the knowledge of other avenues of escape. Like a prisoner in a cell, we bemoan our fate and may even rattle the bars – but never realize that we can forge our own set of keys and be free.

Going out into the world, maintaining that hunger for the world to 'tell me more' is a powerful way of combating destructive isolation. To 'feel the fear and *do it anyway*', seeking knowledge rather than picking up what bits of it drift by, allows us to build a broader picture of what's out there and strengthens us for those times when, by whatever circumstance, we are forced back into ourselves in order to make important decisions.

Today I bind myself more strongly to life by actively seeking life.

The Ideal Man loves to put forth effort, enters boldly on any enterprise, and does not shun work. He can live in the midst of difficulties, bear the brunt of action, and yet keep himself out of contact with it.

Ramdasa

☾

This goes for the Ideal Woman too, of course, and sums up much of what has already been said. In living creatively, which in large part means living deliberately and actively, we live not because we have to, but because we *love* to – this being the defining characteristic between art and technique.

In living with a passion, we exist amidst difficulties but the difficulties don't exist within us. We know what to do and how to do it, guided by our inner voice of wisdom as much as our ability to think carefully and independently towards a solution. We bear the brunt of action by taking what information is useful and significant to us and then incorporating it into a positive picture of the world – one which empowers us and frees us from the less helpful interpretations of others. Thus we 'allow the situation to control our actions' only insofar as it confirms the direction we wish to take. We are not, in this state, at the mercy of circumstance, but its master. Thus we are the Ideal Man or Woman, because life becomes happy and rewarding. And may be so beyond our most utopian aspirations.

Today I put forth effort in the enterprise of life.

Patient, ever patient, is the captain of my ship.
The wind blows, and restless are the sails;
Even the rudder begs direction;
Yet quietly the captain awaits my silence.
And these my mariners, who have heard the choir of
  the greater sea, they too have heard me patiently.
Now they shall wait no longer.
I am ready.

Kahlil Gibran

⑥

When will I ever be ready? When am I sure I 'know what to do and how to do it'? Who am I, for whom the captain of my ship waits so patiently? What is the nature of the restlessness that prompts me to go with the currents of my life? What is the direction of my journey? What is the nature of my destination?

Are these questions 'only in the mind'? Is this the real knowledge by which I act?

Has the time for questioning come to an end?

Today, am I ready?

Some people do not have forty years of experience; they have one year of experience forty times.

Zen aphorism

We need to ask ourselves whether what we count as 'experience' is simply maintaining the illusion of choice on a grander scale. In the same way that information isn't necessarily knowledge, so knowledge is not inevitably woven as experience into the tapestry of the world which our mind is continually creating-and-recreating-anew.

Another danger is that pre-existing perceptions of the world might interpret 'new' experience in the light of unquestioned beliefs, thereby reconfirming what we think we already know. This process, ongoing at all levels, leads inevitably to prejudice, bigotry, narrow-mindedness and all the knee-jerk reactions we see in other people but rarely recognize and challenge in ourselves.

Remember the analogy of the conscious/subconscious mind as a rider on a horse. The rider thinks they're in control, but the horse is actually far more powerful and can be stubborn if the rider 'tugs too persistently on the rein' (which is why, incidentally, will-power works so rarely in breaking habits like smoking).

But if the rider is also caught in the consensus trance of unawareness? Then the illusion of choice is complete, though not, of course, unassailable. Which is why we must consciously, deliberately, creatively seek to interpret experience so that it adds to our view of life, rather than just puts another coat of paint on the tapestry frame.

Today, just another ordinary day, I experience anew.

But words are things, and a small drop of ink,
Falling like dew upon a thought, produces
That which make thousands, perhaps millions, think.

Byron

⑥

Words are things, *but the word is not the thing.*

And yet, by becoming aware of what we say and how we react to what others say, we can use words themselves as new experience to increase our range of outlooks and alternatives.

Dr Brian Roet focuses on what he calls 'negative self talk' and cites several body-oriented examples from his patient files. The words are 'telling', but their message goes unrecognized by the patients themselves. So the grossly overweight patient responds to the doctor's enquiry about her health by saying she's fine, by and large, though a bit fed up. Then there was the alcoholic who, in seeking help, revealed that he constantly bottled up his feelings...

It is surely true in some cases that the language used by the patients simply reflected conditions from which they already suffered, caused by external circumstances or 'hard-wired' genetic defects. But evidence suggests that the reverse might be equally true – that what we say defines what we perceive and what we perceive is the way we come to be.

As Roet says, 'The most important words you will ever hear are those you tell yourself.'

As long as you're listening.

Today I become more aware of the messages in my words.

You are the only person who thinks in your mind.
You are the power and authority in your world.
You get to have whatever you choose to think.

Louise L. Hay

❻

You are the power and authority in your world as soon as you become aware of that fact and use it as 'new' experience. If you automatically think, 'Oh, I've read plenty of these self-improvement books and they all say that. I can't see it myself,' then you are not experiencing the idea anew, but using it (in consensus trance) to reconfirm old habits and patterns which fail to open up the choices available to you.

No one is suggesting that you should simply accept what Louise Hay is asserting. No matter how powerful and persuasive and upbeat a suggestion might be, just to agree smacks of gullibility and the same automatic nature of response referred to above.

But as Louise says, 'The point of power is the present moment.' It is within this moment that experience is in its 'pure' state. What's happening now constitutes the information-that-becomes-knowledge-that-becomes-fresh-experience. Such experience, gained in the clarity of awareness and maximized in the power of open-mindedness, keeps you at the cutting edge of life.

I am never stuck. This is where the changes take place, right here and now in my own mind.

Negaholism is a syndrome in which people subconsciously limit their own innate abilities, convince themselves that they can't have what they want, and sabotage their wishes, desires and dreams.

Cherie Carter-Scott

⑥

Cherie Carter-Scott's fresh and clever angle, in her book *Negaholics*, is to make the idea of negative thinking more 'solid' and believable by making it sound like an illness. 'Negaholism' reminds us of 'alcoholism' or something equally serious. And indeed, the maintenance of old habits and patterns of our thoughts, one symptom of which is to create the false option of an illusion of choice, *is* extremely serious. At the very least we prevent ourselves from moving on to new things, but at worst we actually 'drench' our bodies, minds and spirits with 'can't's, 'won't's, 'don't's and 'haven't's, allowing ourselves to spiral down into hopelessness and despair.

If you are a 'negaholic', you see yourself as *alone*, not as *all-one*. And that inner loneliness has nothing to do with physical solitude.

But to realize, just once, that you are never stuck – *and to act on it* – reverses this destructive trend and allows the greatest of transformations to occur. It's never too late, because the present moment is the point of power. And the present moment is now.

Today I am all-one, not alone.

You deal with a problem either by altering yourself or altering the problem.

Source unknown

ⓑ

Of course, by altering yourself you automatically alter if not the problem itself, then the nature of that problem.

But some problems are entirely beyond our control. In these cases the most we can do is to prepare as best we can, ride the storm and learn as much from the experience as possible. Cherie Carter-Scott offers some sound advice in learning to do this:

Listen to yourself.

Believe in yourself and open your mind to be prepared to believe the impossible.

Make a commitment to yourself to move on.

Treasure who and what you are.

Pursue your 'higher self'.

Reach out when you need help. You are never alone. Some One is always there.

Choose your actions and accept responsibility for them.

Regard life as a mirror and a lesson.

Above all, strive to have fun.

Today, in these ways, I alter myself.

You can choose any colour you like as long as it's black.

Henry Ford

⑥

'I could give up smoking if I wanted to.'

'I'll ask my boss for a rise when the time is right.'

'The diet starts tomorrow.'

'I know I've got problems and as soon as I get the time I'll sit
down and deal with them.'

Such statements embody a problem we often don't realize
we've got: they create an *illusion of choice*. This is more sinister
than the 'ostrich syndrome'. When we use avoidance tactics
and bury our heads in the sand, we do so deliberately and
knowingly. But an illusion of choice can be created slowly and
subtly, so that we might end up actually believing that 'when
the time is right' we really will ask for that rise. Or, if we do recognize the illusion for what it is, we then carry a burden of guilt
or frustration because we aren't doing something about it.

Either way, the result is inaction and a negative outlook
that supports an unhelpful status quo. Brian Roet's advice
when you suspect you are creating an illusion of choice is:

Spend some time each day by yourself, for yourself.

Understand that time and effort are the two basic
requirements for change.

Distinguish between a 'concrete fact' and a 'fixed attitude'.

Summon your courage and look at your 'menu of choices'
frankly and honestly.

Dispense with any alternatives that are not really alternatives.

Today I uncover my illusions of choice.

Change and innovation is a fundamental part of the creative process… You're not prepared to accept the status quo. You want to move things on.

Stephen Bayley

⑥

In a sense, worry is a negative and inappropriate example of the status quo, a single blunt instrument with which we try to batter problems – or if not problems, then ourselves. Which is why chronic worriers say that life's such a headache!

The nature of worry is that it *cannot* change of itself. It does not, by any magical and spontaneous means, transform into something more useful. To metamorphose worry to a state of self-assured endeavour takes energy and the ability to innovate – to change in the face of change. Worry stands stubbornly like a stone in a stream, while all around the water flows. That fluidity is the way of water, and it neither is nor can be anything else.

Problems will come along anyway. We can't alter that. All that can be altered is ourselves, using the deliberate action of adopting certain mental skills to 'bootstrap' ourselves into a new and positive state of competence. It doesn't matter whether those skills initially address the conscious or subconscious aspects of our thinking, because eventually, as Tony Buzan assures us, all areas of our mentality will be improved.

The question remains: 'How do I know I've improved?'

Answer: 'When I'm not prepared to accept the status quo.'

Today I want to move things on.

Everything in this life is worth living for.
Nothing in this life is worth dying for.

> F/O Paddy Finucane,
> DFC, DFM. 1923–42,
> WWII fighter ace,
> RAF Hornchurch, England

ⓖ

All that has been said in these pages implies and celebrates Paddy Finucane's powerful and, given his fate, moving assertion. It is a statement that most 'rational' people would agree with. And yet those same folks allow themselves to be dragged down into the depths of ill-health and unhappiness. 'Stress-related illness' is now both big news and big business, for the pharmaceutical industry as well as the complementary therapies that are flourishing on both sides of the Atlantic.

The source of that stress in most individuals lies not so much in their circumstances or the constitution but in the fact that change is not recognized as a solution, or if it is, then it is not acted upon.

The two parts of the opening quote are synergistic. Everything is worth living for *only* if nothing is worth dying for. And nothing is worth dying for *because* everything is worth living for. Acceptance of this – true, genuine acceptance – demands deliberate and creative action, the precursor to which is deliberate and creative assessment of the situation.

How drastic that action eventually is depends upon how far away you are from life.

Today I ask, what is worth living for?

To those seeking change a great deal of courage is required, comparable to that of a soldier going into battle. They may even be regarded as more courageous than the soldier, by confronting risks more personal and therefore more fearsome and frightening. The soldier cannot run because the gun is pointed at his back as well as his front. The individual trying to grow can always retreat into the easy and familiar patterns of a limited past.

M. Scott Peck

ⓖ

Those 'easy and familiar patterns of [the] past' might prove just too comfortable to stir someone to change. Some boredom, a little frustration, the occasional anger, a low-level background of apathy – even working together these negative forces may not prompt an individual to take the courageous leap into the unknown future.

We get nothing for nothing and deep down realize that real change, fundamental change, necessitates the sacrifice of all or most of what we currently cling on to – in much the same way that the shipwreck victim finds it hard to let go of the sodden driftwood in order to grab the lifeline just out of reach.

But we can learn to know ourselves more fully without having to sacrifice very much. We can, at least, look honestly at ourselves and our circumstances – at the whole picture of our lives – and decide whether or not we're prepared to put up with what we've got, what we've always had, in preference to the implied promises of change.

At this point I ask myself honestly whether I want to change and what I'm prepared to do to achieve it.

Everything you read in the newspapers is absolutely true except for that rare story of which you happen to have firsthand knowledge.

Erwin Knoll

⑥

Erwin Knoll's wonderful little pretzel of a statement sums up many of the points already raised in this book. It highlights the difference between knowledge and experience; the way in which we absorb information that we then use to create an impression of 'the outer world' (which feeds back to help define the inner); the shortcomings of both gullibility and cynicism; and the presence and nature of the 'consensus trance' which maintains the easy and familiar patterns of a limited past – limited, because we have not really experienced it for ourselves firsthand, but vicariously through the filters of the status quo and our own preconceptions.

The ultimate aim of any plan to change – as well as the outcome of self-actualization – is to make the whole flow of our life a 'rare story', so that we may then know the satisfaction and joy of absolute truth.

Today, as well as reading the newspaper, I read myself.

Nothing in life is so exhilarating as to be shot at without result.

Sir Winston Churchill

❁

Many of us spend a great deal of time, effort and money being 'safely frightened', seeking thrills in the knowledge that everything's OK really. We get much pleasure from white-knuckle rides, reading horror novels and watching scary movies, playing ever more realistic arcade and computer simulation games, taking up sports, and so on. Sometimes these activities are so wonderfully exciting that we seem to touch a new, higher level of experience, prompting us to say, 'When I was doing such-and-such, I really felt *alive.*'

In those moments of pure experience, however we may 'engineer' them, we understand something of what it feels like to be shot at without result. Then we return to the easy and familiar patterns of the limited past, refreshed and invigorated for a while.

Facing drastic and profound change in life is like facing the gun, looking as it were into a future that might take us any-whichway. But it can be frightening only because it's unknown, not because, like the pistol, it's about to do us some serious harm.

Real change, designed with care and consideration and enacted with courage, brings the exhilaration that Winston Churchill speaks of, but without the inherent dangers – because we are leaving behind those things with the capacity to kill us.

Today I begin my white-knuckle ride into the future!

When you sit, sit,
When you walk, walk.
If you have to wobble, wobble well.

                    Joshu (adapted by Duncan McColl)

McColl and other teachers call 'consensus trance', or being in the grip of unconscious culture, 'dividedness', the state wherein we do not give ourselves fully to the experience of the moment. That's why white-knuckle rides, etc., are so refreshing and exciting – because they demand our complete attention and awareness, and wake us up to ourselves by hurling life at us, full in the face.

But the idea of 'full attention' exists across a spectrum, it seems to me. We don't need extreme sports or supercomputer-quality graphics to touch this level of true experience. It can be ours in quiet moments or through gentle pursuits. Once we have mastered the knack of giving ourselves over entirely to the situation (i.e., letting the situation control our actions), then our involvement with the moment is complete: it brings to us all that it can and we make of it all that we are able to.

Such a state of affairs – and state of mind – is exhilarating in 1,000 different ways, because exhilaration in this pure sense means not only excitement, but joy, kindness, compassion, serenity, love and so much more.

Today when I walk, I *walk*.

*Happiness is an imaginary condition formerly attributed
by the living to the dead, now usually attributed by adults
to children, and by children to adults…*

Thomas Szasz

(6)

Paul Dickson, in his book *The Official Rules*, quotes Robert O'Brien's 'How to Make Yourself Miserable', which I have here adapted:

Assume that the object of life is to be happy.

Forget the good things in life and dwell on the bad.

Do everything in the name of money.

Think little is worth living for.

Believe you are indispensable to your work, family
  and friends.

Bemoan the fact that you are overburdened and people
  take advantage of you.

Assume that you are exceptional.

Think you can control your nervous system by sheer
  will-power.

Forget the feelings and rights of other people.

Never forget a grudge.

Get mad *and* even.

Fear the future, regret the past, miss the present moment.

Today I rewrite my rule book.

Never speak loudly to one another unless the house is on fire.
                                                    H. W. Thompson

❦

It's easy to shout. Much too easy. Which is why shouting often becomes an automatic reaction, not just to express anger or frustration, but more generally as a way of dominating or manipulating other people or otherwise of projecting the ego. 'Speaking loudly' frequently creates a poor signal-to-noise ratio when it comes to solving problems or making our intended meanings clear. And to compound the situation, we frequently respond to shouting by shouting back. The vicious circle goes round and round, simply getting louder.

Having said this, expressing anger is important. Sometimes we need to show that we are angry and we need other people to feel the effects of our anger, not simply to know that we are angry.

But we probably all remember the poor schoolteacher whose only means of classroom control was to yell. And the more they yelled, the more they *had* to yell to achieve the same effect. But even that effect diminished in the end, as the kids thought of 100 ways of getting that teacher to lose their temper – so that more yelling could go on; so less work had to be done; so the kids could see when the teacher reached snapping point.

Conversely, how effective was the teacher whose technique was to speak quietly and with enthusiasm. The automatic response to someone talking quietly is to listen harder. And when the person *does* speak loudly, you know for sure that they've got something even more important to say.

Today I remember what peace, and purpose, there may be in silence.

Two's company, three's a crowd.
And right now there's you, me and your ego.

Camac II

⑥

The ego is the outward face, the face that resorts to shouting. It represents our sense of self and yet that self exists on the surface of things: it is a skim of oil on deep waters. When egos talk to egos, it is to project themselves and not really to listen to the others. Our egos want people to know what *we* think, how *we* feel, what *our* ideas are... And yet *their* egos want exactly the same thing, perpetuating the talking-but-not-listening cycle of most social intercourse.

Realistically we should not expect anyone else to break that cycle, or even want to break it. We have all sat at parties or other social occasions, finding ourselves perhaps drawn into games of oneupmanship, tossed about like a cork on a stormy sea by the emotional tides of many egos talking, swept from satisfaction at being superior in some way to our neighbour to envy when that neighbour betters us in turn. We are at the mercy of such games, even as we find ourselves deploring them and thinking how petty-minded the whole thing has become.

The answer is to step back from it – not to speak more loudly, but to elevate ourselves to a position of silence, active listening, sincere response. Our achievements speak for themselves, but if we are asked, then we can without false modesty explain what we've done. And if that evokes envy in our listeners, then it's their problem, not ours.

In the realm of my own mind, even two's a crowd
when there's me and my ego.

What's done we partly may compute,
But know not what's resisted.

Robert Burns

ⓑ

Resistance happens at all levels within us. It is a force that meets with counter-force, the conflict setting up tensions inside that emerge and take their toll at the weakest points of our being. What emerges may be thoughts and feelings or more overtly physical responses such as any of that multitude of 'stress-related illnesses'.

Robert Burns is right in part to say, 'We ... know not what's resisted.' But what is not known is rarely unknowable. By becoming sensitive to ourselves, by giving ourselves the time and space for quiet reflection, we become aware of tensions operating within us. We come to realize that *something* is not right.

Whatever that something might be, it is accessible and open to investigation. We may be able to do a great deal for ourselves by utilizing the techniques described in this book as well as others, or we might need to enlist the help of an outside agency.

However we undertake our self-exploration, we are likely to find that by 'computing what's done' we can learn to understand the resistance within and control it by increasing our options for future action.

Today, with my ego subdued, I look calmly for resistance inside me.

*Either the spirit is immortal and we shall not die spiritually,
or it perishes and we will never know we are dead. So live,
then, as though you were eternal.*

André Maurois

⑥

Or, as Marcel Proust said, 'I don't know whether God exists,
but I live as though He does.' The notion of 'living as though' is
an important one which we can use to our benefit. But it raises
dilemmas.

The first is the apparent contradiction between living as
though you were eternal and living for the moment. If we have
an eternity of moments, then the experience of any of them may
be diminished and we might waste time. The answer is not to
entertain or debate this question rationally, but to understand
more profoundly that the essence of eternity is *contained* in each
moment. How we live – now – helps determine the nature of
the infinite future.

Another difficulty comes in going through the motions of
living as though we were eternal. If our progress in life is based
on an empty pretence, then it's no progress at all. But any such
pretence arises from the conscious-centred ego, so we have to
'live as though' on a deeper, subconscious level. The subconscious mind does not deceive or pretend: it responds, based
upon acceptance.

Finally (for the benefit of those conscious minds reading
this!), the spirit may indeed exist and may indeed be eternal.
All we need to do is look quietly for its presence. Failing that,
we can take the principle of 'living as though' and use it as an
affirmation in itself for our empowerment and health.

Today, I live as though...

Only small minds are impressed by the size of things.
                                          Arthur C. Clarke

                          ⑥

I have come to feel that the 'small mind' Arthur Clarke refers to
is the ego-consciousness, familiar as it is to its own everyday
scales of time and space. To this mind – the monkey mind, the
rational mind – the yardstick of space is the size of the human
body, and the yardstick of time is the human lifespan. *Six feet* x
three score years and ten tends to be the formula by which we
measure everything else there is.

Because our rationality is driven by the forces of the ego,
what is smaller than we are tends to be disdained, what is larger tends to be feared, and what is different tends to be met with
confusion, terror and/or the urge to destroy.

Also, 'size' implies purely physical dimensions in space
(and time if the *duration* is added), and is therefore amenable to
the physical senses and processed by the part of the mind that
is impressed (awed, daunted, frightened, etc.) by them.

But looking is not seeing, hearing is not listening, thinking
is not understanding – at least not automatically so. Our truest
and most beneficial perceptions come from every part of us,
from all levels of our being. When this happens, we can at last
begin to appreciate Blake's wonderful vision of 'the world in a
grain of sand, and eternity in an hour'.

**Today I respond to more than surface features,
with more than my surface mind.**

Disequilibrium has a home here.
Nature is balanced only in rhetoric.

James Gleick

⑥

Flip open an atlas and see how neatly your country has been mapped. The picture is familiar and comforting, so familiar that we would have no difficulty recognizing the outlines of the land from space. If we were then to zoom in towards the coastline, we would begin to see finer and finer details: cliffs, beaches, dunes… Soon we could discern the outlines of individual rocks and pebbles. Further still and sand grains themselves would become visible. Then we might wonder where the coast-*line* actually began and realize that reality is never so neat and tidy as our representations make it…

Further in, beyond the microscopic crystalline structure of a single sand grain, we would perceive a chaotic whirl of atomic particles, a seethe of energetic movement wherein boundaries become blurred. We have reached, as it were, the chaotic bedrock of reality.

But chaos on an atomic level does not inevitably mean randomness and meaninglessness in the larger scale of the cosmos. Meaning is not entirely dependent upon physical laws. The sense of rightness, the joy of being here, the enfolded potentials of this correspondence between ourselves and the universe, go beyond looking either at surface features or ultimate physical details. Because while with our instruments we see, ever more clearly, the microcosm and the macrocosm, we need different senses with which to view the meaning.

Today I dispense with the rhetoric and see the reality.

If you work on your mind with your mind, how can you avoid an immense confusion?

Seng Ts'an

❦

It has long been a tantalizing conundrum in the worlds of philosophy, psychology and brain research as to whether 'the mind' (whatever that may be) can know itself. As yet there is no definitive scientific answer to the question, although proponents of the 'computer model' of how the brain works regard the solution as just a matter of time.

But even a complete scientific understanding of the mind by the mind, were that possible, would likely take no account of the spirit, the soul, Cosmic Consciousness, the Overmind, the Superself – and all of the other manifestations of the 'something beyond' the confines of our purely human thinking. In any case, would any amount of such knowledge be of use to us as individuals in our *experience* of life?

As we have seen, there is much that we can do to understand ourselves.

To go further, perhaps we need to allow something other than the mind to lead us towards a fuller understanding. In the same way that we let go with the conscious mind to exploit the powers of the subconscious, so for the next step we need to put the entire mind itself aside to perceive what was there all the time, but that thinking about it blinded us to the fact.

Today, without effort or thought, I let the waters of understanding lap about me.

*Neither a man nor a nation can live without a higher idea,
and there is only one such idea on earth, that of an immortal
human soul; all the other higher ideas by which men live
follow from that.*

Dostoyevsky

❻

The entire meaning of science begins at the instant the universe was created. Scientists tell us that before the moment of the 'Big Bang', there was no space or time, no physical laws. There was nothing at all – not even a somewhere 'full of emptiness'. Science would say, then, that there is no point or purpose in looking beyond the framework of the manifest universe. For it is only what we can perceive and understand with our human minds which exists. The highest idea in all of science begins and ends in a blaze of light and a white-hot seethe of chaotic atoms.

But if, initially in our minds, we allow the possibility of something more, something greater, then ultimately we require something more and greater than our minds to understand it. That 'something' may for convenience be called our soul. And while it informs our path through life (and maybe all the lives which comprise our destiny), it is not amenable to investigation by any amount of clever questions or intellectual debate.

Realization of this does not come through the mind. But like C. S. Lewis, who was 'surprised by joy', the mind is forevermore affected by it and cannot help then but to explain what has happened.

Today I allow the possibility of a higher idea.

God smiles with flowers.

❧

The most powerful telescope cannot peer far enough and the greatest microscope cannot detect enough detail to see God. By the same token, no human mind is clever enough to think the thoughts or ask the questions that will bring the ultimate answers.

Understanding God is not a 'thinking thing', in the same way that finding God is not a 'looking thing'. But paradoxically (to our way of thinking), God is everywhere manifest in the universe of created things. Yet it may be that we are blind for looking, deaf for trying to hear, confused for puzzling, bereft of understanding for our efforts to understand.

What is the sound of one hand clapping?

What is the Buddha? – A pound of flax!

Where do I point to point to God?

The more we think about these statements, the less they mean. Because they are not thinking things either.

How do you get from A to Z without going through the alphabet?

Today I'm closer to knowing than I've ever been before.

There is my truth. Now tell me yours.

Nietzsche

⑥

Becoming what we *most can be* – which is truly ourselves – requires an act of immense honesty. It also means waking up to ourselves, somehow enlivening our senses and perceptions so that we understand our strengths and weaknesses, our boundaries, the far territories of our talent.

Undertaking this process is both a humbling and an empowering experience. It is also vitally necessary if we are to stop pretending, stop living on the empty nourishment of hollow dreams. Yet once we know what is true and what is false for us, the substanceless worries of our 'preawakening' are shown for what they are – meaningless mist quickly dispersing in the new light of realization.

Any progress from here to there – from the 'A to Z of our alphabet' – demands looking for truth and seeing it, listening for truth and hearing it. Then, and only then, once we have shown the world the truth of what we are, will the world reciprocate. Then we will have found out what we've always wanted to know.

Today I tell my truth.

The dissolution of our timebound form in eternity brings
no loss of meaning. Rather, does the little finger know itself
a member of the hand.

C. G. Jung

⑥

Part of the human quest has always been to know everything
that can be known. Until the Renaissance this quest was 'holo-
graphic' in the sense that all means of searching could be
embodied in one person, a person who saw no distinction
between the mystical and the scientific ways of looking.

Since then, specialization and the proliferation of knowledge have caused more than a divergence between these two
great branches of the tree of learning. Now a purely rationalist,
reductionist scientist will have no truck with the woolly thinking of mysticism, while a die-hard transcendentalist would
regard science's endeavours as ultimately empty and profitless,
simple dabbling in the mud of physical creation.

To disdain either river of thought is surely to simplify the
truth that is there to be told? Thus, Jung's assertion is not prov-
able in scientific terms, but can be accepted, believed and lived
upon in the factless knowledge of its certainty.

So while the little finger may or may not know itself to be a
member of the hand (or understand that it cannot point to the
God that exists within), that hand stretches out to the universe
in the purely, fundamentally human gesture of reaching. And
in that act, the universe will never exceed its grasp.

**Today I reach beyond the limitations of my
timebound form.**

Matter is an admirably calculated machinery for regulating, limiting and restraining consciousness, which it encases. Matter is not that which produces consciousness, but that which limits it.

Ferdinand Schiller

⑥

If the universe in some way 'knew we were coming', then it is unfolding as it should in the most profound and wonderful sense. The random churning of subatomic particles didn't *just* happen and will not *simply* end, and our timebound forms are not *merely* here by accident, to be consigned to a pointless oblivion once our genetic information as been successfully (or unsuccessfully) transmitted.

Further, if the cosmos is not *WYSIWYG* (What You See Is What You Get), then our timebound forms are not just one aspect of what we fully, truly, are – but are timebound for the same reason that led to their creation in the first place.

It is no good saying, 'Well, God moves in mysterious ways' or 'What will be will be…' Blind acceptance is not the essence of the truth that the universe has to tell. If we are here for a purpose beyond the purely material, then we need to be 'proactive' to uncover it. The great mythological theme of 'the quest' *requires an act of questing*, a search that will ultimately take us beyond the limits of the flesh and of the ego-consciousness which has both the capacity to wonder and to doubt the source of that wonder.

Today I become sensitive to the greater purposes of my flesh.

Because we are acutely conscious of the signs and symbols of other people, we think we are conscious of everything.

Lynn Margulis

(b)

Such consciousness of everything is a kind of 'ego chauvinism', an arrogance whereby we are led to believe that we are already aware, already in a state of understanding and, therefore, of control.

Even the most cursory examination will dispel the vividness of this illusion…

Our knowledge of the timebound universe is growing exponentially. The whole history of our species' learning curve leads us to realize that we are always in a position of acting out of relative ignorance. Furthermore, the puzzles we solve often throw out a whole new spray of questions, some of which open up vast new avenues of research and understanding.

Even our awareness of the signs and symbols of other people, although in part acutely conscious, is, largely, acutely subconscious, so that we are continually responding to personal, cultural and archetypal cues below the threshold of conscious awareness.

Lynn Margulis also feels that we are 'only dimly conscious', since our senses are limited in comparison with other animals, so that the 'quality of the data' that reaches us is itself restricted to a narrow band of visual and aural frequencies.

We live, then, to some extent, in a state of unknowing.

Today I come to know the limitations of my knowing.

You are given the gifts of the gods:
You create your reality according to your beliefs…
There are no limitations to the self
Except those you believe in.

Jane Roberts

ⓖ

How do we reconcile the state of unknowing from which we seem to suffer with Jane Roberts's assertion that we are 'given the gifts of the gods'? Does sheer belief, without knowing, not lead to self-delusion, wasted effort and missed opportunity? Can acceptance in ignorance ever be anything more than a pathetic lie, created to sustain an existence that is ultimately futile?

Such nihilistic thinking is a kind of worry, one that nibbles away at the roots of a faith that needs to be nurtured and allowed to grow. It may indeed – and has done in so many cases – lead to a 'dark night of the soul', an acute and severe loss of faith that drains the light of existence and turns everything, even 'spaces full of emptiness' into a vacuum of futility.

But the worn adage, 'the darkest hour is just before dawn' is apropos here. Only by suffering the darkness can we truly appreciate the quality of the light. Doubt is as much a part of who we are as is faith. The knight never slays the dragon outright, but struggles with it forever. Balance arises out of conflict.

A gift is only a gift when we do not take it for granted. Though we are creatures of limitation, timebound beings of fragile flesh, we possess, did we but know it, the boon of *becoming greater*.

My reality moves through doubt to understanding.

Whatever you can do or dream you can,
Begin it.
Boldness has genius, magic and power in it.
Begin it now.

Goethe

⑥

We might be unfortunate enough to think of a dream only as something insubstantial and unattainable. Yet dreams, even in the strict 'scientific' sense, are powerful, vital things that affect our lives profoundly.

To use the word 'dream' to mean 'ambition' can make it seem a more solid possibility. We might select from our mental toolkit certain instruments that allow us to break the ambition down into 'bite-size pieces', analyse each one, set our short-term goals as part of an overall strategy and then logically follow our action plan to its conclusion. In theory anyway.

Certainly we should endeavour to become more acutely conscious of what we do. But increased awareness only leads to increased control in our lives if we possess an understanding that goes beyond the purely logical and rational processes of the consciousness.

We can and we must embody our ambitions in behaviour – acting as if there were no question of success. An essential principle of any affirmation is to enact the substance of that affirmation. For dreams define the wish and the potential for change. But only in *beginning it* can we move from the 'A' of dreams to the 'Z' of achievement.

A dream driven by boldness is a reality.

An individual's personality is a passport to his or her success. What do we usually remember about people? More than their physical beauty, the clothes they wear or their voice, we tend to retain an impression of their personality...

Christian H. Godefroy

Thinking about 'personality' is a bit like contemplating 'the soul': as soon as we begin to consider it, we realize we have entered the realm of imponderables and immeasurables. And while psychology can categorize various kinds of personality and go some way to identifying certain factors that make up the personality, the thing itself remains elusive, subtle, astonishingly complex.

All that we can state about the personality *is not the personality itself.* As Godefroy says in his upbeat book *Mind Power*, the personality is an inner quality, which external factors – clothes, voice, physical beauty – reflect but do not define and do not, ultimately, determine.

We can if we wish engage in the labyrinthine nature/nurture argument on the origins and structure of the personality. But while this might be endlessly fascinating, it does seem rather like trying to handle water. Furthermore, does any amount of intellectualization help us to develop, evolve and strengthen our personalities so that life becomes more fulfilling for us?

**Today I don't talk about my personality –
I *live* my personality!**

Life is either a daring adventure or nothing.

Helen Keller

⑥

Christian H. Godefroy, in *Mind Power*, reports, 'A recent study conducted in the USA shows that 85% of people's success depends on their personality.' Leaving aside the ambiguous definition of 'success' and the apparent precision of the percentage result of the survey, the impression is clear that 'personality' counts (and not, I suspect, the slick designer personality advocated by the latest man-management manual).

The inner quality that *is* the personality shines out when it has the opportunity to do so. But the opportunity is not always there. Through petty concerns, egotistical preoccupations (the 'ego' in this sense having little to do with the deeper 'I') and the mechanical thinking that characterizes the worry habit, the light of the essential self is dimmed, as though seen through a grimy window.

Our natural state is one of well-being, health, vitality and positive anticipation. We *need* to be like this, to be strong for the unforeseen circumstances that life brings our way. The fact that we can be 'ground down' to a state of apathy or unhappiness is not something we allow to happen – we simply drift into it and in the end accept it as being the reality of the situation.

But reality is what we make it. Through mental skills, determination and deliberate action, we can dare to be ourselves. That is nothing more than allowing the personality to shine in everything we think, feel and do. Then we will have an '85%' chance of whatever success we envision.

Today I dare life's adventure.

*True education establishes associations of ideas and actions,
such that much of what we wish to do becomes automatic
and, consequently, during its performance we can attend to
other things.*

J. Louis Orton

🌀

We probably all remember our first driving lesson (or, if you don't drive, swimming lesson, typing lesson, cycle lesson, etc.). There was so much to remember, to learn, to concentrate upon… I clearly recall paying so much attention to steering that I forgot about changing gear and when I needed to concentrate on the foot pedals – which meant looking down at them, of course – my steering went haywire!

By the time I passed my driving test (on the second attempt), I had assimilated enough information to feel that the skill was something of which I was capable, if not adept. My instructor congratulated me on my success and said, 'Well, now that you've passed your test, you can start learning to drive.'

Having gone through the process of being taught, I could then begin my true education – that of making driving automatic.

There is absolutely no difference, it seems to me, between learning to drive and learning to be confident and banish worry. We are 'taught', we pay attention to the separate elements of the process, we practise the skills… And at some point our true education begins, so that worry *automatically* ceases to trouble us, and life *automatically* becomes a daring adventure to relish.

Today I begin my true education in life.

The secret of control of oneself is easy assumption, and that the harder one tries to bring about a phenomenon whilst under the conviction of inability, the more pronounced is the failure.

J. Louis Orton

⑥

The conviction of inability can go deep. It starts for many in early childhood, when comments made by parents and teachers begin to define the child's self-image. Further experiences are then interpreted in the light of what the individual believes to be true, so that a weight of attitude solidifies, as adulthood approaches, into what seems to be an unshakable certitude.

The 'easy assumption' to which Orton refers is a mechanism, a technique for accessing the true education which is everyone's right. Yet, although professional counsellors, therapists and other assorted authority figures are all available as guides, the only sure way of realizing, affirming and reaffirming the positive aspects of ourselves is to practise them in the context of daily living.

This means 'letting go' of negative thoughts and feelings to give today's experiences – and tomorrow's – a fair chance of being interpreted in a different, positive way. It does not mean struggle or effort; it is not analysis or endless conscious deliberation, but an ease of faith into a state where we will honestly and simply say, 'I can do this!'

Today I do not *deliberate on the secret of control of myself...*

When I wish to compose I sit down at the piano, shut my eyes, and play what I hear.

Ernst Hoffmann

❻

Our creativity can express itself in particular ways – music, writing, art, sport – or more generally in and through life itself. The hardest and yet least satisfactory form of creative expression involves conscious struggle, as if to force an outcome, to 'bully something into being'.

Our conscious minds, while they shine in certain ways, do not have the capacity or power (the processing power, if you like) to assimilate the lessons and meanings of life fully enough for us to adopt the easy assumption that we have a purpose – a purpose that involves the daring adventure of the journey as much as it does any imagined destination.

The art of living is nothing we can learn from an instruction book. Instructions are simply other people's opinions and definitions of how something should be done. They may be useful to us, but we must always expect to adapt from them what we can, discard what seems inappropriate and disdain whatever leads us down the negative road. We do this by 'easing up' on ourselves and letting go of preconceptions and damaging beliefs (which often go unchallenged, despite the successes and triumphs we achieve), thereby giving life, and ourselves, a chance to work in our favour.

Today, sitting quietly, I 'play what I hear'.

There is no such thing as an imaginary complaint, though there are complaints of the imagination.

Source unknown

⑥

Even hypochondria, though it exists in the mind – indeed, *because* it exists in the mind – is as real as a broken leg. Our bodies reflect what our thoughts tell us every moment of our lives. And while these thoughts are conscious during the waking hours, our subconsciously held beliefs are always active, interpreting all that happens to us according to their nature.

To dwell on complaints of the imagination compounds the problem, and intensifies any negative state we may have assumed. Attention is synonymous with 'a-tension', so that if we keep reflecting on worry, that worry will reach our every cell and fibre – and the body mirrors that worry with a frightening array of illnesses which are anything but imaginary.

The natural tendency of the body is towards health and strength. When its own healing and self-strengthening processes work in harmony with a mind that looks to the positive, the effects are startling – truly transformational. But to learn to look to the positive, we must resist the automatic impulse to view things negatively. Even unpleasant experiences can empower us if we allow them to form part of our true education.

The 'ease of faith' we have in ourselves, like driving a car, is something we first make an effort to do consciously. But this is a temporary phase, becoming, as we learn in light of what we do, a process which is simple, natural, completely automatic.

Today I set about eradicating complaints of the imagination.

I congratulate you!

Goethe

✆

The story goes that Goethe, one of the greatest poets of his time, would exploit a state of mind that exists on the way to sleep. This state, between waking and sleep, is the realm of self-hypnosis. Here, the conscious and subconscious parts of the mind can 'talk' to each other more effectively. The daytime volume of consciousness has become subdued; thoughts, images, feelings ebb and flow like waters lapping a gentle shore. We are relaxed, not paying particular attention (a-tension) to anything. We have eased off, let go the day's preoccupations. Now we are able to connect with our deep beliefs in a purer, more influential way...

Goethe used this quiet time by conjuring up a picture of a friend walking towards him. The friend would always have a beaming smile on his face and would always proclaim, 'I congratulate you!' The image would send a wash of positive feelings through Goethe's body, providing an affirmation of the achievements and successes of the day. Moreover, the effect of this practice was *cumulative*, producing a kind of mental ratchet effect, so that the thousandth repetition of the image would be many times more powerful than the first.

Such 'mental cinema' is an ancient, tried and trusted path towards true education. It is not self-delusion: Goethe was not kidding himself that he'd done well. He worked hard to fulfil the purpose to which he'd dedicated himself – and simply told himself so in a particularly effective manner.

Tonight, in my quiet time, I congratulate myself for a day's work well done.

One may not reach the dawn,
Save by the path of the night.

Kahlil Gibran

&

Insist, to yourself and others, that you *will have* your quiet at the end of the day. Build it in to your regular routine and approach that time with a sense of pleasant anticipation of what will ensue:

Feel free to ring the changes on the affirmation you make –
you don't need to have the *same* friend congratulating you
each time! You can vary the form of the affirmation, though
its essential nature will remain unchanged – as positive as
possible.
Your daily affirmations are in themselves progressive, but
you can enhance this by adding, for example,
'I congratulate you! Day by day you are becoming more
confident/relaxed/happy' etc…
Make the affirmation simple and straightforward, whether
you choose to convey it in words, pictures or whatever.
Part of that simplicity is to focus on one
suggestion/affirmation at a time. Thus, if you wish to target
self-confidence, repeat the affirmation daily until you think,
feel and behave with greater confidence *automatically*. Then
you can switch to a different suggestion of your choice.

Today I use the night to reach the dawn.

Summer grasses,
all that remains
of soldiers' dreams.

Bashō

⑥

A haiku poem, traditionally three lines and 17 syllables, is gone almost before it begins, like an insect drifting past the window or a stranger's face in a crowd, fleetingly glimpsed. Its ephemeral nature reflects the profound but obvious fact of our own temporary state.

Leaving aside the consideration that the evanescence of our lives may be intentional, we can 'flip the coin' of our attitude and decide – deliberately at first, but at last naturally and automatically – to make the most of whatever time we may have. And it's more than the worried mind thinks – millions of 'nows' all there to be fully exploited and enjoyed.

Thinking this way is no mere game of bluff. Because life is brief, problems are brief – and they too exist only in a context that is largely of our own making. When they appear, question them, make them justify themselves and the hurt they are doing to you now. Ask:

Why is this so?
How is this so?
Where/when is this so?
Who said this is so?

Summer grasses outlive both problems and dreams.
Today I turn in my time to dreams.

In the first part of your journey you may [try] out many methods. Don't consider these changes ... a weakness. Each person has to be very honest and honour his or her stage of evolution. Nobody can live another's life. You've got to live your own.

Ram Dass

ⓖ

Curiosity, honesty, independence – these are the great corner-stones of Ram Dass's advice. And the foundation on which they are built is not to *think* your life through, but to *live* it through. Only in the living is the meaning to be found.

Worrying delays and distorts the honest, independent living of life – as does envy, hatred and regret. Through these filters we see things as we wish they had been, or hope they will be, or hope they will not be ... but rarely as they are. Our honesty to ourselves is to take these things as they are and make of them the best we can. Our integrity demands it and our humanity depends on it.

The 'many methods' Ram Dass refers to are the multitude of pathways that lead towards the inevitable destination of death. *Any* forward path is better than walking backwards, or in circles, or stopping to bury your head in the sand. We still reach the end just as quickly, but not so enjoyably.

Thus, whichever path we finally choose, having gained the experience of many, we do so on the guiding principle that 'This is my journey and I want the view to be spectacular!'

Today I listen to my heart and be truthful with myself.

In circles, in cities, in groves, in streams, in waking and
sleeping dreams, in words, in motion, in a flow of music, in
poetry, in an opening art, in a day and a night, in struggle,
in hunger, in joy, in quickening, in milk, in wine, in the
blink of an eye, in a breath, in love – a seed is planted.

Starhawk

⑥

Starhawk continues: 'But I am forced to consider the question, "Will it have time to take root and grow?" '

The entire thrust and purpose of planted seeds is towards growth. But in the same way that the demands of modern life place a burden on the Earth, on its soil and air and water, so they do on the flow of our inner existence, on the soil of our imagination. Our happiness, dreams, our fondest hopes can be and are stifled by contaminants and pollution.

A seed has an opportunity for growth. In the outer, natural world it will take that opportunity if it can – seeds are exquisitely designed down to the last detail to survive and grow and flourish. Not so, perhaps, the seeds of opportunity that are planted moment by moment in our lives. Many of them lie unrecognized and uncherished, wasted until we see them for what they are – and until we see *ourselves* for what we are: cultivators of our own individual path.

Seeds will fail to grow inside us until we make that transition and see anew. Then, in the light of spring morning consciousness, the shoots of fresh life will appear.

Today, in the blink of an eye, in a breath, in love,
a seed is planted.

…words don't fall exactly; they hang in there
In the heaven of language, immune to gravity
If not to time, entering your mind
From no direction, travelling no distance at all,
And with rainy persistence tease from the spread earth
So many wonderful scents…

Robert Mezey

⑥

Words are not immune to time in the conscious mind. An insult, the beauty of a poetic line, the force and influence of a well-structured argument – all fade and are lost to conscious recall unless an effort is made to record them, revisit them, appreciate them anew when the need or the wish arises. Keeping a record of words that have moved you is a useful way of exploiting the powertool of language.

Worry chants the same old mantra mindlessly. Whatever words are used to symbolize the bleak grey landscape of the worried mind are often left unchallenged and in this state remain unvarying. We talk to ourselves in negatives as though these were the only things available, not considering the chronic drain they place on our energies, not realizing that language, carefully chosen and applied, lifts us from its first touch to a new level of understanding and control.

Words, simple words, carry the wisdom of ages and the freedom of choice, if we but take the time and trouble to seek them out…

Today I understand that when I was born the words which will save humanity had already been written and the only thing lacking was action.

'From a drop of water,' said the writer, *'a logician could infer the possibility of an Atlantic or a Niagara without having seen or heard one or the other. So all life is a great chain, the nature of which is known whenever we are shown a single link of it.'*

Sir Arthur Conan Doyle

ⓖ

Life is not so much a chain as a web – a network of chains – and is itself part of the greater interconnectedness of all created things. And logic, it seems to me, is not the only tool with which to infer, if not the details of its completeness, then its vastness and diversity.

We explore possibilities with our hearts as much as with our minds. Inference comes no more from sifting data than from using intuition and leaps of the imagination to ascertain the 'factless knowledge' available to us but not amenable to the analytical skills of the conscious mind. We may logically deduce the presence of Niagara from a water drop, but this feat does not inevitably lead us to be awed by its thunder. For that, we need to let go of logic. We must move beyond words and be led from the depths of our being to the heights of true understanding.

Today, from what is small and insignificant, I infer the presence of greatness.

He his Fabric of the Heav'ns
Hath left to their disputes, perhaps to move
His laughter at their quaint Opinions wide
Hereafter, when they come to model Heav'n
And calculate the Starrs…

John Milton

⑥

Here in *Paradise Lost* the angel Raphael tells Adam that God has allowed Man to quarrel over the nature and meaning of the stars, perhaps to laugh at Man's quaint attempts to model the reality underlying them.

It is not reality itself, and – so far in humanity's long garnering of knowledge – has only ever been a partial picture. *How much more* lies beyond what we see now is an unknown quantity. But from the drops of water we hold in our hands, we at least entertain the possibility of Niagara!

This is our heritage from all who have lived before us. And we tend, as a species, not to be satisfied with what we've already got, whether that be a gathering of possessions or the latest theory of life, the universe and everything. We are driven by the boundless curiosity of our hearts. We are not built to sit around and vegetate.

So how *unnatural* it is to let the stale despair or chronic nagging of a problem stifle what we are fully and truly born to be. What can we infer of the greater picture from what worry tells us? How can we even begin to look up and 'calculate the stars', when the weight of worry keeps us down?

Today, whatever my 'quaint opinion' of life might be, I demand the right to model Heaven.

*People are born willing to listen, but after many years of
being put down, a person may stop being willing to listen.
People are also born willing to be wrong. But after an
invalidator points out constantly what we do wrong, we
may stop being willing to be wrong about anything.*

Jay Carter

⑥

Jay Carter's pithy book *Nasty People* is subtitled 'How to stop
being hurt by them without becoming one of them'. And that,
of course, is the great danger of any self-reinforcing system.
Those who tell us we are wrong – the invalidators – reinforce
their own arrogance or desire to dominate at our expense. We
may eventually come to believe, purely from their opinion of
particular incidents, that our entire lives amount to one great
failure. Beyond that, we transfer our anger and frustration and
hatred to others ... by becoming invalidators ourselves.

This amounts to 'self-invalidation'. And once we reach this
state, we never think to lift ourselves out of it, because now we
have an escape, a temporary release, which is to invalidate the
efforts of others. Even if we are forced to listen to some home
truths, these may not mean much, because we have passed the
point of being told that we're wrong.

Jay Carter's advice, when confronted by the manipulations
of an invalidator, is to stand your ground, insist upon your
assertive rights – or disconnect from the source of the trouble as
quickly, cleanly and permanently as possible.

**Today I am willing to be wrong – but not to believe
automatically someone else's *opinion* that I am
wrong.**

If you hate someone very intensely and want to work on that, you have to personify your hate and talk to it, and not the living person.

Marie-Louise von Franz

⑥

Hatred is an extreme emotion, and for one person truly to hate another intensely and over a long period is probably quite rare. But all of us might suffer from 'flashes' of hate or more commonly from its precursors: anger, envy, resentment, revulsion…

Although the source of these emotions is an external one – the person who has generated them within us – the problem is ours and is internal. Our reasons for hating, envying, etc., might be very good ones. Perhaps the person we hate *deserves* to be hated. But even so, we need to bear in mind that hate's acidity burns inward, perhaps even to the delight and satisfaction of the one who has caused it.

In *Shadow and Evil in Fairy Tales* Marie-Louise von Franz suggests, 'If you wish to work on a relationship with a real person … then talk to your own personified affect; but you must keep it within the vessel of your own personality and not draw in the outer person.'

And in dealing with the personification of your hatred, defuse it by not generalizing or judging, blaming or insinuating. Don't make it personal, don't act out your hatred and the attendant feelings of anger, don't feel guilty as a consequence of hatred or attempt to make the one you hate feel guilty in turn.

The bottom line is that while you probably don't have control of another person, you can and do have control of yourself.

Today I take positive steps away from hatred, anger, resentment…

Rich and poor are not functions of how much money we have, but rather of whether or not we are content with what we have.

Brian Bruya

ⓖ

Contentment is not the same as feeling satisfied at any one moment. Immediately after a good meal we feel satisfied, but know full well that we'll be hungry again around the next mealtime.

So it is, I contend, with everything else in our lives. True contentment comes in realizing that the world is unfolding as it should, coupled with the knowledge that we are cropping its rich harvest of opportunity; savouring its pleasures and beauty; living deliberately and in a balanced way; adapting to change while remaining true to our essential selves...

Today I reflect on whether I see the cost of things or their value.

Let each man believe and hope what he can.

Charles Darwin

❻

Beliefs can destroy us or be our salvation. The difference lies in the absence or presence of hope. Hope is the great driving force that gives shape to our imagination, engaging the latent energies we all possess to fuel the realization of our dreams.

But while hope is an incredibly powerful force, it can also be a subtle one. As an overcast sky will block out the sun, so a setback, a crisis or a nagging worry can veil the light of hope, leading us to say, 'The situation is hopeless.'

Even when we come to that pitch, we should remember that while a *situation* might be hopeless, *we* are not. Even if nothing of value is salvaged, it seems, from the darkest hour, at least – at best – we can come through it with hope. In fact, it might well be true that we *only* come through it with hope.

We believe and hope what we can. That is the most we are able to do. Our actualization as individuals, fully engaged in the life wherein we find ourselves, is possible and sustainable only when we discover our capacity to hope. Out of that, our beliefs will follow. And they will all be positive.

Today I ask, 'What can I believe, how can I hope?'

*When people succeed in isolating ... that inner significant
structure of truth which is the same in all climes and in all
races, then there will emerge the universal religion ... that
unified though not uniform approach to God.*

Alice W. Bailey

⑥

Alice Bailey's rather contentious, though powerful and optimistic, views define a process of ongoing change in the world
which, she feels, will lead to a unified approach to God. She
cites the new discoveries of science and the emergence, partly
through them, of the 'intellectual mystics' who tend not to
belong to any organized religion, but who cohere through the
same body of essential beliefs. These she says, form the 'subjective background of the new world', the spiritual nucleus, the
unifying principle.

We all need a body of essential beliefs drawn from the subjective background of our lives. And hope, as the positive foundation of all that we are able to do, requires verification and
reaffirmation. No one can hope in a vacuum.

Wherever we go for our verification, whatever we do, the
crucial act of assimilation needs to happen within. That said, it
may be triggered by external forces: the smallest and apparently most insignificant of incidents can lead to the most fundamental of transformations. The 'starting conditions' for vast
and vital changes might be mere minutes or seconds away. Or
they might be here right now.

We become our own spiritual nucleus, our own unifying
principle.

**Today, in hope and for hope, I gather together my
essential beliefs.**

Using your original natural energy does not mean entering into a weak, mindless trance. Relaxing does not mean going limp. The secret of the art of internal strength is to rediscover and release the powerful energy that is dormant and blocked.

Master Lam Kam Chuen

ⓖ

Master Lam Kam Chuen's book *The Way of Energy* sets out the principles and practice of the Chinese system of exercise, Chi Kung, in its most powerful form: Zhan Zuang, 'standing like a tree'. It is a manual for the cultivation of inner strength, a way of balancing the forces of body and mind so that they can be utilized to their fullest and most positive extent.

While hope might be triggered by the minutiae of life, its power depends upon our overall state of well-being and health. Indeed, hope and well-being are inextricably linked and mutually supportive. Hopelessness, however it arises, can drag us quickly into a state of ill-health, lassitude and depression: our energies ebb away, drained by the conflicts and tensions inside. Similarly, if we are already weakened physically, mentally and spiritually, the spark of hope will set our lives alight only with difficulty.

Paying attention to ourselves, ensuring that we are balanced and centred, creates the best possible conditions for the emergence and strengthening of hope, together with its attendant forces of optimism and joy.

Today I look to the task of using my original, natural energy.

No snowflake falls in the wrong place.

Zen saying

⑥

There is personal hope and there is universal Hope.

If we have no personal hope, then we might feel that no snowflake falls in the *right* place... And trust it to snow today, of all days! If there is no universal Hope, then the snowflakes just fall, winter comes and goes, things merely happen.

Personal hope and universal Hope grow one out of the other. Indeed, they are so closely connected that there is no difference between them. As a leaf derives its existence from the tree, so the tree can only live by putting forth its leaves.

Personal hope by itself sustains a life, but never goes beyond the confines of that life. Those who are hopeful reap its day-to-day benefits. They are snowflakes falling in the right place. But those who are Hopeful see the purpose of the snow.

Today I consider how the snowflakes fall.

When one is living there is no acceptance,
there is only living.

J. Krishnamurti

⑥

Children playing in the snow evoke many feelings, many thoughts. Perhaps we think back to when we were younger; perhaps we muse on the innocence of childhood and how valuable that foundation of innocence is when the doors of experience swing open. Maybe we accept that children have to grow up, but wish with all our hearts this were not so – or at least that childhood should not be brought to a premature close by the concerns and conflicts of the adult world.

Children playing in the snow... Perhaps we would love to be able to play with such unselfconscious joy, to let ourselves go for once and indulge in the pure pleasure of unashamed fun. Perhaps, when no one is looking, we will! But for now we relish by proxy the fun these kids are having.

Children playing in the snow ... their shrieks of laughter echoing in the brittle air. One falls, twists an ankle, cries, gets up a moment later and joins in the game again. Two of them quarrel, a third breaks it up, they carry on playing.

These children don't accept or reject. And they're doing more than playing. They're *living* – no differently from the way we can live, right now.

Today I don't accept or reject. Today I live.

–

An impeccable hunter makes his weakness his prey.

Carlos Castaneda,
quoting Don Juan Matos

⑥

Living is a process. And we are not the product of our living, but the core of the process itself. If there were no snow, the children would play among the leaves and the grass, or in the streets, in the house, at the table, in their heads.

Whatever stops us from living in this way, living whether the snow falls or not, is a weakness. Part of the process of such living is to seek out the source of the weakness and eradicate it.

Usually it is the external circumstances of our lives which trigger a response which prevents the flow of creative, elegant living. The boss gets on our nerves. We can't eradicate the boss. We can't quit the job. We can't change the way our circumstances are arranged. All that's left to change is our anger and frustration – which is the weakness that blocks the free flow of the process of living.

Seek out the inner source of the anger. It started for a reason, but the reason may now no longer be valid. Indeed, it is certainly *not* valid if your aim is to live deliberately, yet spontaneously, as the children play in the snow...

Today I resolve to become an impeccable hunter.

I must lose myself in action, lest I wither in despair.

Tennyson

❻

Becoming an impeccable hunter does not mean dwelling on the reasons for your worries, even if the intention is to wipe them out of your life. As Krishnamurti expresses it, 'The eagle in flight does not leave a mark.' And when it strikes, it strikes quickly, cleanly, decisively – and moves on.

Our 'hunting skills' amount to clear-sighted analysis and the self-confidence to act, followed by the clean enactment of our decision:

What is my problem/weakness?

What is the *cause* of that problem/weakness?

What are the possible options for change

  i) in myself;

  ii) in my circumstances?

Which option(s) will bring me the most benefit?

  Why? How? When?

What exactly must I do to bring about this change?

What will be the cost of bringing about this change?

Am I prepared to meet that cost?

What is the worst that can happen if I take this option?

Am I still prepared to make this change?

If the answer is 'Yes' – then act. If it's 'No', go back to the start of the cycle.

Action is change *and the preparation for change.* And while you lose yourself in such action, you will find yourself there too.

Today I find myself in action.

Dwell not on the past.
Use it to illustrate a point,
then leave it behind.

Eileen Caddy

⑥

The past is always active inside us. Everything I have experienced has contributed towards what I am at this moment. Tiny incidents combine and run like little sub-programs in the head. So how can we leave it behind? There are of course specific techniques to enable the 'reprogramming' of specific events to take place, as we have seen, but does this resolve this apparent dilemma?

Yet Eileen Caddy's advice is still sound. Dwelling on the past is different, especially if, as is the implication here, the incidents upon which we dwell are negative, painful, damaging. When we indulge, for whatever reason, in such backward-looking behaviour, we are neither losing ourselves in action nor hunting the sources of weakness impeccably. Celebration of past triumphs, joys and successes is one thing; maudlin reminiscence or bitter recrimination is quite another.

If we are to look back, let us do so in order to move forward more effectively. What is done is done. But what we understand and learn from what is done is always open to change.

Today a glimpse of the past illustrates the point of the present.

Even if my marriage is falling apart and my children are unhappy, there is still a part of me that says, 'God, this is fascinating!'

Jane Smiley

⑥

Dwelling on the past rehearses future failure, unless it's used to illustrate a point and then left behind. It also contributes towards establishing an attitude of negative self-reflection, so that even when new events are unfolding, we anticipate unfortunate outcomes *yet still don't prepare to meet them positively.* We fail, in this state, to look at options for action or change. Instead, we gravitate towards the worst that can happen, treat it as inevitable and stand helplessly in the face of its imminence. This is not impeccable hunting.

Jane Smiley's perception touches upon several threads developed in this book. The part that finds fascination in unfortunate circumstance is the part that plays like a child in the snow, that inner guide which sees the snowflakes falling and recognizes that none fall in the wrong place. It is the part that does not accept or reject, but just lives. It is the part that stirs and uses our original natural energy to allow us to shine in life. It is the part that builds the inner significant structure of truth on which our purpose relies. It is the part that believes and hopes what it can...

Recognizing the source of that fascination celebrates and empowers what we are. Given such power, it is unlikely that our marriages would fall apart or our kids be unhappy!

Today I find fascination in my life.

The chess-board is the world; the pieces are the phenomena of the universe; the rules of the game are what we call the laws of Nature. The player on the other side is hidden from us.

T. H. Huxley

⑥

Huxley goes on: 'We know that his play is always fair, just and patient. But we also know, to our cost, that he never overlooks a mistake, or makes the smallest allowance for ignorance...'

The need for a god is deep-rooted. Whatever cynical intellectualization we bring to bear on the issue, the urge to believe in omniscience is overwhelming. So is the despair or bitterness that arises when circumstances seem to deny the presence of a caring deity.

And still, *and still*, the force of faith – yet to be or withered on the vine – compels us to try to invest all that we see with the ultimate meaning.

Organized religions may or may not be helpful. For the path to meaning is a personal one. Whether we regard the world as a chess-board or a playground depends upon how we have lived and what we have learned. But if God is 'out there', then He is 'in here' too, and we are equal participants, if not in the creation of the universe, then in the creation of meaning as it evolves.

As the old rabbinic story has it, 'Without me,' says God, 'you would not exist.'

'But without me,' Abraham replies, 'You would not be known.'

Today I attend to the force of faith. The task of making God known to me is mine.

If it is said that [God is] concealed by the existence of the
world, then who is it that blossoms in the form of the world?

Jnaneshwar

⑥

If you are in touch with your spiritual self, then this question is
neither meaningless nor naïve. To say 'No one blossoms in the
form of the world; the world just *is*' automatically closes off
the possibility of considering God, reducing all that can be
known to a certain kind of knowing about a particular kind of
cosmos. Shutting out purpose beyond ourselves only narrows
our range of options for change.

But even when we might have made that leap – not of faith
necessarily, *but of the possibility that faith has some basis* – then to
apply our 'old ways of looking' to a new way of understanding
blunts our sensibilities and leaves a veil drawn across the
vision.

To look, therefore, for God 'behind' the laws of physics or
as some hidden player in the chess game of existence misses the
point of His, and our, participation in the life we lead here and
now.

Jnaneshwar quotes Krishna: 'So there is no need to draw
the curtain of the world away in order to have my vision,
because I am the whole panorama.'

**Today I wonder whether my eyes conceal what is
right in front of them.**

Teach your children what we have taught our children, that the earth is our mother. Whatever befalls the earth befalls the sons of the earth. If men spit upon the ground, they spit upon themselves.

From Chief Seattle's Message

⑥

Reverence for the living world around us has nothing to do with superstition or paganism. Does the living world conceal God or reveal Him? This is a question asked by the conscious mind. In looking for answers, that conscious mind must also wonder, 'When do we ever know enough to know for sure?'

We can never 'know for sure' in the way the conscious mind would like. Our egos must ultimately put up with different kinds of knowing that arise in us 'irrationally', without going from the A-of-asking to the Z-of-being-shown. There is no logical path from atheism to faith, only the opening out of yourself to greater possibilities.

But *in the process*, we can begin to connect with the highest and most subtle emotions of which we are capable: awe, reverence, mindfulness, respect. These forces, whether God-given or not, lift us above petty matters and concerns and allow us to see the whole panorama – even if we don't recognize the hand of the painter at work.

Today I reflect that the rocky crests, the juices of the meadows, the body heat of the pony and mankind all belong to the same family.

No-one wants advice, only corroboration.

John Steinbeck

⑥

Said of the conscious mind, by the conscious mind. And as long as this cynical statement holds true for any one of us, then we will find all the corroboration we need and disdain the advice that comes our way.

One symptom of this malaise is the 'yeah-but' syndrome, the tendency some have to counter any advice that fails to corroborate their egocentric view of life. Look back over some of the advice given in this book and note how many times the 'yeah-but' reaction kicked in.

The point has already been made that one function of the conscious mind is to test 'reality', but because we are subjective beings who live by our interpretation of what's real, we tend to test reality by the picture of reality that we already hold in our heads. Thus, the 'yeah-but' reflex acts as a distorting flaw through which we see the panorama of the world.

Cultivating an attitude of open-mindedness, even if it's open-minded scepticism, begins to dilute the force of the 'yeah-but' response. We then no longer automatically counter an argument, a perception, a piece of advice, with an unconsidered reply that corroborates our own world view.

And at some point, as 'yeah-but' gives way to 'well-maybe', we begin to see that the only advice worth taking is that which corroborates our wish to change and grow.

Today, what is my reaction to advice?

Have faith in Allah – but tie up your camel.

Old Arabic saying

⑥

There is a wonderful passage (among many) in George Orwell's book *Animal Farm* where the two pigs, Napoleon and Snowball, put forward their political vision of the future. Each pig has a certain gift for rhetoric, each is highly persuasive. And the animals find themselves in the strange position of favouring Napoleon while Napoleon is speaking, then favouring Snowball while Snowball is speaking. Both pigs offer visions that seem equally tempting; both come forward with solutions to all the animals' problems.

Yet, is their position so strange? We live in a world of varied and often contradictory persuasions. Utopia, a diversity of nirvanas, a spectrum of solutions, any one of a multitude of answers can be ours for the price of a stamp and an unthinking commitment thenceforth.

Unquestioning acceptance makes us vulnerable and weak. Grasping at an attractive package of fast-food belief, swallowing the sugar pill of an easy answer, denies us the basic entitlement we have to see for ourselves. Changing our minds means making up our own minds. Snatching at corroboration is just as self-depriving as cynically disdaining any new option.

Deciding upon positive and beneficial change means looking at what's on offer and carefully listening to every aspect of ourselves.

Today I look at the quality of offered advice.

If liberty means anything at all, it means the right to tell people what they do not want to hear.

George Orwell

⑥

Liberty also means the right not to listen when people try to tell you what you do not want to hear! But it is also the case that what is meaningful and significant to us might be unpalatable. The truth, in other words, might hurt – but perhaps the pain is worth the gain, if it allows us to grow and move on.

Significant truths don't always come from other people. What we tell ourselves, in the form of sudden insights or a conscious, longer-term dialogue, might not be what we particularly wanted to hear. Facing up to flaws or weaknesses, coming to terms with guilt or shame, shining a light on past actions we regret and taking responsibility now for what we've done is the most important and beneficial kind of listening. And although, perhaps, we might not find it in our hearts to forgive the damaging actions of others, as a starting-point we should at least be able to forgive ourselves.

Listening is also making meanings from what we hear. If we wish to embrace beneficial change in ourselves, we must accept the process of change – the consequences of discovering what we need to do, to become who we want to be.

If liberty means anything at all, it means breaching the inner walls of self-deception.

Today, I start to liberate myself.

There comes a time when one must stop suggesting and evaluating new solutions, and get on with the job ... of implementing one pretty good solution.

Robert Machoc

⑥

If liberty means sometimes having to listen, then it also means reaching a time when listening must end. Otherwise it would be so easy to let listening become a delaying tactic so that we don't actually get round to *doing* anything about change. The process of suggesting and implementing – of exploring options for change – can slowly and subtly become another version of the 'yeah-but' syndrome. We end up rejecting some pretty good solutions in our quest for the grail of perfect happiness, ignoring the little voice inside that tells us wisely there is no such thing.

When we listen selectively to ourselves in this way, we might as well not bother listening at all. Because for every pretty good solution we suggest, there are any number of pretty good reasons why it won't work. Thus we are caught in a stasis of indecision, weighing up the evidence while life goes by and we grow inexorably older.

Whatever solution we opt for, implementing it makes it better. A solution is no solution if it remains a theory untested, nothing more than an abstract 'good idea'. Living deliberately means more than deliberate thinking: on occasions we need simply to get on with the job.

Today the end of listening approaches.

Doubt has devoured the whole world,
but no-one has ever eaten Doubt.

Sākhī

❻

Doubt is the great divider, separating intention from action, keeping apart suggestions and evaluations, and their implementation in deliberate living.

It is well said that doubt has devoured the whole world, because it seems that in so many areas, trust is an uncommon commodity which is growing rarer. What a sad but sinister paralysis, when pretty good solutions fail to be implemented because of doubt.

Most sinister of all is when we doubt ourselves, maybe on the basis of missed opportunities and unaccepted challenges, or because of the reasons, equally abstract, of why we might fail, or through a basic lack of trust in our abilities and strengths...

Of course we might fail. Perhaps the 'good solution' turns out to be nothing of the sort and collapses beneath us in a very short time. What then? Do we give up entirely and return to the safe old way of things (while that little voice inside tells us, unheeded, that things aren't safe and cosy at all)?

To be devoured by doubt is the antithesis of liberty. It means the abrogation of the right to listen and judge. It means opting for the non-solution of sitting tight in a situation that is far from satisfactory, putting up with it in order to reduce the risk of failure.

Can we find happiness that way? I doubt it.

Today I swallow my doubts. I don't let doubt devour me.

We labour on and think, and carve our idols, and the pen never ceases from its labour; but the lapse of the centuries has left us in the same place.

Richard Jefferies

⑥

It is a useful exercise to compare the way we, as a species, are now with the way we were 10, 50, 100 years ago. We soon come to see that there is no small wisdom in Richard Jefferies' rather frustrated, rather disappointed declaration. The endless cycle of suggestion, evaluation and doubt has left us in the same place in so many areas of human endeavour.

But we cannot take the burdens of the world on our own shoulders. All we are able to do – the least and the most – is to offer what help we can, given our resources and circumstances. Unless dedicating ourselves to a general cause is our chosen path, then the global failings of humanity should not be allowed to cast too dark a shadow over our lives.

Instead, let us compare the way that we as individuals were five or 10 or 20 years ago with the way we are now.

Comparisons are invidious only when used to judge unfairly – we compare to celebrate success, not to highlight failure. So look back and use the past to pinpoint how you've changed, how successfully you've changed and how you want to change further. Face up to the areas where the lapse of years has left you in the same place. Consider where you want to be. Consider how to get there and the consequences of your actions.

Today, after labour and thought, comes the liberty of action.

Total surrender to the demands of the human spirit;
be attentive, be intelligent, be reasonable, be responsible,
be in love.

Bernard Lonergan

⑥

It might seem strange to suggest that liberty comes through surrender. But the human spirit is no enemy and it is more, much more, than a friend. It is the source of our greatest strengths, including the strengths of reasonableness and responsibility and love.

The quintessence of our intelligence comes in realizing that intelligence is limited, that the control it imposes on ourselves and our world is at best a partial, fragile dominion.

Beyond thought, and the labour of staying in the same place, we need action driven by another power, one that resides in the depths of the human spirit. My wife makes the distinction between love and 'being in love'. Love, she says, is the foundation and bedrock of the years, an accumulation of happiness. Being in love is the excitement of the moment, that sharp blade of exhilaration which cleaves through the seconds and makes the world sparkle.

Our human spirit knows that we don't need to limit being in love to another. Being in love can encompass ourselves (this is no mere egocentricity), the world, life itself. Such on-the-moment love demands involvement, compels us to drink of the essence of our living. In this state, suggestions and evaluations seem like maps scribbled on paper – while around us stretches the glory of the whole panorama.

Today, without negotiation, I surrender to the demands of the human spirit.

*That's what learning is... You suddenly understand
something you've understood all of your life, but in a
new way.*

Doris Lessing

ⓖ

The human spirit has always been making demands upon us,
though as most of us grow older its subtle insistence is stifled
by the louder urge to be 'in control', 'covering ground', 'getting
on'. We lose sight of the step we take now as we contemplate
the tortuous pathway into the future and thus learn nothing.

Surrendering to the demands of the human spirit makes
learning an inevitability. We suddenly understand! And more,
we realize that we have always understood, yet so rarely listened. But now, by an inner process of change, or perhaps by
the shock of suddenly different circumstances, we are jolted
into a new realization. Now we are attentive, reasonable with
ourselves, responsible (at last) for what we do. Now we are in
love with the life we have been given anew and doubt has vanished entirely.

Today, I live with conviction.

It is absolutely essential for me to be loved or respected by almost everyone I encounter.

Clive Wood

⑥

This is one of a number of irrational beliefs that Clive Wood highlights in his book *Say Yes to Life*, together with, 'I should be thoroughly competent, adequate and achieving in everything that I do if I am to be considered worthwhile' and 'Human unhappiness is caused by outside factors and we have little or no ability to control our sorrows or distress.'

In the clear light of day, we can look at these statements and easily dismiss them. But their essence may have percolated into our subconscious over the years, so that now, deep down, we feel them to be true.

Wood goes on to describe the work of psychotherapist Albert Ellis who, in the 1950s, evolved the concept of Rational Emotive Therapy. This pivots on the notion that a person who is not living in a way that achieves their basic goals is acting 'irrationally' (because of unquestioningly held irrational beliefs). The mechanism of RET is called 'the ABC formula'. A – the action/activity that causes us to feel disturbed; B – the belief that causes the inner/outer conflict; C – the consequence of our interpretation of the action.

Ellis sums this up as 'the tyranny of the shoulds' and quotes Epictetus: 'People are disturbed not by the things which happen, but by their opinions of those things.' In other words, by what we feel *should* happen. The solution, according to Ellis, adds D and E to the formula. D – dispute irrational beliefs. E – dispute them effectively and *feel* the benefits.

Today I break the 'tyranny of the shoulds'!

It is not enough to have a good mind.
The main thing is to use it well.

Descartes

ⓖ

Albert Ellis would say perhaps that 'a good mind' is aware of the intimate cycle of thought/belief – attitude – feeling – action – thought and effectively disputes irrational beliefs, thus breaking the tyranny of the shoulds.

But there are other ways of using the mind well. Many are described in Michael D. Chafetz's book *Smart for Life*, which is a compendium of activities, games and techniques for improving thinking skills at all levels. They include:

Imagine shapes and objects and move/distort/swell/
shrink/re-colour them in your mind's eye.
Remember 10 facts from the morning paper.
Go on 'mental journeys'. Whiz along your route to work or in
imagination visit a much-loved holiday resort.
Look out for ambiguous sentences and paradoxes, such as
'Flying planes can be dangerous' or 'I always tell lies'…
Create your own.
Review the day's events. Look for examples of irrational
beliefs, circular thinking, ambiguity, generalization, bias, etc.
Pick a picture at random and make up a story in which to
embed it.
Ask 'What if?' questions and speculate on possible answers.

Today I use my mind well.

*Out yonder there is a huge world, which exists independent
of us human beings and which stands before us like a great,
eternal riddle.*

Einstein

❧

'The contemplation of this world,' says Einstein, 'beckons like a
liberation.'

One of the games I use in my creativity workshops is called
'Parallel World'. I tell the participants that, in a few moments,
we will be stepping through a door in the imagination to a
world that is just like this one – with one essential difference. It
might be small and apparently insignificant or glaringly obvious and overwhelming, but either way, its consequences are
likely to be pervasive. Some of the parallel worlds I use are:

> In this world, people (who have a characteristic shared by
> some of the group – dark hair, are women, etc.) can turn
> invisible whenever they wish.
>
> In this world (ignore the mechanics!) babies are born big and
> people shrink as they become older. The elderly are two
> inches (five cm) tall.
>
> In this world, everyone, once a day, can look briefly into the
> mind of another person.
>
> In this world, we all have the right be given the full and
> truthful answer to one question each year – but must base
> the subsequent year's living on its consequences.

Today, contemplation of the world beckons.

The most wasted of all days is that on which one has not laughed.

Nicholas Chamford

⑥

Does your contemplation of the world include or generate laughter?

We need often to remind ourselves of the value of seeing the funny side of things, for, as Nietzsche once said, 'Perhaps I know best why it is man alone who laughs; he alone suffers so deeply that he had to invent laughter.'

The capacity to laugh is ingrained in our attitudes and beliefs. It does not imply, as Bertolt Brecht suggested, that we 'haven't heard the bad news yet'. Bad news is all around us and it would be a clever person who managed to avoid it even for a day.

The ambiguous nature of reality, the riddle of the huge world yonder, can sustain interpretations which make us laugh. But like all interpretations, these are created within. They are the outcome of our proclivity to look at the wider panorama and to react to what we see with a wide repertoire of responses.

Thus, our laughter need not be cruel, blind or unfeeling. We might find ourselves giggling like children at a piece of unintentional slapstick or smiling wryly at the poignancy of some event, or indeed moved to tears by circumstance, which then turn to tears of laughter as we realize that this is the creative life-giving response to misfortune.

As the old proverb has it, 'Let them laugh that win.'

Today I make sure my day is not wasted.

Millions long for immortality who do not know what to do with themselves on a rainy Sunday afternoon.

Susan Ertz

⑥

This beautiful little quote sums up what might be called not the 'tyranny of the shoulds', but the 'tyranny of the I-wish-could-bes'.

To spend time in idle hope does nothing to strengthen the mind or the personality, or indeed go any way towards engineering our circumstances to optimize our chances for success.

Achievement comes by setting realistic goals – that is, short-term goals which are like steps toward the greater dream. Simply to wish that we could have already arrived devalues the journey and brings the eventual destination not one day closer.

More than that, by wishing for what we can never even have may create a cynical backlash that cuts deep into our self-esteem and our enjoyment of those things we do possess. We take for granted or disdain life's treasures, never making the best of them *right now* because in our minds they pall against the dazzle and glitter of the unattainable.

Wishing is not even an irrational belief. Much better to decide now what we can do next Sunday afternoon.

Today I see that 'I wish' is the flipside of the 'yeah-but' coin.

The reward of a thing well done is to have done it.

Emerson

❧

Emerson's words remind us that the *only* realistic short-term goal is to do today's work superbly today. In that, we not only enjoy the journey, but celebrate the fact that we are alive to undertake it. And whatever the outcome of our efforts, we know in ourselves that we have done what we can, given our fragile mortality, free of irrational beliefs, free of the mental candyfloss of wishful thinking…

In doing things as well as we are able, we view the riddle of the world from a perspective grounded in achievement. 'I did it and have survived' becomes the basis of our laughter and our tears. It is an inner force, a liberating power, an understanding that has always been with us, but which is suddenly realized.

Living is doing. There is nothing else, nothing more. There is only the immediacy of action, which ultimately becomes its own accomplishment and reward.

Today I reap the rewards of my living.

I figure you have the same chance of winning the lottery whether you play or not.

Fran Lebowitz

⑥

Do you play the lottery? Examine your reasons why or why not. Separate out the simple frivolous pleasure of 'having a flutter' from any irrational beliefs such as 'Life owes me some luck' or 'How is last week's millionaire winner different from me? What have they done that I haven't?' or 'Someone up there is on my side (or not!)'

Most of us, having been told the chances of a big win are 14,000,000-to-1 against (or whatever), never really expect to hit lucky. Our hopes are modest, amounting to a quiet background thrill as the numbers are drawn. When we find ourselves tossed on the tide of strong emotion, however – the passion of superstitious faith, the anger of not winning, the envy of seeing someone who has – then we are in dangerous waters and need to work on a healthier attitude towards the vicissitudes of fate.

Do you play the lottery of life? Examine your reasons why or why not. Consider whether you are a fatalist, believing that whatever will be will be (and if so, does that belief extend to your inner state?), or whether you are strongly determinist in thinking some outside agency, an omniscient force, controls our every experience. If this is what you believe, then reflect on whether this is not, in fact, just another kind of fatalism...

Today I wonder whether I am a loser by chance or a winner by design.

Go home and make a net if you desire to get fishes.

Chinese proverb

⑥

The whole thrust and purpose of this book has been to suggest that beneficial change is eminently possible, to outline a number of techniques to bring it about and to refer to a number of sources where further guidance can be sought. The pivot of its whole position is encapsulated in the formula:

Awareness – understanding – control.

Awareness amounts to realizing our capacity to change ourselves, if not initially our circumstances.

Understanding comes as the desire for change is embodied in direct and deliberate action.

Control of ourselves *and* our circumstances increases as we live more creatively, with greater enjoyment, dignity and success – which in turn leads to deeper awareness that further change can then be brought about.

Any net is made of many strands, none of which is useful by itself. But those strands, woven together carefully and artfully, form a whole much greater than the sum of its parts.

Today I go home and prepare to catch fishes.

A long life may not be good enough,
But a good life is always long enough.

Anonymous

⑥

There are some things over which we have no control. We are mortal, for example, and our lives will end. Whether this inevitability is built into the deep fabric of reality, painted in by the hand of the Creator, or is merely the result of the blind forces of physics matters not. The fact of our ephemeral flesh is not altered in any way.

If we 'know what to do on a rainy Sunday afternoon' – if every moment is treasured because of its brevity and because it is one of a finite number of moments that compose our limited lives – then death, the ultimate fact and finale of life, will fail to terrorize. In the glow and bustle of a life that is good, because we have worked to make it so, we don't dwell morbidly on death or what might lie beyond. If we suspect there is nothing beyond, then that force should turn us back to life, should impel us to celebrate every single precious second.

And if this flicker of existence is part of a greater plan, then a fundamental part of that plan must be for us to experience it as fully as we can, in a way that is most beneficial to our own growth of understanding.

Today I ensure my life is a good one, however long it may be.

If you wish your merit to be known, acknowledge that of others.

Japanese proverb

ⓖ

There is a natural tendency in most people to talk about their achievements. At its pettiest this consists of brash boasting, coupled perhaps with a belittling of what other people have done. To become a braggart is to enter a vicious circle of negativity, where the self is inflated through invidious comparisons with others. Compliments become barbed, oneupmanship and point scoring are rife, the knives are always out and back-stabbing is the preferred method of social murder...

At this point you are possibly thinking, indignantly and justifiably, that this does not in any way describe yourself. But still, the public acknowledgement of personal merit is important. We like people to know what we've done.

Use that force positively, by accepting that people like to talk about themselves. Listen attentively and with sincere interest. Be honest in your praise if you feel that praise is due and well deserved. Other people's achievements do not, of themselves, diminish your own – only their bad attitude and yours can do that.

Break the circle of malicious competition in this subtle and elegant way. Better still, don't get into the ring in the first place.

Today I acknowledge my own merits and praise other people's.

The only golden rule is that there is no golden rule.

George Bernard Shaw

⑥

I have heard this delightfully mischievous paradox in several versions, attributed to different people. Somerset Maugham supposedly said, 'There are three golden rules to the secret of successful writing – and nobody knows what they are.' I quote this early on in every creative writing class I run, much to the amusement, and sometimes consternation, of the students.

The belief in golden rules takes many forms, but in all cases seems to amount to a desire to be given an easy answer. Also, and more damaging, while we chase the grail of 'the secret' of being more attractive to women/men, making a million pounds, living longer, looking younger, increasing our 'brain power', or whatever, we don't bother to look for more practical ways of achieving these things – or cut our losses and abandon the vain dream entirely.

When my students ask, 'So how do I get better at writing?', I tell them to sit down and write a million words. Then they'll be better than they are now and in a position to make the *second* million better still, then the third, then the fourth, then the fifth…

So it is with life itself. Live the next million moments, then the next million, taking them for what they are and using them to improve the quality of however many moments are to follow.

Today I discover the secret of the only golden rule.

Nothing, I am sure, calls forth the faculties so much as being obliged to struggle with the world.

Mary Wollstonecraft

✿

We live as much by our weaknesses as we do our strengths. It might be even argued that to know our weaknesses is our greatest strength, for we are then in a position to eliminate them or, if not, then adapt to them to minimize their effect.

There is nothing new in desiring success or peace of mind or freedom from worry. In recent times libraries of books on 'self-improvement' have been written, all dressing up ancient wisdoms in current clothes. The answers go back as far as the questions. The 'golden rule' of successful living has been set down by sages and in religious and spiritual texts all through the centuries, right across the world.

Throughout history, people have had to 'struggle with the world'. And to do this is to engage with life fully and honestly for what we are. We laugh, we cry, we succeed, we fail, we rage, we forgive. We are never perfect. We are always mortal. We are free only within the limits of our humanity.

But that struggle to be as much ourselves as we can calls forth our faculties most effectively and answers the deepest, oldest questions of our kind.

Today I am answered in my struggle with the world.

Mind Games are education, ecstasy, entertainment, self-exploration, powerful instruments of growth. Those who play these games should become more imaginative, more creative, more fully able to gain access to their capacities and to use their capacities productively.

                                        Jean Houston and R. E. L. Masters

                                        ⑥

Jean Houston and R. E. L. Masters' book *Mind Games* is subtitled 'The guide to inner space'. First published in 1972, it is now part of a large and growing corpus of material broadly categorized as 'self-improvement'. Most of the important ideas that occur throughout the literature are made in Houston's and Masters' work, which advocates a progressive exploration of your own mind through a range of structured techniques carefully assembled into an overall programme.

But we all play 'mind games' anyway and most of what has been said in *this* book amounts to an underscoring of that point, together with the equally vital assertion that we can become much more effective players through awareness, understanding and control.

Worry itself is a 'mind game', albeit an unpleasant one that takes us round in a circle rather than leading us towards any satisfactory resolution. As we know, its effects can be devastating to all aspects of our lives. And they can sometimes be fatal. So although worry, like other mind games, is 'all in the head', it is unquestionably 'real' and 'physical', with consequences that affect us profoundly.

Today I become a more effective player of mind games.

Efficiency is the power of producing the effect intended,
active, competent power, competence for one's duties.

F. Addington Symonds

❻

In a sense, efficiency means 'calling forth the faculties', to use Mary Wollstonecraft's phrase. Worry is the height of inefficiency because its effects are never *intended*. There is no 'competent power' in it.

F. Addington Symonds, in *Teach Yourself Personal Efficiency*, assembles a varied menu of mental techniques for improving our ability to produce the effect intended. These include:

looking at yourself and your circumstances

taking measures to prevent ill health

becoming more sensitive to your emotions (listening to yourself)

examining ideals and values, aims and purposes

boosting self-confidence and self-determination

developing memory skills

improving creativity (and, together with the above, intuition)

dealing with other people and improving social skills

improving time management and other organizational skills

Only by sustained effort – though a gentle discipline – and quiet determination can we hope to produce in ourselves an active, competent power.

'Only those who have the patience to do simple things perfectly will acquire the skill to do difficult things easily.' (Schiller)

Not the cry, but the flight of a wild duck leads the flock to fly and follow.

Chinese proverb

⑥

All the words of wisdom in the world are of little value if they are not embodied in practice. Practice, whether it is a mind game 'in the head' or direct involvement with 'outside reality', is essential for success.

No matter how many books you read or 'gurus' you listen to, no matter how many experts impart the fruits of their own experience, no matter how earnestly you cling to these bits of wisdom offered by 1,000 hands and use them to tell yourself 'Yes, I can do it' – unless you start to do it, nothing will change and the weight of worry will bear down on you once again.

In another context, but with the same principle in mind, I achieve my aim of being a writer by sitting down every day to write 2,000 words. Ten years ago I was involved with a writers' workshop, the organizer of which was 'researching' his first novel. In the past decade I have written several million words, while my colleague has yet to finish (indeed, I suspect, even begin) his book.

I now call this the 'I-am-starting-to-think-of-beginning-to-contemplate-wondering-about-commencing-my-action-plan' syndrome.

Do you suffer from it? How long will you put up with that situation?

Today I am moved by the flight, not the cry to action.

We think of acting so as to bring about a good result, or a bad result, when in fact every action has a multitude of results, some of them good and some of them bad.

Dorothy Rowe

⑥

Dorothy Rowe's vast and powerful book *Wanting Everything* has many pertinent things to say about action and results.

Nothing we ever do (as opposed to what we think we want to do) can guarantee success. However efficient we become, circumstances might still militate against us so that life is hard and, we might once have been tempted to say, unfair.

Achieving competent power comes down to gaining control over the link between our intentions and subsequent actions. We do what we set out to do and take responsibility for that, but in an uncertain world, where at each moment new 'starting conditions' come into existence, we are never able to predict precisely what tomorrow will bring.

Thus, perhaps the most useful mind game of all is that of adaptability. For us to be flexible as the future rushes upon us at a rate of 60 seconds per minute, we need to understand that no regime or system or programme can be expected to meet all contingencies and our every requirement, all the time. Everything changes.

And so, if we set out on the path towards personal change, we need to follow that path wherever it takes us. We must keep changing, keep adapting in this inconstant world, so that while we can never say, 'I'm here!', we can always proclaim, 'I'm getting there!'

Today, as I practise the art of happiness, I expect the unexpected.

Help thy brother's boat across, and lo! thine own has
reached the shore.

Hindu proverb

⑥

An old Zen story tells of a time in Japan when paper lanterns were commonly used, with a candle burning inside. The friend of a blind man who had visited him that night offered him such a lantern for the journey home.

'I need no lantern,' the blind man proclaimed. 'Darkness and light are all the same to me!'

Nevertheless, his friend urged him to take a lantern for the journey home and eventually, though with some bad grace, the blind man agreed.

'I'm glad you've decided to do this,' said the friend. 'For although you make no distinction between darkness and light, others do. If you had no lantern, someone might run into you.'

The blind man grumbled his thanks as he took the lantern and set off home. He had not gone very far when someone bumped into him, sending him stumbling.

'Hoi there, look where you're going!' exclaimed the blind man. 'Can't you see my lantern?'

'I cannot,' the stranger replied. 'Your candle has blown out, brother...'

In expecting the unexpected, I listen to advice, help others along the way – and carry a bell as well as a paper lantern!

One of the reasons we have such a problem with happiness is that we confuse it with a life untouched by such negative feelings as anxiety, rage, sadness and doubt.

Jerome Burne

⑥

None of us is perfect. Nobody does or can live a life untouched by negative feelings. It is our capacity for anxiety, rage, sadness, doubt and a host of others that combines to make us what we are.

In seeking to make the best of ourselves, we should not deny the worst in us. Our aim, ultimately, is to learn by whatever we experience, to use life in all its colours, with all its pain and limitation, as a positive force for change. Though we rage, though we doubt, though we inevitably feel the pangs of anxiety, we should endeavour not to let these things control us. If we are at the mercy of negative feelings, because they have no mercy, we will be carried away in the tides of their passion and be lost.

We cannot live in a vacuum, cloistered away in some utopian safe haven of perfect peace and happiness. If we could, if we did, what scope could there be for excitement and enthusiasm? What joy would we find in a world of flawless light, when unending rapture itself became as bland as the same meal eaten a million times over?

Happiness is not static and uniform. It is a dynamic, arising out of the context of our lives, with all their sham, drudgery and broken dreams.

Today, whatever my labours and aspirations in the noisy confusion of life, I strive to keep peace with my soul.

If you can't enjoy a walk around the block, you won't enjoy going to Hawaii or Paris.

Barbara De Angelis

(6)

Happiness is generated by the normal, ordinary things in life. How else could it be? A normal, ordinary life is all that most of us have. Some people strike lucky in the lottery, some people develop a life-threatening illness. But there is no absolute correlation between these things and our state of happiness.

Whatever we're looking for, we're unlikely to find it if we can't come round to seeing that it's here with us now. Otherwise, we spend our time in a state of profitless regret or anticipation, believing the grass is somehow magically greener on the other side of the hill.

Barbara De Angelis points out that whatever has caused anxiety, doubt, rage or sadness does not taint our every waking moment. There are many instances in our lives that can be enjoyable – small and simple experiences like a memory, an aroma, a kind word or gesture, a humorous incident... During these moments, we are absorbed. Just fleetingly, existence has no other purpose than *to be there for what's happening*. If only, if only we but realized it. 'Having particular experiences won't make you happy,' says Barbara De Angelis. 'What will is knowing how to live them with full awareness.'

Full awareness means simply becoming conscious of how you're feeling as these experiences occur. Let's get to know what happiness feels like, instead of allowing it to go mindlessly by, so that it becomes diluted by the times we're bored or frustrated, sorrowful or hurt.

Today I enjoy a walk around the block.

It is sobering to consider that when Mozart was my age he had already been dead for a year.

Tom Lehrer

❻

Do you ever compare yourself unfavourably with another person in this way? Do you suddenly find yourself shocked to realize that people 'who are your age' are already dead, with all of life's achievements behind them?

Tom Lehrer's wonderfully wise, beautifully bittersweet words say so much, point out so many of our frailties.

There will always be those who are great, who stand as icons of their age, whose shadows are cast far into the future. The accomplishments of such people cannot be matched by ordinary folks like you and me, as far as the rest of the world is concerned. But as far as *we're* concerned, what we do can bring as much satisfaction and happiness to us as Mozart's music brought to the man himself. The flame of achievement burns as hot whether it is a candle or a bonfire.

But yes, it is sobering to think that life is passing us by, if we have not yet achieved what we want. So now is the time to strive for those achievements – using that sobering thought to become drunk on the joy of living.

Today I drink a deep draught of experience.

I want to be what I was when I wanted to be what I am now.

Graffiti

⑥

I occasionally find myself thinking how good it would be to return to childhood, or college days, or to relive that first date with the girl who became my wife...

We all indulge in this kind of wishful thinking, I'm sure, from time to time. But in my case at least, I always want to go back *armed with the knowledge and experience I possess now*. It is, I suppose, a gentle kind of regret – but a pointless one, too, because then I was what I was, now I am what I am. And as the years go by, I will with no shadow of a doubt become what I am going to be.

How tempting it is to create a mental montage of our perfect selves enjoying the limitless excitement of childhood adventures, the freshness of youth, the knowledge of maturity, the wisdom of old age. If only we could be that, all wrapped up in one neat package.

But it can never happen and we should not allow the wish for it to be so to be any more than an occasional frivolous flight of fancy. What we are is the outcome of what we were. What we will be will arise as the result of what we do now.

Today, I want to be what I am as completely as I can.

The meaning of life is wrapped up in what will remain after we depart. The meaning of life is to help create a better future.

Simon Wiesenthal

◉

Without meaning in life, we are not truly alive. And although we may discover meaning in the jewels of tiny memorable moments, celebrating, however modestly, our life as we live it, there is meaning to be found also – and possibly greater meaning too – in the altruism of helping to create a better future.

Remember 'Old men are very dangerous, because they don't care what happens to the world'? There is a terrible sadness in the thought that we use and abuse the world, paying no heed to the consequences of our actions because we will be gone, be dead and buried, by the time the full damage is done.

Creating a better future is one of the most civilized and civilizing endeavours a person can undertake. It is a thoroughly humanizing activity.

Whatever we do in our lives, some part of it should stand as our legacy. We do not need to produce monumental works; we do not in any way need to cast the shadow of Mozart across the years. Ordinary people doing ordinary things will be enough, because there are millions of us.

So, in seeking to live life completely through mindful awareness, we can enrich our experience by giving some thought, some time, some kindness, to the sons and daughters of destiny.

Today, on this particular day, I think of the untold tomorrows.

One had to find out what things were not necessary, what one really needed. A little music and liquor, still less food, a warm and beautiful but not too big roof of one's own, a channel for one's creative energies and love, the sun and the moon…

T. H. White

⑥

To find out what is not necessary is as useful, and may be far easier a task, than discovering what we really need. 'More is the devil,' as they say, and the whole tendency of our society – and thus of our way of thinking – is to want more, to equate more with success, achievement, superiority and happiness.

Take a closer look. Break down into 'thought-sized portions' what it is exactly that you need more *of*. Look at what is not necessary. Look at what you might have to exchange to get more of what you really need.

You get nothing for nothing. There is always a trade-off, though we shirk from this idea because we believe that to relinquish anything in which we've invested time, money or effort is somehow to take a step backwards. But this is a fallacy you can prove for yourself. Play the mind game of imagining life with what you really need and *only* what you really need. How much do you miss what wasn't necessary? What are you sacrificing simply to accumulate more of these things?

How do you go about rearranging your life to have it the way you want it?

Today I recognize that riches come in all forms.

...there was no moon, the sky was very clear. Neither of us spoke ... partly, I think, because the beauty of the starry heavens had taken hold upon us both, filling our hearts with thoughts too big for words.

J. Meade Falkner

⑥

When the mind reaches its limits, the heart still has the capacity to appreciate and to understand. As a species we were alive before we were able to think. And it may be (though the scenario might horrify some) that we will evolve beyond thought, our 'cerebral phase' being nothing more than a fleeting transition to something greater.

There comes a time in our individual lives also, in our tumble of busy days, when there is an end to losses and gains, a brief cessation of rational thought and struggle and even hope. We move beyond it, stunned into stillness, to a realm where only the heart is at home. Here words are pointless, because they are utterly inadequate to express our extremity of awe or reverence or passion. True love, profound and boundless, is an inarticulate thing.

The little irony here is my attempt to define the indefinable with the little tools of language. Go out and find what you may think I may be talking about! Open yourself up to it. Let whatever beauty is out there take hold of you.

Today my heart fills with thoughts too big for words.

I would rather that my spark should burn out in a brilliant blaze than it should be stifled by dry rot. I would rather be a superb meteor, every atom of me in magnificent glow, than a sleeping and permanent planet.

Ian Fleming

☙

The greatest sadness and the most misguided of motives is to want more of time rather than more of life. 'Quality not quantity' is the watchword here, though a high quality of life often brings the bonus of increased longevity.

For the spark to burn in a brilliant blaze does not mean living 'on the edge'. We don't need to indulge in extreme sports, to eat more, drink more, meet more people or see more places. 'Quality time' can also be spent in silence, in modest achievement, in the minutiae of daily existence, if you are truly yourself in such moments. Then every atom of your being glows magnificently.

Ian Fleming also said that the proper function of life is to live – it is a verb, not a noun; a process, not a thing. 'I shall not waste my days trying to prolong them,' he declared. 'I shall use the time.'

Today I shall use the time to ignite my spark of life.

Where art though, beloved tomorrow?
When young and old and strong and weak,
Rich and poor, through joy and sorrow,
Thy sweet smiles we ever seek –
In thy place – ah, well-a-day!
We find the thing we fled – Today.

Shelley

⑥

If we run away from today, drawn on by the false promise of a brighter future, we will never blaze like a meteor. Rather, the dry rot of vain hope and bitter regret will stifle us at last. Our only thoughts, trapped in the head, will be meagre ones. We will dream small, and live smaller. There will be nothing of note in the journey, and no destination worth speaking of. We will have existed and died, and left no legacy in the form of a life lived to capacity.

There is only today. Here it is in this flickering instant when the future becomes the past. It slips by so quickly, so subtly; gone before we know it.

Today I replace tomorrow with today.

What is life? It seems that I cannot thoroughly understand it… I just paint because I want to… My father shares this view. I guess the sun and moon in his mind are rounder and brighter. Maybe this is what can be called his love for life.

Wang Yani

❦

Wang Yani, who was China's most famous child artist, recalls that his father smiled at his painting paper and was enchanted by mountains, the crowd and flowers.

In this case, these men, father and son, had found a specific outlet for the expression of their love. But when we love life, we express it anyway in all that we do: we cannot help but communicate the love, which is the final reason for being, the ultimate context, the journey and the destination all aglow within the present moment.

Wang Yani declares that when he paints, he feels free. It is a freedom from so many of the things so many people flee from. It is a freedom, not from problems and worries, but from their tyranny. It is the freedom to be all, and only, what we can be.

Today I live because I want to.

We do not see things as they are. We see them as we are.

Anaïs Nin

◉

In other words, the world is what our thoughts make of it. From this truth spring many of our biases, prejudices, worries and fears. Also, it must be said, the world reflects our joys and ambitions, our dreams and the source of our happiness.

Our perceptions begin to form from the moment we are born – or even before. How else could it be? We need to know what the world is about in order to survive.

But our growing world picture is uniquely ours and that is a weakness as well as a strength. A problem we fail to solve, an unhappy relationship we cannot salvage, a run of misfortune, and so on, all help to build it up. The danger is that we will come to see the world more and more surely and unalterably as a cold and uncaring place or even as a general rule as somewhere positively hostile and dangerous. And to whatever extent the world may or may not be perilous or heedless of our hurt, the idea that it is will grow inside and haunt us forever. From a few specific incidents, we will have generalized a view of our entire existence.

The first step towards breaking this vicious circle lies in realizing that our view of things is inside, not somewhere out there.

The next step is to understand that there's no big mystery in changing who we are. It's not a secret. It's not hard. People are doing it every day. Start right here, right now. Do you remember what Marcel Proust said? 'Voyages of discovery are not made by going to new places, but by seeing with new eyes.'

Today I will attempt to see something with new eyes.

I stopped very gently and sat upon the Time Machine, looking around.

H. G. Wells

ⓖ

To sit upon the saddle of such a machine must be the dream of every child – and probably most adults – at some time or another. To see what would be happening in 10 years, 50, 100, 1,000… To witness the unfolding story of humanity and to say, 'So that's the answer' or 'I told you so' or, more prosaically, to jump forward a day to spot the winning horse of a race yet to be run. Or, more darkly, to venture forward in trepidation and fear to the moment of our own death. The temptation would be overwhelming…

And maybe that's why, as far as we know, time travel doesn't exist. But most people, even without a time machine, focus their attention almost exclusively on the future… 'By this time next year I'll have paid off this loan.' 'In another week this cough will have gone.' 'Where will I be in 10 years' time?' 'Will I ever be rich or famous or happy or…?'

So it goes on. But by living for the future, we miss out on the present.

So in our minds, let's jump on board that time machine, push the lever forwards and zoom into our imaginary future. Let's look back on our lives and wonder where those worries went. Let us see what we have achieved, what hopes came true, what successes we enjoyed.

Can our lives really be like that? Why not – there's still time to do something about it.

Today I will enjoy my journey into the future, at a speed of one second per second.

in Just-
spring when the world is mud-
luscious…

E. E. Cummings

ⓖ

How many times have we told our children to stop jumping in puddles or admonished them because they came home muddy? Then how many times have we thought, 'But that's how *I* used to be,' and smiled fondly to remember those simple and innocent joys?

The child-like and the wise live in a world of uniqueness. For them, there's not merely 'spring', but 100 startling shades of spring as that season unfolds. There is the day of the year's first snowfall, and the last, and the day of the first snowdrop, the day when the final leaf drops from the old lime tree at the bottom of the garden. There is the day of Just-spring …

Are these distinctions of any consequence, we may ask – or rather, the grown-up and businesslike part of our mind might ask. And if we let it, it will supply its own answer, which may be the wrong one. It may say that today's the day when the gas bill arrived, when the car broke down, when the roof sprang a leak, and so on.

These are not instances of uniqueness. These are the dreary and habitual thoughts that make one day as grey and forgettable as the next, or the last. These are not things to celebrate, but things to solve and have done with, so that the true uniqueness of this day can be seen with eyes newly opened.

Today I will not simply look, but see what makes this day unique and wonderful in my life.

The same fire purifies gold and consumes straw.

Italian proverb

❦

When it comes to the problem of worry, we are quick to point the finger of blame at strangers, at motorists, at pedestrians, at the government, at pollution, at the youth of today, at the boss, at friends, at our husbands and wives, at our children.

By laying the blame elsewhere, we suggest to ourselves that the problem is someone else's fault and that it is beyond our personal control. And yet oddly, when we recognize a fault within ourselves, many of us still feel that nothing can be done: 'It's just the way I am' or 'Well, it's a mistake that anyone could have made.'

Yet the same fire is within us all. Rather than apportioning blame, we should ask ourselves for what purpose are we using it?

This proverb also reminds us that what we want and wish for is already there, within. We know the answer to the problem. We possess the cure to the illness. We have already reached the destination.

Today I will use my fire well.

There is surely a piece of divinity in us, something that
was before the elements, and owes no homage unto the sun.

Sir Thomas Browne

We are creatures of flesh and blood alive in a world of metal, glass, wood, stone and earth. We consume the flesh of other creatures and plant material and metabolize this in the oxygen-burning factories of our bodies in order to survive from one second to the next, to the next.

Yet we would not dream for a moment that we are only brute engines, existing as a blind component in the self-perpetuating pointlessness of creation... The very fact that we can dream for a moment belies this idea.

We are driven by thoughts which are shaped by our experiences. Those experiences accumulate to form beliefs, truths and perceptions. Our perceptions texture our attitudes, which then affect our bodies in a multitude of ways.

Worrying is part of that 'feedback loop' between body and mind. Many people fall ill because of something as subtle as a thought. So, what is subtle can also be powerful.

There are many techniques for affecting the mind–body dialogue in positive, beneficial ways. Some of them are essentially of the body, while others address the powers of the mind. But beyond both lies something vastly more subtle, incomparably more powerful. And because it is all-pervasive, sometimes our thinking is too narrow and our seeing is too specific to see it. Opening out, letting go, initiates a greater dialogue – between the body–mind and the spirit.

Today I will search out my divinity.

Beware the ghosts that haunt you
And the demons who will taunt you –
Always there, but rarely seen;

They are the spirits of despair
And the wraiths of couldn't-care
The phantoms of perhaps-I-will,
The shades of might-have-been.

Stephen Bowkett

Further Reading

Aitchison, Jean, *Words in the Mind*, Blackwell, 1994

Appleyard, Bryan, *Understanding the Present*, Pan Books, 1992

Bach, Richard, *Jonathan Livingston Seagull*, Book Club Associates, 1973

—, *Illusions*, Pan, 1977

Bailey, Alice W., *A Treatise on White Magic*, Lucis Press, 1974

Bashō, *On Love and Barley: Haiku of Bashō*, trans. Lucien Stryk, Penguin, 1985

Bentham, Jeremy, ed., *Collins Gem Dictionary of Quotations*, William Collins, 1970

Bentine, Michael, *The Shy Person's Guide to Life*, Grafton, 1986

Best, S., and Smith, C., *Electromagnetic Man*, Dent, 1989

Bettelheim, Bruno, *The Uses of Enchantment*, Penguin, 1991

Bierce, Ambrose, *The Devil's Dictionary*, Sagamore Press Inc., 1957

Bloch, Robert, *The Best of Robert Bloch*, Ballantine Books, 1977

Bloom, William, ed., *The New Age*, Rider/Channel 4, 1991

Boyd, Malcolm, *Rich with Years*, HarperCollins, 1994

Brady, Maureen, *Mid Life: Meditations for women*, HarperCollins, 1995

Brooks, C. Harry, *The Practice of Autosuggestion*, George Allen & Unwin, 1922

Buzan, Tony, *Use your Head*, BBC Books, 1993

Campbell, Joseph, *The Masks of God*, Secker & Warburg, 1960

Carnegie, Dale, *How to Stop Worrying and Start Living*, World's Work Ltd, 1972

Carter, Jay, *Nasty People*, Contemporary Books, 1989

Carter-Scott, Cherie, *Negaholics*, Century, 1989

Cassettari, Stephen, *Pebbles on the Road*, Angus & Robertson, 1992

Chafetz, Michael D., *Smart for Life*, Penguin, 1992

Chuen, Master Lam Kam, *The Way of Energy*, Gaia Books, 1991

Collings, Jillie, *Life Forces*, New English Library, 1991

Conrad, Joseph, *Heart of Darkness*, Bantam, 1969

Cummings, E. E., *Selected Poems 1923–58*, Faber, 1977

Daintith, John, and Stibbs, Anne, eds, *Quotations for Speeches*, Parragon Books, 1994

Darbishire, Helen, ed., *Journals of Dorothy Wordsworth*, Oxford University Press, 1958

Darling, David, *After Life*, Forth Estate, 1995

Dass, Ram, *Journey of Awakening*, Bantam, 1985

Deehan, Geoff, and Evans, Peter, *The Keys to Creativity*, Grafton Books, 1988

Deveraux, Bob, *Be Green*, Ark Press, 1975

Dewhurst Maddock, Olivia, *The Book of Sound Therapy*, Gaia, 1993

Dickson, Paul, ed., *The Official Rules*, Arrow Books, 1980

Edwards, Betty, *Drawing on the Artist Within*, William Collins, 1987

Edwards, E. D., ed., *The Dragon Book*, William Hodge & Co., 1944

Eliot, T. S., *Four Quartets*, Faber

Falkner, J. Meade, *Moonfleet*, Puffin Books, 1978

Ferguson, Marilyn, *The Aquarian Conspiracy*, Paladin, 1981

Franz, Marie Louise von, *Shadow and Evil in Fairy Tales*, Shambhala, 1995

Friend, David, and the Editors of *Life*, eds, *More Reflections on the Meaning of Life*, Little, Brown & Company, 1992

Fromm, Erich, *To Have or To Be?*, Abacus, 1979

Gibran, Kahlil, *The Prophet*, Pan, 1980

Gleick, James, *Nature's Chaos*, Sphere Books, 1991

Godefroy, Christian H., *Mind Power*, Piatkus, 1993

Gollancz, Victor, ed., *A Year of Grace*, Penguin, 1955

Gooch, Stan, *The Paranormal*, Wildwood House, 1978

Gordon, David, *Therapeutic Metaphors*, Meta Publications, 1978

Graham, Helen, *A Picture of Health*, Piatkus, 1995

Greig, Sue, Pike, Graham, and Selby, David, *Greenprints*, Kogan Page/WWF, 1989

Hall, Carol and Eric, and Leech, Alison, *Scripted Fantasy in the Classroom*, Routledge, 1990

Hall, Edward, *Beyond Culture*, Anchor/Doubleday, 1976

Hay, Louise, L., *You Can Heal Your Life*, Eden Grove Editions, 1988

Hayward, Susan, *A Guide for the Advanced Soul*, In-Tune Books (PO Box 193, Avalon NSW 2107, Australia), 1986

Heider, John, *The Tao of Leadership*, Wildwood House, 1986

Herrigel, Eugene, *Zen in the Art of Archery*, Vintage Books, 1971

Hopkins, Gerard Manley, *Poems & Prose*, ed. W. H. Gardner, Penguin, 1970

Hughes, Ted, *Season Songs*, Faber & Faber, 1976

Hunt, Morton, *The Universe Within*, Simon & Schuster, 1982

Jefferies, Richard, *The Pocket Richard Jefferies*, ed. A. H. Hyatt, Chatto & Windus, 1911

Jeffers, Susan, *Feel the Fear and Do It Anyway*, Arrow Books, 1991

Jung, C. G., *Memories, Dreams, Reflections*, Fontana, 1963

Kenyon, J., *21st Century Medicine*, Thorsons, 1986

Krishnamurti, J., *The Flight of the Eagle*, Harper & Row, 1973

Laing, Ronald D., *The Divided Self*, Tavistock, 1960

—, *Interpersonal Perception*, Springer, 1966

Lawrence, T. E., *The Seven Pillars of Wisdom*

Long, Barry, *Meditation: A foundation course*, The Barry Long Foundation (BCM Box 876, London WC1N 3XX), 1992

Macleod, Fiona, *The Birds of Angus Og*, Messrs Chapman & Hall, 1910

Manning, Mary, *Help Yourself to Mental Health*, Columbus Books, 1988

Matthews, John and Caitlín, *The Little Book of Celtic Wisdom*, Element Books, 1993

May, Rollo, *The Courage to Create*, Bantam, 1985

McColl, Duncan, *The Magic of Mind Power*, Gateway Books, 1989

Miller, Jonathan, *States of Mind*, Pantheon Books, 1983

Milne, A. A., *Winnie the Pooh: The complete collection of stories and poems*, Methuen, 1994

Milton, John, *Milton: Poems and selected prose*, ed. Marjorie Hope Nicholson, Bantam, 1966

Nietzsche, Frederick, *Twilight of the Idols*, Penguin, 1968

Parfitt, Will, *The Elements of Psychosynthesis*, Element Books, 1990

Parrinder, Geoffrey, ed., *Collins Dictionary of Religious and Spiritual Quotations*, HarperCollins, 1992

Pearson, John, *The Life of Ian Fleming*, Pan Books, 1967

Peck, M. Scott, *The Road Less Travelled*, Hutchinson & Co., 1983

Perls, Frederic, *In and Out of the Garbage Pail*, Bantam, 1972

Postman, Neil, and Weingartner, Charles, *Teaching as a Subversive Activity*, Penguin, 1972

Prévert, Jacques, 'The Dunce' in *Every Man Will Shout*, Oxford University Press, 1984

Reps, Paul, ed., *Zen Flesh, Zen Bones*, Pelican, 1980

Rinpoche, Dharma-Arya Akong, *Taming the Tiger*, Dzalendara Publishing, 1987

Roberts, Jane, *The Nature of Personal Reality*, Prentice Hall, 1974

Roet, Dr Brian, *All in the Mind?*, Optima, 1987

Rowe, Dorothy, *Wanting Everything*, HarperCollins, 1991

Russell, Peter, *The TM Technique*, Routledge & Kegan Paul, 1979

Sagan, Carl, *Other Worlds*, Bantam, 1975

Sahtouris, Elisabet, *Gaia: The human journey*, Pocket Books, 1989

Seed, John, Macy, Joanna, Fleming, Pat, Naess, Arne, *Thinking like a Mountain*, Heretic Books, 1988

Shah, Idries, *The Exploits of the Incomparable Mulla Nasrudin*, Jonathan Cape, 1966

Shaughnessy, Susan, *Meditations for Writers*, Aquarian, 1993

Skolimowski, Henryk, *Eco Yoga*, Gaia Books, 1994

Sky, Michael, *Breathing*, Bear & Co., 1990

Smith, Manuel J., *When I Say No I Feel Guilty*, Bantam, 1975

Spindler, Stephanie, *Learn to Live*, Element Books, 1991

Star, Jonathan, ed., *Two Suns Rising*, Bantam, 1992

Starhawk, *The Spiral Dance*, Harper & Row, 1989

Stephens, Elaine, *Whispers of the Mind*, Harper & Row, 1989

Stock, Gregory, *The Book of Questions*, Workman Publishing Company, 1987

Stryk, Lucien, and Ikemoto, Takashi, eds, *Zen Poetry*, Penguin, 1985

Thomas, R. S., *Selected Poems* 1946–1968, Granada Publishing, 1977

Lao Tzu, *Tao Te Ching*, trans. D. C. Lau, Penguin, 1984

Sun Tzu, *The Art of War*, trans. Thomas Cleary, Shambhala, 1991

Ueland, Brenda, *If You Want to Write*, Element Books, 1994

Watts, Alan, *Tao: The watercourse way*, Pelican, 1981

Watzlawick, Paul, *How Real Is Real?*, Vintage Books, 1977

Wells, H. G., *The Short Stories of H. G. Wells*, Ernest Benn Ltd, 1941

White, T. H., *The Goshawk*, Penguin, 1973

Wilson, Colin, *The Directory of Possibilities*, Book Club Associates, 1981

—, *The Occult*, Granada, 1983

—, *Mysteries*, Granada, 1983

Wilson, Ian, *Superself*, Sidgwick & Jackson, 1989

Winokur, Jon, ed., *The Portable Curmudgeon*, Gollancz, 1989

Wood, Clive, *Say Yes to Life*, Dent, 1990

The Wordsworth Dictionary of Film Quotations, Wordsworth Reference, 1991

Yalom, I. D., *Existential Psychotherapy*, Basic Books, 1980

Yanagi, Soetsu, *The Unknown Craftsman*, ed. B. Leach, Kudasha International, 1978

Of further interest...

Healing our Hearts and Lives
Inspirations for Meditation and Spiritual Growth
Eileen Campbell

The true meaning of healing is to become more whole. None of us escapes pain and suffering and we all have to deal with healing our hearts and lives. Healing ourselves is a first step towards healing our relationships, our communities and our world.

In the process of healing we need to focus on what is uplifting and inspiring, for we are responsible for our thoughts, whatever our outward circumstances may be. We also need to let go of the past; forgiveness of ourselves and others is a vital aspect of the healing journey. Through the wisdom of forgiveness we will find lasting peace.

Love and Relationships
Inspirations for Meditation and Spiritual Growth
Eileen Campbell

To achieve love which is everlasting and truly satisfying, each of us must strive to cultivate love as a state of mind, and in giving love, we will receive it. Unconditional love knows no barriers and overcomes all difficulties. It is the only lesson we have to learn.

This anthology of quotations on love and relationships has been gathered from a wide variety of sources from both East and West. It is an inspirational guide to the perennial wisdom of the heart.

101 Ways to Joy
Freeing your Spirit, Dancing with Life
Charlotte Davis Kasl

In this insightful yet light-hearted guide Charlotte Davis Kasl offers readers 101 simple yet profound ways to focus on the positive and bring joy into their lives, relationships and communities.

Dip into these brief, creative reflections, and discover how to free up your mind to find self-acceptance, openness and truth. *101 Ways to Joy* will take you on a path away from guilt, hurt, self-criticism and depression towards a new sense of happiness and peace.

Charlotte Davis Kasl is a psychologist and the author of several successful books.

A Little Book of Comfort
An Anthology of Grief and Love
Anthony Guest

Grief is never mild. In its early, intense stages it threatens to overwhelm and extinguish all hope. This has been the experience of men and women down the centuries, in all cultures. But so too has the healing which follows. Slow, imperceptible, yet inevitable, it is a personal affirmation we each receive of the triumph of life over death and the indestructibility of love.

From Dante and Shakespeare to Emily Bronte, Robert Graves and C S Lewis, this anthology draws together a selection of the most moving, comforting and inspiring writings of all time on the themes of loss and love.

HEALING OUR HEARTS AND OUR LIVES	1 85538 436 1	£7.99 ☐
LOVE AND RELATIONSHIPS	1 85538 502 3	£4.99 ☐
101 WAYS TO JOY	0 7225 3030 7	£6.99 ☐
A LITTLE BOOK OF COMFORT	0 551 02968 4	£5.99 ☐

All these books are available from your local bookseller or can be ordered direct from the publishers.

To order direct just tick the titles you want and fill in the form below:

Name: _____

Address: _____

_____

_____

Postcode: _____

Send to Thorsons Mail Order, Dept 3, HarperCollins*Publishers*, Westerhill Road, Bishopbriggs, Glasgow G64 2QT.

Please enclose a cheque or postal order or your authority to debit your Visa/Access account —

Credit card no: _____

Expiry date: _____

Signature: _____

— up to the value of the cover price plus:

UK & BFPO: Add £1.00 for the first book and 25p for each additional book ordered.

Overseas orders including Eire: Please add £2.95 service charge. Books will be sent by surface mail but quotes for airmail dispatches will be given on request.

24-HOUR TELEPHONE ORDERING SERVICE FOR ACCESS/VISA CARDHOLDERS — TEL: 0141 772 2281.